A VINDICATION

OF THE DOCTRINE OF

THE CHURCH OF ENGLAND

ON THE VALIDITY OF THE ORDERS OF THE SCOTCH AND FOREIGN NON-EPISCOPAL CHURCHES:

IN THREE PAMPHLETS ON THE SUBJECT.

CONTAINING

I. A GENERAL REVIEW OF THE SUBJECT.

II. A REPLY TO ARCHDEACON CHURTON AND CHANCELLOR HARINGTON. (SECOND EDITION.)

III. A REPLY TO THE BISHOP OF EXETER'S LETTER TO THE ARCHDEACON OF TOTNES. (THIRD EDITION.)

BY

W. GOODE, M.A., F.S.A.,

Rector of Allhallows the Great and Less, London.

NEW YORK:

A. D. F. RANDOLPH, 683 BROADWAY.

1853.

ADVERTISEMENT.

The three following pamphlets have been called forth, as their contents will show, by a recent controversy in the Church of England respecting the validity of the Orders of the ministers of the Foreign Non-Episcopal Churches. They are now put together in the hope that they will supply the reader with sufficient materials to enable him to judge of the genuine doctrine of the Church of England on the subject of a Non-Episcopal ministry; especially with regard to those Foreign Protestant Churches that were placed in less happy circumstances than our own Church in the struggle for their emancipation from the yoke of Popery. A semi-Popish party—the seeds of which have been perpetuated even from the times of the Reformation, and have ever since, at fitting opportunities, germinated with more or less luxuriance and vigor—has recently sprung up in our Church, which would fain limit the ministry of the Christian Church to those who have been ordained by Bishops episcopally consecrated, and deriving their episcopal commission through an uninterrupted line of episcopally consecrated bishops from the Apostles, denying to all others the power both of preaching and administering the sacraments; and which maintains, that the Church of Christ, properly speaking, consists only of those who are in communion with ministers so ordained. And, extraordinary as it must appear to those who are at all acquainted with the early history of our Reformed Church, it is farther asserted by this party that such is the doctrine of our Church.

It may be fairly supposed that, in the various publications to which a reply is given in the following pages, all the arguments that can with any semblance of reason be adduced to prove such a theory to be the doctrine of our Church have been brought forward; and, consequently, that the reader may here see this question fully discussed, and the arguments on both sides carefully stated and thoroughly sifted.

It is to be regretted that our Church has not, in her Articles, spoken more clearly and definitely on the point; though the fact that she has not done so entirely negatives the idea of her holding the "High-Church" view. No doubt, in the case of a national Church, it is well that room should be given for some difference of opinion. But unfortunately the tendency in all independent bodies of men, and not the least in those of an ecclesiastical kind, is, to magnify their own importance, and stretch to the utmost the rights and privileges of their order. The consequence is, that, in every *established* Church, the stream of opinion among the *Clergy* will, before long, however it may have commenced, run in the direction of the exclusive principles of what is called "High-Church" doctrine. And this, we may observe by the way, shows the importance of a State not allowing such a body to have, unnecessarily, any opportunities of tampering with the code of doctrine originally laid down at its establishment.

The subject is one of no little importance. It is no light matter to excommunicate from the Church of Christ by far the largest portion of its professed Protestant members. And they who do so should take good heed that they have the authority of its great Head, for fulminating such a sentence against those who, to all appearance, are equally devoted followers of Him as those who are pronouncing an anathema against them.

The author of the following pages is as little inclined as ever to give up the doctrine that the Episcopal form of Church government was of Apostolical institution; but he is equally indisposed to maintain that it is indispensable to the existence of a valid Christian ministry and Christian Church; still less, that the Christian ministry can only be perpetuated by bishops episcopally consecrated in an uninterrupted line from the Apostles. Had it been so, the Church would not, he believes, have been left without some definite precept to that effect in the Holy Scriptures; and certainly, in the absence of such a precept, no man, or body of men, has a right to lay down such a rule. And however strong may be the claims of Episcopacy, both from its superior efficiency, *cæteris paribus*, and from its Apostolical institution, he believes that it is entirely contrary to the spirit of the New Testament Scriptures to deny the validity of every ministry but that which is derived from the Episcopal succession.

In the following pages, however, the sole question is as to the doctrine of the Church of England on the subject; and he trusts he has been enabled to prove that her genuine doctrine is very different from that exclusive view that has lately been so vehemently contended for by some of her members. That there may be many cases in which ministerial orders may be perfectly *valid*, though in our view somewhat *irregular*, and ecclesiastical communities be true Churches, in real communion with Christ, though not constituted in the best way, is, he hopes, here clearly shown to be the doctrine of our Church; and the notion that such communities and their ministers are outcasts from the family of God, proved to be entirely opposed both to her creed and practice.

W. G.

LONDON, Oct. 21, 1852.

THE DOCTRINE

OF

THE CHURCH OF ENGLAND

ON

NON-EPISCOPAL ORDINATIONS:

OR,

THE QUESTION BETWEEN

THE PRIMATE AND THE TRACTARIANS

FULLY DISCUSSED.

Reprinted from the "Christian Observer" for November, 1851.

NEW YORK:
A. D. F. RANDOLPH, 683 BROADWAY.
1853.

THE DOCTRINE

OF THE

CHURCH OF ENGLAND

ON

NON-EPISCOPAL ORDINATIONS, &c.

The Exclusive Validity of Episcopal Ordinations Vindicated. A Sermon. By Rev. G. L. BIBER, LL.D., Perp. Curate of Roehampton. London: Rivington.

Continuation of Ditto; in Two Sermons. By the same.

A Few Words on the Correspondence between the Archbishop of Canterbury and Mr. Gawthorn. By Rev. W. B. BARTER, Rector of Highclere, &c. London: Rivington.

OUR readers have probably often viewed with interest the action of a sea, lashed into fury by a sudden tempest, upon a rock firmly imbedded in its bosom. Beating, roaring, foaming, the waves seem as if the very immovability of the obstacle presented to their course had exasperated them to a state of frenzy. The rock meanwhile, with placid steadfastness, remains utterly unshaken; covered, it may be, at times, with the boiling surge and foam, but only to reappear in undisturbed repose, and quietly make manifest the impotency of its assailants.

We have been irresistibly reminded of such a scene by what has been lately taking place in our Church. The cause of truth and sound Church of England principle has been exposed, in the person of the Archbishop of Canterbury, to a storm of vituperation and invective such as few but Tractarians would be willing to raise against the Primate of their Church. These worshippers of Episcopacy and the Apostolical Succession have discovered, apparently, that such only of the "successors of the Apostles" are entitled to respect, as maintain their views, and that, however in theory it is essential to hold "the grace of the Apostolical succession," practically they for whom this grace is claimed may be treated as if there was nothing of the kind.

Meanwhile the Primate, having calmly maintained his position, and vindicated the genuine doctrine of the Church of England, has left his assailants to fret, and fume, and rage to the top of their bent; not, doubtless, without much grief at seeing such a display in the bosom of our reformed Protestant Church, but without solicitude as to the result, either for the cause of truth or of his own character with the public.

A certain Mr. Gawthorn, a befitting convert to Romanism, recently took upon himself to put into undisguised practice the principles of his Jesuit instructors; and, *ad majorem Dei gloriam*, endeavored, under a false name, to draw the Archbishop of Canterbury into a correspondence respecting his views on the validity of the Orders of the Foreign Protestant Non-Episcopal Churches, conscious that a public statement of his well-known sentiments would be sure to excite the indignation of a certain party lately arisen in our Church; and thus a burning torch would be thrown into the Church of England, which could hardly fail, he supposed, to do some mischief there. The Primate, having nothing to conceal, freely imparted his views to his unknown correspondent; but not wishing to give occasion for a public controversy on the subject, marked his note *private*. The worthy disciple of the Jesuits had thus gained his end to the utmost extent of his wishes. He had obtained the desired expression of the Archbishop's sentiments, and the mark *private* was an additional boon, that might be turned to considerable account, and pointed at as indicating that his Grace did not wish his views to be known; though, to use the language of the *Guardian* itself (which, to do it justice, has been much more temperate on this occasion than its brethren of the same school), the opinion expressed in his note was "*the opinion which* ALL THE WORLD *has for years known him to entertain.*" (*Guardian* for Sept. 17.)

The note was of course as soon as possible made public. And as it is short, we must again place it before our readers. The Gawthorn epistle we leave to grace the annals of Jesuitism.

"(Private.)

"SIR: You are far too severe in your censure of the Bishop of London, though I wish that his Lordship had explained himself more fully. But in his original letter to Lord Cholmondeley, he *expressly* stated that *they could not by law minister in our churches*, but that every endeavor would be made to provide places where they might celebrate Divine worship according to their own form. I hardly imagine that there are two Bishops on the Bench, or one Clergyman in fifty throughout our Church, who would deny the validity of the orders of those Pastors solely on account of their wanting the imposition of Episcopal hands; and I am sure that you have misunderstood the import of the letter which occasioned your addressing me, if you suppose that it implied any such sentiment in the writer's mind.

"I remain, sir, your obedient and humble servant,

"W. FRANCIS, Esq." "J. B. CANTUAR."

The immediate consequence of the publication of this note was such as, no doubt, to afford the accomplished pupil of the Jesuits unmixed gratification. The interests of our Church have been lately taken under the special patronage of certain agitating clubs, called Church Unions, having the same aspect towards the legally appointed authorities of our Church that certain Parisian clubs had towards their appointed rulers, resolved upon giving them, unsolicited, the most strenuous assistance in the discharge of their duties—an assistance which may, perhaps, produce ultimately the same happy consummation which has followed the labors of their predecessors in another country. And still more recently an important ally has been added to their ranks, in the person of one who almost daily favors us with his oracular decisions on all points of Ecclesiastical doctrine, government, order, and discipline, sometimes to the emendation of all historic records we ever met with, and settles without difficulty, and to the infinite satisfaction of himself and all who agree with him, all disputed points. If our Primates would only establish an electric telegraph between their residences and the Strand, they might save themselves all farther trouble on Ecclesiastical matters. D. C. L. and his fellow-laborers are ready to teach them the true and genuine doctrine of the Church of England, on all points whatsoever, at the shortest notice. And this, not as speaking their own sentiments merely, but those of everybody, always, everywhere, according to the venerable Canon of St. Vincent of Lerins, worthy of any notice, including, of course, the present generation of English Churchmen.

We confess that, sometimes, when we have been reading the magniloquent effusions of D. C. L. and his coadjutors, in their various organs, in which they address us as the exclusive representatives of orthodoxy in our Church, and the genuine expounders of the mind and feelings of all the clergy worth being listened to, we have been strongly reminded of the three tailors of Tooley Street, who prefaced their lucubrations with the words, "We the people of England." But it becomes not us to dive too deeply into the mysterious recesses of the oracular abodes of these "Catholic" evangelists, or publicly to lift the veil under which these *great unknown* have chosen to shroud themselves. D. C. L., for aught we know, may have a million arguments for putting himself forward as the great instructor of the Church, and establishing his super-Primatial authority at 332 Strand.

Such, however, being the protection under which the interests of our Church have been placed, it was not to be expected that such a letter as that of the Archbishop, in favor of the Orders of certain foreign non-Episcopal Churches, should be allowed to pass without notice.

What! that a set of rebellious, schismatical, heretical communities such as these, should be spoken of by the Primate of the Church of England as having any among them entitled to preach the word of God and administer the sacraments, to the edification of any soul among them!—that a set of persons, who, if ever they *do* find mercy at the hand of God, must obtain it in a way that nobody ever heard of, or can conjecture its nature—since it is not found in the Divine covenant—should be spoken of by the Archbishop of Canterbury as though they really formed part of Christ's Catholic Church!—this was intolerable. To suppose that the grace of God could flow through any other channel than Bishops canonically consecrated, was a notion stamped and sealed with the brand of heresy by "Catholic consent." And then, to be a Bishop, and belong to a Church having the Episcopal form of church government, and think that Divine grace was communicated to the world by any other medium than a Bishop, what inconsistency, what treachery, as well as heresy! And of all others, the Archbishop of Canterbury, who is the exclusive channel of all Divine grace for everybody in his Province, for he consecrates all the bishops, the bishops ordain all the ministers, and from the ministers, so ordained, alone (Mr. Keble would tell us*), can we derive "sacramental grace" and "mystical communion with Christ!" Could any words be too strong to denounce such impiety!

Such were the outpourings of wrath which D. C. L. and his fellow-laborers in Church Unions, and newspapers, and magazines, heaped upon the devoted head of the Primate. Anything like *proof* that the Primate had uttered what was contrary to the doctrine of our Church, it was far beneath the dignity of these self-constituted authorities to offer; or if any was vouchsafed by a more humble laborer, it was a sufficient condescension to inform the Primate, that when our Church required its ministers to be episcopally ordained, it declared the exclusive validity of Episcopal ordination for all churches, places, and times. Could it indeed be doubted, that what "Catholic consent" had established, what everybody, always, everywhere, worth notice, had maintained, what all the decently-respectable divines of our Church had, with one voice contended for, was the true doctrine of our Church? And that all this was the case, D. C. L., and many other equally infallible authorities were prepared to maintain against all comers, and enforce the belief with all the means which the deplorable spirit of these liberal times might permit.

Amidst the storm thus raised, and while the assailants of the Primate—as if they had, after all, some awkward misgivings as to the strength of their cause—were endeavoring to fortify it by the most gross misrepresentations of the real meaning of the note, came a well-meant attempt to give the Archbishop an opportunity of authoritatively disowning the views which his unscrupulous adversaries had been laboring to fasten upon him, which gave rise to the following correspondence:—

"Whitchurch Canonicorum, Sept. 17, 1851.

"My Lord Archbishop: Having seen in the public journals a letter addressed by your Grace to Mr. Gawthorn, and being under the impression that the purpose and meaning of that communication have been in some degree misunderstood, I venture most respectfully to inquire of your Grace: first, whether the letter in question is to be considered as an official and authoritative document, or as an informal expression of private opinion; and, secondly, whether it was your Grace's intention, in that letter, to state that

* Pref. to Hooker, p. lxxvii.

the Bishops and Clergy of the Church of England generally are of opinion that Episcopal ordination is simply non-essential to the validity of Orders, in which case it might be dispensed with amongst ourselves; or whether your Grace meant to include, in the majority of which you spoke, those who would be reluctant to pronounce positively on the invalidity of all ordinations to the ministry performed in foreign parts, where Episcopal ordinations could not be obtained, though they would not consent that such ordinations should be introduced into the Church of England, or recognized as conveying power to officiate in that Church? — I have the honor to be, my Lord Archbishop, your very humble servant in Christ,

"WILLIAM PALMER.

"His Grace the LORD ARCHBISHOP OF CANTERBURY."

"ADDINGTON, Sept. 19, 1851.

"REVEREND Sir: A letter addressed to me in a spirit of Christian candor would be entitled to attention, independently of the advantage which it derives when contrasted with other notices which have been taken of the communication fraudulently obtained from me by Mr. Gawthorn.

"In regard to that communication, I take the opportunity of mentioning, that it is not unusual for me to receive inquiries from persons unknown to me respecting matters connected with the Church; to which I consider myself bound to reply, when there appears no ground for suspecting the motive of the writer. Mr. Gawthorn's letter came to me as one of these; and whether concocted by himself, or with the assistance of others, I cannot think that it was otherwise than cleverly composed, or contained anything to excite suspicion.

"My answer was expressed in a manner which I certainly should not have adopted 'in an authoritative or official document,' or if I had believed that I was writing any other than a private letter. Still, inferences have been drawn from it for which it furnishes no ground whatever. Otherwise you could not ask me whether 'it was my intention to state that I myself, or the majority of our Clergy, look upon Episcopal ordination as non-essential to the validity of Orders, so that it might be dispensed with among ourselves,' and so that any others than those episcopally ordained could 'have power to officiate in our Church.' This was no part of Mr. Gawthorn's inquiry. His inquiry was, whether in 'my opinion or that of the majority of my brethren, these foreign clergymen were not truly pastors of the Church of Christ, but were to be considered as mere laymen.' This I thought equivalent to the question, whether we hold that no person, in any country, or under any circumstances, will be entitled to minister in the Church of Christ except through the imposition of Episcopal hands.

"I replied that I imagined this to be as far as possible from the general opinion, either among our bishops or clergy. I knew that neither our Articles nor our Formularies justified such an opinion. I knew that many of our ancient divines had disclaimed such an opinion; and I know that such an opinion would amount to declaring that no valid sacrament or other ministerial act had ever been performed, except under an Episcopal form of government. And therefore I could not believe, and I still do not believe, that many of our clergy would venture seriously to maintain such an opinion.

"To be convinced that Episcopal government, and therefore that Episcopal ordination, is most agreeable to Scripture, most in accordance with primitive practice, and is in itself the 'more excellent way,' is perfectly consistent with the judgment of Hooker, that 'the lineal descent of power by apostolical succession is not, in certain cases, to be urged absolutely, and without any possible exception.' (Book vii. clause 14. See also Book iii. clause 11.)

"Unable as I am to account for the misrepresentations to which I have been subjected, I am glad to find so proper an opportunity of correcting them as your letter affords.

"And I remain, Reverend Sir, your faithful servant,

"Rev. WILLIAM PALMER." "J. B. CANTUAR."

We give these letters that our readers may have the whole of the case before them. And we see from them that the Archbishop calmly maintains his ground, and distinctly reasserts his first statement. Whether or not his Grace took too favorable a view of the sentiments of his brethren, we are not disposed to inquire; but whether his doctrine or that of his assailants has the best claim to be considered the Doctrine of the Church of England, we shall presently endeavor to determine, not by assertion, but by proofs.

We must first notice, however, the effect which the publication of this letter had upon the movement against the Primate, which was somewhat remarkable. It had apparently been found, that the furious onslaught made by D. C. L. and his fellow-laborers had fewer sympathizers than was expected. Even the *Guardian*, though certainly not, as its pages continually show, remarkable for its regard for the reputation of the Primate, prudently warned its party against following such extreme counsels, honestly confessing, that from "the actual language" of the note, could only be gathered the doctrine, "that Episcopal ordination is not absolutely *essential* to a true Christian ministry in any sense of the word;" and asking, "Have the gentlemen who are going to raise an agitation on this note cleared up their own minds on this question; so that they will determinately say that under no circumstances whatever can any ordination deviating from the Episcopal one, receive the Divine blessing, and be accompanied with grace?" (Sept. 17.) And the Editor had previously intimated his opinion to be, "that the Episcopal organization of the Church is not so essential, but that there may be, though not so completely, real Christian means of grace and ministries without it."

We hail the expression of such sentiments in such a quarter, and are at a loss to understand what cause of quarrel a maintainer of such views can have found in the Archbishop's note, and regret that party-feeling should have led him to make the remarks in which he has indulged. Well might a certain Archdeacon, and others of the party, complain of it as treason in the camp. But treason evidently there was, and consequently great risk of certain threatened protests turning out to be failures. And so this second letter of the Archbishop was represented to the public as a *retractation*. Yes, wondering reader, in the face of the Archbishop's express reiteration of his former view, and declaration of his adherence to it, the Metropolitan Church Union had the courage to put forth the following statement:—

"At a special meeting of the Committee of the Metropolitan Church Union, held on Friday the 26th of Sept. 1851, a letter from his Grace the Archbishop of Canterbury, to the Rev. W. Palmer, having been read, *Resolved*, That forasmuch as the indispensable necessity of Episcopal ordination to the validity of holy orders appears to this Committee to be recognized by his Grace in the above letter, no farther steps be taken to procure signatures to the Protest issued by this Committee, and that the Petition to Convocation on this subject now in draft be dropped."

And the trustworthy *Morning Chronicle*, under the oracular guidance apparently of D. C. L., indulges itself in the following—we should suppose, perilous—experiment upon public patience and credulity:—

"The Primate has clutched, not without evident relief, at the three thin and unsubstantial straws with which Mr. Palmer has had the charity to offer to conduct him out of a very Serbonian-looking bog. In a word, the imprudent letter is for all substantial purposes, in fact—whatever even now is his Grace's lamentable misconception of the true theory of ordination—DISAVOWED AND RETRACTED; and, so far as this goes, of course it is a matter of congratulation. Everybody, all sorts of journals, organs of every class [everybody, always, everywhere, so that it must be a 'Catholic' truth] agreed in drawing an inference from the Archbishop's letter, for which we are now assured 'there is no ground whatever.' Common consent has for once, we suppose, been wrong."

We pause to point out to our readers the happy illustration this writer has afforded us of the real value of the everybody-always-everywhere argument, the true meaning of the Tractarian plea of "common consent."

We will add but one passage more from this production, for, in all seriousness, it is heart-sickening to transcribe such a tissue of misrepresentations and calumnies as are contained in that single article. "We are not exaggerating the value of his Grace's last letter, if we pronounce *the retractation of his note to Gawthorn to be inferentially complete.*" And with characteristic self-complacency and love of truth, the writer broadly intimates, that the public are indebted to himself and his fellow-laborers for having frightened the Archbishop into taking such a course.

These gentlemen are apt disciples of their quondam leader, Mr. Newman, whose open avowal of his having been in the habit of making certain statements, simply because they were "necessary for his position" in the part he was then playing in the Church of England, has probably not yet been forgotten by the public. Mr. Gawthorn has at least the satisfaction of finding that there is a considerable body, even of those professedly of the Church of England, whose love of truth appears to be scarcely more rigid than his own. Indeed it may be doubted, whether a single act like that of Mr. Gawthorn is not a less offence, and less injurious to morality, than the conduct of those who professing to be what they are not, sincere members of a Protestant Church, are constantly laboring to "unprotestantize" it.

The true character of the representation they have given of the Archbishop's second letter may be best learned by contrasting it with the statements of other writers of their own school. The remark of the *Guardian* on this letter, when it appeared, was, "We cannot pretend to say that" it "much changes the posture of affairs for better or worse," (Oct. 1.) And the Bristol Church Union has published a resolution, in which they distinctly maintain, that the Archbishop's "published explanation of the said letter, in his reply to the Rev. W. Palmer, has only served *more fully to elucidate the fact* that his Grace does not deem the imposition of Episcopal hands in all cases necessary to valid ordination," and protest against it accordingly. (*Guardian*, Oct. 15.)

And such is clearly the case. The Archbishop simply repudiated the views that had been falsely charged upon him, and reaffirmed his original statement, adding arguments in favor of it; and consequently, as any fair opponent would see, left the matter precisely as it stood before.

We have here, therefore, a remarkable proof of the fitness of these self-constituted ecclesiastical authorities for guiding the Church, when, in a matter so clear as this, they are thus contradicting and opposing one another.

But the truth is, that it was "necessary for the position" of certain of the Archbishop's opponents, that they should make out his second letter to be a retractation, for they had rashly committed themselves to an agitation which, it was evident, would be a failure. The Archbishop's repudiation of the views attributed to him would otherwise have produced not the slightest effect; for the imputations, being utterly without ground to rest upon, had evidently been made for the mere purpose of bringing disgrace upon him more readily than by calling him into question for what he really had said; which, however obnoxious to *them*, would have afforded them a poor handle with the public. He was to be punished for having spoken against the Tractarian doctrine; but this was not sufficiently popular for them to make it their professed ground of attack; and, therefore, according to the well-known tactics of many in this party, he was to be charged with maintaining something which might more plausibly be objected to. And no repudiation on his part of such views would for a moment have prevented their proceeding with their protests, if only there had been a chance of success. The ground of their quarrel lay much deeper than what was their nominal pretext for the assault. It was in fact the view he really held, that was the object of their attack, not the misrepresentation which for their own ends had been palmed upon him.

There is nothing more painful perhaps in the whole Tractarian movement, than the frequent disregard to truth by which, throughout its course, it has been characterized. Men entertaining Tractarian views are in *a false position* in our Church, and consequently are continually driven into all sorts of inconsistencies and offences against truth. And no declamatory asseverations of their doctrines being the genuine doctrines of the Church of England can deceive any who give the slightest attention to the subject, and desire to know the truth. They commenced with a profession of slavish submission to bishops; and their doctrine demands it of them. Their conduct is the very reverse, to a degree that makes us compare it with thankfulness with that of the supposed undervaluers of the Episcopate, the, to use the ordinary name, Evangelical body, towards other prelates in past times. Their *Catenas* parade with the most unblushing effrontery the names of divines who have directly and clearly opposed their views, as of advocates in their favor. The interpretation they are compelled to give to our Articles and Formularies (to say nothing of the veil of secrecy thrown over their practices) is such as to make the more honest among their disciples writhe under the consciousness of the duplicity of the course marked out for them. This is not the mere accusation of an opponent; it is the confession of those who have belonged to them. Witness (to refer to no other authority) the pamphlet, not long since published, entitled *The Morality of Tractarianism.* Whenever they have tried their ground before a public tribunal, they have been utterly defeated. In the face of facts like these, frothy declamations, protesting that they are the true exponents of the doctrine of the Church of England, will deceive none but those who wish to be deceived.

But to the point more immediately before us.

The great question raised in this controversy, is simply this: Whether it is a doctrine of the Church of England, that Episcopal ordination is a *sine qua non* to constitute a valid Christian ministry? *In what cases* Non-Episcopal Ordinations may (if ever) be valid, *is a farther question not now under consideration*, except so far as concerns the Foreign Churches referred to in the Archbishop's note.

The Archbishop holds the negative, his assailants maintain the affirmative of this question. And we are glad that the violence of the Tractarian party has brought the matter prominently before the public, as it affords a good opportunity of impressing upon the public mind the real doctrine of our Church on the subject, and of showing how grievously that party are misrepresenting it. The more such questions are publicly discussed, the better will it be for the cause of truth and sound Church-of-England principles. We have to thank the Tractarians for having *unintentionally* done good service to the cause of truth on more than one occasion, by giving an impulse to such investigations. The public would never have had such a complete conviction of the opposition of the doctrine of our Church to the Romish sacrifice in the Eucharist, and still less a Judgment respecting it, if the Tractarians had not attempted to force upon us stone altars. And certainly, for the public having become far better acquainted with the doctrine of our Church on the effects of Baptism, and for a Judgment of no ordinary value respecting it, we are greatly indebted to them. And it would give us no little pleasure, to find them again blundering into a court of justice in support of some other of their anti-Protestant dogmas.

In discussing the question now at issue, we shall point out—

I. The ground taken on this subject by our early divines.

This, in the absence of any definite statement on the subject in our Formularies, is clearly the best indication we can have of the mind of our Church respecting it, and of the meaning of any indirect notices touching it in our authoritative documents.

Let us first hear what Mr. Keble himself is compelled to admit on this point. Thus he writes :—

"Since the Episcopal succession had been so carefully retained in the Church of England, and so much anxiety evinced to render both her Liturgy and Ordination services strictly conformable to the rules and doctrines of antiquity, it might have been expected, that the defenders of the English hierarchy against the first Puritans should take the highest ground, and challenge for the bishops the same unreserved submission, on the same plea of exclusive apostolic prerogative, which their adversaries feared not to insist on for their elders and deacons. It is notorious, however, that such was not in general the line preferred [it was never adopted, as is *confessed* presently] by Jewel, Whitgift, Bishop Cooper, and others, to whom the management of that controversy was intrusted during the early part of Elizabeth's reign. They do not expressly disavow, but they carefully shun, that unreserved appeal to Christian antiquity, in which one would have thought they must have discerned the very strength of their cause to lie. It is enough, with them, to show that the government by archbishops and bishops is ancient and allowable; they never venture to urge its *exclusive* claim, or to connect the succession with the validity of the holy sacraments; and yet it is obvious, that such a course of argument alone (supposing it borne out by facts) could fully meet all the exigencies of the case. It must have occurred to the learned writers above mentioned, since it was the received doctrine of the Church down to their days; and if they had disapproved it, as some theologians of no small renown have since done, it seems unlikely that they should have passed it over without some express avowal of dissent; considering that they always wrote with an eye to the pretensions of Rome also, which popular opinion had in a great degree mixed up with this doctrine of apostolical succession." . . . . "Farther, it is obvious that those divines in particular who had been instrumental but a little before in the second change of the Liturgy in King Edward's time, must have felt themselves in some measure restrained from pressing with its entire force the ecclesiastical tradition on church government and orders, inasmuch as in the aforesaid revision they had given up altogether the same tradition, regarding certain very material points in the celebration, if not in the doctrine, of the holy Eucharist. . . . . It should seem that those who were responsible for these omissions must have felt themselves precluded, ever after, from urging the necessity of Episcopacy, or of anything else, on the ground of uniform Church tradition."*

Such a passage as this presents many topics for remark; and we may observe, in passing, that the doctrine of the necessity of Episcopacy seems to be confessedly rested on *tradition.* But the object for which we have quoted it, is to show the difficulties in which Mr. Keble confessedly finds himself involved in dealing with the views of our early divines on this subject. He admits, that they "never venture to urge the *exclusive* claim of the government by archbishops and bishops, or to connect the succession with the validity of the holy sacraments." But then it is

* Keble's Pref. to Hooker, pp. lix.—lxii.

hinted, that they *may* have held it, because they have not given an "express avowal of dissent" from it.

Now we hope our readers have too good an opinion of the honesty and fair dealing of those venerable men, not to feel assured, that, if they had held the doctrine of the absolute necessity of the Episcopal form of church government, they would have said so. Can we suppose that, in the midst of that intimate intercourse and communion they maintained with the Foreign Non-Episcopal Churches, they would never have admonished them of the fatal effect which their want of the Episcopal form of church government entailed upon their ministrations? Would they have acknowledged their ministers in the way they did, as fellow-laborers in the Church of Christ?

But in fact we shall find, from their own words, that they *do*, virtually at least, if not more expressly, *disavow* the doctrine advocated by Mr. Keble and his party. There was no necessity, at a time when no one in our Church thought of upholding such a doctrine, for them to write formally and expressly against it. But they do *disavow* such a notion, writing in a way irreconcilable with their holding it. And we must add farther, that it will be found that the authors whom Mr. Keble quotes as having first advocated his exclusive doctrine in our Church, bear witness against it.

Having thus seen how much our opponents are compelled to concede, let us proceed to consider the following testimonies:—

And we may notice, first, that even in the time of Henry VIII., at the very dawn of the Reformation, the bishops and clergy of our Church put forth a document containing the very doctrine on which the validity of Presbyterian ordinations has been chiefly rested, namely, the parity of bishops and presbyters, with respect to the ministerial powers, essentially and by right belonging to them. In the *Institution of a Christian Man*, put forth by the bishops and clergy in 1537, we read as follows:—

"As touching the sacrament of holy orders, we think it convenient that all bishops and preachers shall instruct and teach the people committed unto their spiritual charge, first, how that Christ and his apostles did institute and ordain, in the New Testament, that besides the civil powers and governance of kings and princes (which is called *potestas gladii*, the power of the sword), there should also be continually in the Church militant certain other ministers or officers, which should have special power, authority, and commission, under Christ, to preach and teach the word of God unto His people; to dispense and administer the sacraments of God unto them," &c. &c.

"That this office, this power and authority, was committed and given by Christ and his apostles unto certain persons only, that is to say, unto priests or bishops, whom they did elect, call, and admit thereunto, by their prayer and imposition of their hands."

And, speaking of "the sacrament of orders" to be administered by the bishop, it observes, when noticing the various orders in the Church of Rome: "*The truth is, that in the New Testament there is no mention made of any degrees or distinctions in orders, but only of deacons or ministers, and of priests or bishops.*" And throughout, when speaking of the jurisdiction and other privileges belonging to the ministry, it speaks of them as belonging to "priests and bishops."

Again, in the revision of this work set forth by the king in 1543, entitled *A Necessary Doctrine and Erudition for any Christian Man*, in the chapter on "the Sacrament of Orders," priests and bishops are spoken of as of the same order. For after having spoken of Timothy being "ordered and consecrated priest" by St. Paul, and remarked, "whereby it appeareth that St. Paul did consecrate and order priests and bishops by the imposition of his hands; and as the apostles themselves, in the beginning of the Church, did order priests and bishops, so they appointed and willed the other bishops after them to do the like, as St. Paul manifestly showeth, in his Epistle to Titus, saying, &c., and to Timothy, &c.;" it subjoins, shortly after: "Of these two orders only, that is to say, priests and deacons, Scripture maketh express mention, and how they were conferred of the apostles by prayer and imposition of their hands."*

Now this view certainly goes far to remove the difficulty as to recognizing the validity of Presbyterian ordination in the absence of bishops; and this view we see was entertained by the leading bishops and clergy in this country at the very dawn of the Reformation; and those who are at all acquainted with Ecclesiastical history, know that this view had long been advocated by many of the divines of the Church of Rome, especially among the scholastic divines, including their great founder, Peter Lombard, the Master of the Sentences.

Our opponents are fond of speaking of these early documents, published at the very dawn of the Reformation, as authoritative proofs of the doctrine of our Church. The above extracts may perhaps show them, that, however pleasant the first taste may be, there are some sours mixed up with the Romish sweets which these works contain; and if they will have the one, they must be satisfied to take the other.

We decline, for the sake of a momentary gain, to make any such illegitimate use of these documents. But this we do say, that if even *then* the Tractarian doctrine of Episcopacy was not held by our Church, much less is it conceivable that it was held after the current of our theology had taken a course so much more decidedly Protestant, and our divines were recognizing the ministers of the Foreign Non-Episcopal Churches as their colleagues in the ministry. In these extracts, we see the views on this subject with which our divines *commenced* the work of Reformation; and it will hardly be urged that, when they went forward on every other point, they retrograded in this.

But we have still stronger testimony to the views of the leading

* See Formularies of Faith, &c., pp. 101, 105, 278, 281. Oxford, 1825.

divines of the English Church at this period. In the autumn of 1540, certain questions were proposed by the king to the chief bishops and divines of the day,* of which the tenth was this: "Whether bishops or priests were first? and if the priests were first, then the priest made the bishop." With the wording of this question we have nothing to do, and should certainly be sorry to be made answerable for it; but our object is to see what views were elicited in the answers. Now to this question the Archbishop of Canterbury (Cranmer) replied: "The bishops and priests were at one time, and were not two things, but both one office in the beginning of Christ's religion." The Archbishop of York (Lee) says: "The name of a bishop is *not properly a name of order, but a name of office*, signifying an overseer. And although the inferior shepherds have also care to oversee their flock, yet, forsomuch as the bishop's charge is also to oversee the shepherds, the name of overseer is given to the bishops, and not to the other; and as they be *in degree* higher, so in their consecration we find difference even from the primitive Church." The Bishop of London (Bonner) says: "I think the bishops were first, and yet I think it is *not of importance, whether the priest then made the bishop, or else the bishop the priest;* considering (after the sentence of St. Jerome) that in the beginning of the Church there was none (or, if it were, very small) difference between a bishop and a priest, especially touching the signification." The Bishop of St. David's (Barlow), and the Bishop elect of Westminster (Thirlby), held that bishops and priests "*at the beginning were all one.*" Dr. Robertson, in his answer, says: "Nec opinor absurdum esse, ut sacerdos episcopum consecret, si episcopus haberi non potest." Dr. Cox (afterwards Bishop of Ely) says: "Although by Scripture (as St. Hierome saith) priests and bishops be one, and therefore the one not before the other, yet bishops, as they be now, were after priests, and therefore made of priests." Dr. Redmayn, the learned Master of Trinity College, Cambridge, says: "They be of like beginning, and at the beginning were both one, as St. Hierome and other old authors show by the Scripture, whereof one made another indifferently." Dr. Edgeworth says: "That the priests in the primitive Church made bishops, I think no inconvenience (as Jerome saith, in an *Epist. ad Evagrium*). Even like as soldiers should choose one among themselves to be their captain; so did priests choose one of themselves to be their bishop, for consideration of his learning, gravity, and good living, &c., and also for to avoid schisms among themselves by them, that some might not draw people one way, and others another way, if they lacked one Head among them." With respect to the other answers, which are from the Bishops of Rochester (Heath) and Carlisle (Aldrich), and Drs. Day, Oglethorp, Symmons, Tresham, and

* These questions and answers are given by Burnet, in his *History of the Reformation*, and Collyer, in his *Ecclesiastical History*.

Coren, it is difficult to judge what the views of the writers would have been on the point we are now considering.

All the leading divines, therefore, whose testimonies we have just quoted, were of opinion that bishops and priests were, properly and strictly speaking, of the same *order*, though differing in *degree.*

Nay, more; we find by the answers to the next question, that, even at that time, some were prepared to take the next step, and grant to presbyters, under some circumstances, the power to ordain presbyters; and that most of them replied uncertainly to the question. The question was this: "Whether a bishop hath authority to make a priest by the Scripture or no? *And whether any other but only a bishop can make a priest?*" The reply of Cranmer, Archbishop of Canterbury, goes much beyond what we should wish to plead for, and is as follows: "A bishop may make a priest by the Scripture, and so may princes and governors also, and that by the authority of God committed to them, and the people also by their election: for as we read that bishops have done it, so Christian emperors and princes usually have done it; and the people, before Christian princes were, commonly did elect their bishops and priests." The answers given by the rest to the latter part of the question were to the following effect. Dr. Cox (made in 1559 Bishop of Ely) and Dr. Tresham openly admit, that, in a case of necessity, others may ordain besides bishops. The Archbishop of York says: "That any other than bishops *or priests* may make a priest, we neither find in Scripture nor out of Scripture;" clearly implying that priests may make a priest. The Bishops of Rochester and Carlisle, the Bishop elect of Westminster, and Drs. Redmayn, Symmons, Robertson, Leighton, Curren, Edgeworth, and Oglethorp, reply only, that they have *never read* that others besides bishops assumed the power of ordaining. The Bishop of London and Dr. Day give no reply to this part of the question. So that not one ventures to determine definitively that the power of ordination belongs exclusively to bishops.

Such was the doctrine of the leading divines of our Church at this period on the subject. We may therefore safely leave it to the reader to determine, whether, when in 1549 they put forth the Ordinal, with a Preface in which they speak of the "three orders" of the Christian ministry, they meant to assert, that the Episcopal and Priestly orders were so completely two distinct orders, that the special duties for the performance of which bishops had been set apart could under no circumstances be performed by priests; and were not rather using the word "order" in a large and general sense; especially when we find that the Services never apply the word *order* or *ordering* to the making of bishops, but only in the case of deacons and priests, and speak of the *consecration* of bishops; and that most of our early divines, as, for instance, the most distinguished among the earliest defenders of our Church against the Puritans, Archbishop Whitgift held (as we shall show presently) that bishops and priests are, strictly speaking, of the same order.

Let us proceed to the divines of Queen Elizabeth's reign, when our Formularies were finally constituted and established as (with a few exceptions) they now stand.

Unfortunately, the question now at issue was not so brought into controversy at that period as to enable us to find many direct testimonies upon the subject; for no one but a professed Romanist dreamed of throwing a doubt upon the validity of the Orders of the divines of the Foreign Non-Episcopal Churches. We are therefore thrown upon their incidental notices of the matter. But even where the witness is not direct, it is sufficiently plain to indicate the doctrine held. And, in fact, the ground then taken on this subject by our leading divines was much lower than what the lowest of the (so-called) Low Churchmen of modern times have ordinarily maintained; for they expressly defend the position, that the form of church government adopted is a matter of indifference, left to the free choice of each Church for itself.

We give the precedence, as the order of time demands, to the learned Bishop of Exeter, Dr. Alley, who in his Prælections upon 1 Peter, read publicly in St. Paul's, in 1560, says:—

"What difference is between a bishop and a priest, S. Hierome, writing ad Titum, doth declare, whose words be these: 'Idem est ergo presbyter, qui episcopus,' &c.; a priest, therefore, is the same that a bishop is, &c."

And having given Jerome's words in full, he adds:—

"These words are alleged, that it may appear priests among the elders to have been *even the same that bishops were.* But it grew by little and little that the whole charge and cure should be appointed to one bishop within his precinct, that the seeds of dissension might utterly be rooted out." (Alley's *Poor Man's Library*, 2d ed. 1571, tom. i. fol. 95, 96.)

It could hardly be doubted, then, by one who held this, that if the circumstances of the Church required it, Presbyterian ordination would be valid.

About the same period, namely, in 1563, we have a much stronger testimony from Dr. Pilkington, then Bishop of Durham:—

"Yet remains one doubt unanswered in these few words, when he says, that 'the government of the Church was committed to bishops,' as though they had received a larger and higher commission from God of doctrine and discipline than other lower priests or ministers have, and thereby might challenge a greater prerogative. But this is to be understood, that *the privileges and superiorities, which bishops have above other ministers, are rather granted by men for maintaining of better order and quietness in commonwealths, than commanded by God in his word.* Ministers have better knowledge and utterance some than other, but their ministry is of equal dignity. God's commission and commandment is like and indifferent to all, priest, bishop, archbishop, prelate, by what name soever he be called. . . . . St. Paul calls the elders of Ephesus together, and says, 'the Holy Ghost made them bishops to rule the Church of God.' (Acts xx.) He writes also to the bishops of Philippos, meaning the ministers. . . . . St. Jerome, in his commentary on the 1st chapter *Ad. Tit.*, says that 'a bishop and a priest is all one.'. . . . A bishop is a name of office, labor, and pains." (*Confut. of an Addition. Works*, ed. Park Soc. pp. 493, 494.)

Both these were among the bishops who settled our Articles, on the accession of Queen Elizabeth.

Our next witness shall be Bishop Jewell, of whose standing in our Church it is unnecessary to add a word. On the parity of order in priests and bishops, he says :—

"Is it so horrible a heresy, as he [Harding] maketh it, to say, that by the Scriptures of God a bishop and a priest are all one? or knoweth he how far, and unto whom, he reacheth the name of an heretic? Verily Chrysostom saith : 'Between a bishop and a priest in a manner there is no difference.' (In 1 Tim. hom. 11.) S. Hierome saith. . . . 'The apostle plainly teacheth us, that priests and bishops be all one.' (ad Evagr.) S. Augustine saith : 'What is a bishop but the first priest; that is to say, the highest priest?' (In *Quæst, N. et V. Test.* q. 101.) So saith S. Ambrose : 'There is but one consecration (ordinatio) of priest and bishop; for both of them are priests, but the bishop is the first.' (In 1 Tim. c. 3.) All these and other more holy Fathers, together with St. Paul the apostle, for thus saying, by M. Harding's advice, must be holden for heretics." (*Def. of Apol.* Pt. ii. c. 9. div. i. *Works*, p. 202. See also Pt. ii. c. iii. div. i. p. 85.)

But there is a passage in his writings still more strongly bearing on the point in question. Harding had charged our Church with deriving its orders from apostate bishops, &c. Jewell replies :—

"Therefore we neither have bishops without church, nor church without bishops. Neither doth the Church of England this day depend of them whom you often call apostates, as if our Church were no Church without them. . . . . *If there were not one, neither of them nor of us left alive, yet would not therefore the whole Church of England flee to Lovaine.* Tertullian saith : 'And we being laymen, are we not priests? It is written, Christ hath made us both a kingdom and priests unto God his Father. The authority of the Church, and the honor by the assembly, or council of order sanctified of God, hath made a difference between the lay and the clergy. Where as there is no assembly of ecclesiastical order, the priest being there alone (without the company of other priests) doth both minister the oblation and also baptize. Yea, and be there but three together, and though they be laymen, yet is there a church. For every man liveth of his own faith.'" (*Def. of Apol.* Pt. ii. c. v. div. i. p. 129.)

It is needless to point out how much this passage implies.

We proceed to Archbishop Whitgift.

And first, as to the parity of order in bishops and priests, he speaks thus:—

"Every bishop is a priest, but every priest hath not *the name and title* of a bishop, in that meaning that Jerome in this place [*Ad Evagr.*] taketh the name of a bishop . . . Neither shall you find this word *episcopus* commonly used but for *that priest that is in degree over and above the rest*, notwithstanding *episcopus* be oftentimes called *presbyter*, because *presbyter* is *the more general name.*" (*Def. of Answ. to Adm.* 1574, fol. p. 383.)

"Although Hierome confess, that by Scripture *presbyter* and *episcopus* is all one (AS IN DEED THEY BE *quoad ministerium*), yet doth he acknowledge a superiority of the bishop before the minister. . . . . Therefore no doubt this is Jerome's mind, that a bishop *in degree and dignity* is above the minister, though he be one and the self-same with him in the office of ministering the word and sacraments." (*Ib.* pp. 384, 385.)

Secondly, as to the form of government to be followed in the Church. His adversary Cartwright, like the great body of the Puritans, contended for the exclusive admissibility of the platform of church government he advocated; and, like Archdeacon Denison, maintained that "matters of discipline and kind of government are matters necessary to salvation and of faith." And this is Whitgift's reply:—

"I confess that in a church collected together in one place, and at liberty, government is necessary in the second kind of necessity; but that any one kind of government is so necessary that without it the Church cannot be saved, *or that it may not be altered into some other kind thought to be more expedient,* I utterly deny, and the reasons that move me so to do be these. The first is, because *I find no one certain and perfect kind of government prescribed or commanded in the Scriptures to the Church of Christ,* which no doubt should have been done, if it had been a matter necessary unto the salvation of the Church. Secondly, because *the essential notes of the Church be these only; the true preaching of the word of God, and the right administration of the sacraments:* for (as Master Calvin saith, in his book against the Anabaptists): 'This honor is meet to be given to the word of God, and to his sacraments, that wheresoever we see the word of God truly preached, and God according to the same truly worshipped, and the sacraments without superstition administered, there we may without all controversy conclude the Church of God to be:' and a little after: 'So much we must esteem the word of God and his sacraments, that wheresoever we find them to be, there we may certainly know the church of God to be, although in the common life of men many faults and errors be found.' The same is the opinion of other godly and learned writers and the judgment of *the Reformed Churches*, as appeareth by their Confessions. So that notwithstanding government, or some kind of government, may be a part of the Church, touching the outward form and perfection of it, yet is it not such a part of the essence and being, but that it may be the Church of Christ without this or that kind of government, and therefore the kind of government of the Church is not necessary unto salvation." (*Ib.* p. 81.)

"*I deny that the Scriptures do . . . . set down any one certain form and kind of government of the Church to be perpetual for all times, persons, and places without alteration.*" (*Ib.* p. 84.)

And speaking of the platform of church government contended for by Cartwright, he says:—

"Yet would I not have any man to think that I *condemn any churches where this government is lawfully and without danger received*; only I have regard to whole kingdoms, especially this realm, where it cannot but be dangerous." (*Ib.* p. 658.)

In *Tract* 17, c. iv. he undertakes expressly to prove: "That there is no one certain kind of government in the Church which must of necessity be perpetually observed." (*Ib.* p. 658.) And he remarks in it:—

"It is plain that any one certain form or kind of external government perpetually to be observed, is *nowhere in the Scripture prescribed to the Church;* but the charge thereof is left to the Christian magistrate, so that nothing be done contrary to the word of God." (*Ib.* p. 659).

The equality of bishops and presbyters *jure divino*, was also expressly maintained at this period by the learned Dr. W. Whitaker, Reg. Prof. of Div. at Cambridge. Among other remarks on the subject, he says, referring to Jerome's words in his *Commentary on Titus*, c. i.:—

"Si Episcopi *consuetudine* non *dispositione Dominica* presbyteris majores sunt, tum humano non divino jure totum hoc discrimen constat." (*Resp. ad Camp. defens. adv. J. Duræum.* lib. vi. *Op.* tom. i. p. 149.)

And to the reference of his opponent to Jerome's Epistle to Evagrius, showing that the power of ordination had been placed in the hands of the bishop, he replies:—

"Quod autem affers ex eadem Epistola, ad humanam non divinam constitutionem pertinet. Etsi enim ortu suo iidem erant ambo, *postea tamen* (inquit Hieronymus) *unus electus est, qui cæteris præponeretur;* atque inde natum est illud episcopi ac presbyteri discrimen." (*Ibid.*)

Of course, then, that which owed its origin to human appointment might, by the same authority, in any individual church, be laid aside.

Our next witness shall be Hooker, in himself a host. And when our readers have perused the extracts we are about to give from his writings, they will be able to judge of the honesty with which his name has been used in favor of the exclusive doctrine of the Tractarians, both in their Catenas and in their recent onslaught on the Primate.

"Now whereas hereupon (he observes) some do infer that no ordination can stand, but only such as is made by bishops which have had their ordination likewise by other bishops before them, till we come to the very Apostles of Christ themselves; in which respect *it was demanded of Beza* at Poissie, 'By what authority he could administer the holy sacraments, &c.' [Our readers will observe *the instance cited,* the very case now in question between the Archbishop and his assailants.] . . . . To this we answer, *that there may be sometimes very just and sufficient reason* TO ALLOW ORDINATION MADE WITHOUT A BISHOP. The whole Church visible being the true original subject of all power, it hath not ordinarily allowed any other than bishops alone to ordain; howbeit, as the ordinary course is ordinarily in all things to be observed, so it may be, in some cases, not unnecessary that we decline from the ordinary ways. Men may be extraordinarily, yet allowably, two ways *admitted unto spiritual functions in the Church.* One is, when God Himself doth of Himself raise up any . . . . . Another . . . . when the exigence of necessity doth constrain to leave the usual ways of the Church, which otherwise we would willingly keep." (*Eccl. Pol.* vii. 14. See also iii. 11.)

Here is a direct assertion of the validity of such orders as those of Beza.

And in a former passage of the same book, he distinctly admits the power of the Church at large to take away the Episcopal form of government from the Church, and says:—

"*Let them* [i. e. *bishops*] *continually bear in mind, that it is rather the force of custom, whereby the Church, having so long found it good to continue under the regiment of her virtuous bishops, doth still uphold, maintain, and honor them in that respect, than that any such true and heavenly law can be showed by the evidence whereof it may of a truth appear, that the Lord himself hath appointed presbyters forever to be under the regiment of bishops;"* adding, that "*their authority*" is "*a sword which the Church hath power to take from them.*" (*Ib.* vii. 5. See also i. 14, and iii. 10.)

And, therefore, though he admits the office and superiority of bishops to be of Apostolical institution, and takes much higher ground on the subject than most of his contemporaries, yet all that he expressly undertakes to prove on the subject is, that such superiority is "*a thing allowable, lawful, and good.*" (*Ib.* vii. 3.)

We will take next the testimony of Hadrian Saravia; of whom Mr. Keble writes thus:—

"Saravia is a distinct and independent testimony to the doctrine of *exclusive* [the Italics are ours] divine right in bishops. . . . . And since Saravia was afterwards in familiar intercourse with Hooker, and his confidential adviser when writing on nearly the same subjects, we may with reason use the recorded opinions of the one for interpreting what might seem otherwise ambiguous in the other." (*Pref. to Hooker*, p. lxvii.)

Now certainly Hadrian Saravia took very high ground in his defence of Episcopacy, maintaining that the Episcopal authority was of Divine institution and Apostolical tradition, and was taught as well by the word of God as the universal consent of all Churches;* yet in the same work he speaks thus:—

"In our fathers' memory Luther, Bucer, Œcolampadius, and others, had no other calling than that which they had received in the Church of Rome; and when it happened to them to be called before Cæsar, no question respecting their calling could ever be justly raised; and if it had been, they had an answer ready more fit in my judgment than that which was made at the Conference at Poissy. . . . . For although all who had assembled there before the king had not the same kind of ordination, and some were ordained by bishops of the Church of Rome, *others by the Reformed Churches, none of them ought to have been ashamed of his ordination.* They might, so far as I can see, without any danger, have professed that they had been *ordained and called*, some by bishops of the Church of Rome, *others by orthodox presbyters*, in the order received in the Churches of Christ, after an examination of their morals and doctrine, and with the authority of the magistrate and consent of the people, with the imposition of hands and prayer. Although I am of opinion that ordinations of ministers of the Church properly belong to bishops, yet necessity causes that when they are wanting and cannot be had, *orthodox presbyters can in case of necessity ordain a presbyter;* which thing, although it is not in accordance with the order received from the times of the Apostles, yet is excused by the necessity of the case, which causes that in such a state of things a presbyter may be a bishop. Moreover, although the act is out of the usual order, the calling is not to be considered extraordinary." [And then, having remarked that no one ought to receive orders from an heretical bishop, and that the Romish bishops were all heretics, he adds:] "This also is true, that in such a state of confusion in the Church, when all the bishops fall away from the true worship of God unto idolatry, without any violation of the government of the Church, the whole authority of the Episcopal ecclesiastical government is devolved upon the pious and orthodox presbyters, *so*

* Episcopalem authoritatem Divinæ institutionis et Apostolicæ traditionis esse defendo, et id tam Verbo Dei quam universali omnium Ecclesiarum consensu doceri.—(*Defens. Tract. de div. Ministr. Ev. gradibus: In Epist. dedicat.*) Op. 1611.

that a presbyter clearly may ordain presbyters. . . . . There is one God, one Lord Jesus Christ, one Church, one Baptism, one Ministry. The difference there is between presbyters and pastors of the Church of Christ consists in the authority of Ecclesiastical government. And this is not violated, when the higher orders being in any way removed, those who are of the lowest grade alone remain, with whom, consequently, *the whole power of the keys of the Church then resides.* . . . . But where all the bishops are become impious heretics, the orthodox presbyters are freed from their jurisdiction, and ought to vindicate to themselves the power of the keys which they have received in their ordination. . . . . I certainly know not by what necessity Master Beza should have been compelled to resort to an extraordinary calling. *For I do not think that either he, or Nicholas Galasius, or any other that may have been then present, not ordained by Romish bishops, took upon themselves the ministry of the Word without a legitimate calling received in the Churches of Christ.*"*

Nor did he hold that the Foreign Non-Episcopal Churches were bound to seek Episcopacy from some Reformed Episcopal Church, for he says: "If they call in the aid of our men, and wish to use their advice, they can; but if they do not, they ought not to arrogate to themselves any authority over them and their churches, but to rejoice, and congratulate them upon their conversion, and offer them communion (*offerre societatem*)."†

So that here again we have a direct testimony in favor of the validity of the ordinations of the Foreign Non-Episcopal Churches.

Let us take next the testimony of Dr. John Bridges, then (1587) Dean of Salisbury, afterwards Bishop of Oxford. He, as we shall see, agrees with Archbishop Whitgift, that the form of church government is a matter left to the discretion of each church. He speaks of it, indeed, in language which we cannot reconcile with the respect we feel due to the primitive form of church government; but yet he was one of the most able and distinguished prelates of that period.

With respect to the question of *order* in the case of bishops and priests, he expressly maintains that bishops are superiors, "*not in the office of their order*, yet in the office of their dignity;" (*Defence of the Government Established in the Church of England*, 1587, 4to. p. 287); and he speaks of the Episcopal state as "a high calling, not so much of superior dignity, as of superior charge in governing of God's Church." (*Ib.* p. 288.)

And on the subject of the Episcopal government of the Church—opposing the notion of the Puritans, against whom he was writing, that one certain form only was allowable—he writes thus:—

"If now, on the other side, this be not a matter of necessity, but such as may be varied, being but a form and manner of Ecclesiastical government, as the observation of this feast and these fasts were of accustomed order, not of necessity; then, so long as it is used in moderate sort, without tyranny or pride, nor anything contrary to the proportion of faith and godliness of life

* Defens. Tract. de div. Ministr. Ev. gradibus, &c. ch. ii. pp. 32, 33. We translate from the Latin.

† Ib. p. 18.

necessarily maintained thereby (for otherwise, if those fasts or this feast had been used to be kept superstitiously, it had been so far forth to be condemned), there is no reason why we should break the bond of peace, and make such trouble in the Church of God, to reject the government *that in the nature thereof is as much indifferent as the solemnizing this or that day the memorial of the Lord's resurrection.* And yet we celebrate the same on the Sunday only, as those Bishops of Rome at that time did. Which I hope we do without all offence, though we have no precept in Scripture for it. And therefore, as Polycarpus and Anicetus, differing in that point, notwithstanding did not violate the peace and unity of the Church, so, according to Irenæus's rule, while no such excessive superiority is maintained of us, as the Pope since that time hath usurped, but such as we find practised in the primitive Church and in the very apostles' age, *we ought neither to condemn, nor speak, nor think evil of other good Churches that use another Ecclesiastical government than we do;* neither ought they to do the like of ours. Not that every person *in one and the same Church* should use this liberty of difference, without controlment and restraint of the superior in that Church wherein he liveth. For, though it were lawful for one Church to differ from another, being not so tied to uniformity, as to unity; yet is it not meet for one Church to differ from itself; but to be both in unity, and be ruled also by uniformity. Especially where law binds them to obedience." (*Ib.* pp. 319, 320.)

Another of the most able prelates of our Church, and defender of it against the Puritans, was Dr. Thomas Cooper, Bishop, first of Lincoln, and afterwards of Winchester. In the year 1589, he published an *Admonition to the People of England*, in answer to the attacks of the Puritan party. And thus he defends in this work the form of church government established in this country :—

"As touching the government of the Church of England, now defended by the bishops, this I say. When God restored the doctrine of the Gospel more sincerely and more abundantly than ever before, under that good, young prince King Edward VI. . . . . by consent of all the States of this land, this manner of government that now is used was by law confirmed *as good and godly*....... As for this question of church government, I mean not at this time to stand much on it.... *Only this I desire, that they will lay down out of the word of God some just proofs, and a direct commandment, that there should be in all ages and states of the Church of Christ one only form of outward government.*" (Ed. Lond. 1847, pp. 61–63.)

So that, far from maintaining the necessity of the Episcopal form of church government, he, on the contrary, challenges his opponents to prove that any particular form of church government is necessary. And he adds :—

"Surely, as grave learned men as most that have written in this time.... do make good proof of this proposition. *That one form of church government is not necessary in all times and places of the Church*, and that their Senate or Segniorie is not convenient under a Christian magistrate."

And after pointing out the different forms of church government that prevailed in the Foreign Non-Episcopal Churches, he says :—

"All those churches in which the gospel in these days, after great darkness, was first renewed, and the learned men whom God sent to instruct them, I doubt not but *have been directed by the Spirit of God to retain this liberty* that in external government and other outward orders, they might choose such as they thought in wisdom and godliness to be most convenient for the state of their country and disposition of the people. *Why, then, should this liberty that other countries have used under any color be wrested from us?*" (*Ib.* p. 66.)

"*The reason that moveth us* not to like of this platform of government is, that when we on the one part consider the things that are required to be redressed, and on the other the state of our country, people, and common-weal, we see evidently, that to plant those things in this Church will draw with it so many and so great alterations of the state of government and of the laws, as the attempting thereof might bring rather the overthrow of the gospel among us, than the end that is desired." (*Ib.* p. 67.)

This of course disposes of the doctrine of our opponents, root and branch.

We will add but one more authority for the reign of Queen Elizabeth. We began with the Bishop of Exeter; we will end with one of whose high authority as the proper expounder of the doctrine of our Church we have lately heard much—the Dean of the Arches. We beg the attention of our opponents to the following statement of the very learned and able Dean of the Arches in 1584, Dr. Richard Cosin. It occurs in his answer, "published by authority," to a Puritan work entitled *An Abstract of Certain Acts of Parliament.* He is opposing the notion that "a set form" of "external policy of discipline and ceremonies" is "set down in Scripture," and he says:—

"Are all the Churches of Denmark, Sweveland, Poland, Germany, Rhetia, Vallis, Tellina, the nine cantons of Switzerland reformed, with their confederates of Geneva, of France, of the Low Countries, and of Scotland, in all points, either of substance or of circumstance, disciplinated alike? Nay, they neither are, can be, *nor yet need so to be;* seeing it *cannot be proved, that any set and exact particular form thereof is recommended unto us by the word of God.*" (*Answer to an Abstract, &c.* 1584, 4to. p. 58.)

Such are the statements of some of the best authorities for the doctrine of our Church in the time of Queen Elizabeth, in whose reign our Articles and Formularies were settled (with slight exceptions) in their present form. *And we now challenge the Archbishop's assailants to produce their authorities for the same period.* Can they bring even one for *their doctrine?* We do not believe it. And upon the testimonies of this period, be it remembered, must rest the proof of the original and genuine doctrine of our Reformed Protestant Church. That there was a declension from that doctrine afterwards, in many of our divines, is freely confessed. But that proves nothing. It can neither alter nor add to the doctrine of our Church, as laid down in her Formularies drawn up in the time of the divines from whom we have been quoting. And we shall give presently a series of testimonies, from their times to our own, showing that their view has, in the main, been held by a large proportion of our greatest divines ever since; and farther, that even the highest among our eminent High Church divines (as they are called), have never advocated the extreme notions maintained by the Tractarians.

The ground taken by our early divines, as shown by the testimonies above given, was, that the Episcopal form of Church government is the best and the most scriptural, and comes recommended to us by the practice of the Church even from the times of the Apostles, but has not been authoritatively laid down by Christ or his Apostles as of indispensable obligation, and therefore is not binding upon all Churches.

They did not oppose the early Nonconformists, on the ground of the absolute necessity of the Episcopal form of Church government, still less of a succession of bishops consecrated by bishops, to constitute a Church. They left such notions to the Romanists. But they found fault with them, as throwing a well-constituted Church into confusion and disorder, as causing needless schisms and divisions, and as sinfully disobeying the ordinances of the Supreme Power in the State, which had established a Christian Church agreeable to Holy Scripture and Apostolic practice. The high-flown claims of our Tractarian High Churchmen to the *exclusive admissibility* of one system of Church government, were the weapons, not of the divines of our Church, but of their opponents the Nonconformists. The Genevan platform of Church government, was with the Puritans that which alone was conformable to the word of God. Every other, but especially the Prelatical, was to be eschewed as an abomination. And, as to the power of the civil ruler in religious matters, they spoke of it—much as the Tractarians now speak of it; except that under Elizabeth they muttered in the dark what under Victoria is proclaimed in the market-place.* Thus it is that extremes meet.

Precisely in accordance with these views of our early divines are:—

II. *The Articles and other Formularies* which were drawn up by the school of theologians to which they belonged.

Thus, in the Article of our Church on the subject of the ministry, we find it carefully worded, so as not to limit a lawful ministry to those that have Episcopal ordination.

"It is not lawful (says the Article) for any man to take upon him the office of public preaching or ministering the sacraments in the congregation, before he be lawfully called and sent to execute the same. And those we ought to judge lawfully called and sent, which be chosen and called to this work by men who have public authority given unto them, *in the congregation*, to call and send ministers into the Lord's vineyard." (Art. 23.)

It should seem hardly possible for one acquainted with the circumstances of those times, to read this Article and not see that it

* Hence we may remark, by the way, that when we are considering the events of that period, and the apparent (and to some extent real) absence of those principles of toleration now so happily established among us, it must not be forgotten, that the object of the early Nonconformist was, not the mere toleration of their own system, but the utter subversion of the system of church government then established by the consent of the sovereign, the clergy, and the people, and the substitution of their own in its stead. This was notoriously and confessedly their aim; and this it was which infused so much wrath and bitterness into the controversies of the period.

is carefully worded, so as not to exclude the ministry of the Foreign Non-Episcopal Churches.

But a more authentic interpretation of this Article can hardly be conceived than that given by Thomas Rogers, chaplain to Archbishop Bancroft, in his *Exposition of the Articles*, published in 1607, as "perused, and by the lawful authority of the Church of England allowed to be public," and which the Archbishop ordered all the parishes in his province to supply themselves with. He deduces from the Article the six following propositions :—

"1. None publicly may preach but such as thereunto are authorized. 2. They must not be silent who by office are bound to preach. 3. The sacraments may not be administered in the congregation but by a lawful minister. 4. There is a lawful ministry in the Church. 5. They are lawful ministers which be ordained by men lawfully appointed to the calling and sending forth of ministers. 6. Before ministers are to be ordained, they are to be chosen and called."

And then, proceeding to point out the testimonies we have in favor of the truth of these propositions, he observes upon each, as he comes to it, that the Foreign Reformed Churches maintain it. On the first: "All this is acknowledged by the Reformed Churches;" referring to the Helvetic, Bohemic, French, and other Confessions. On the second: "Hereunto bear witness all the Churches of God which be purged from superstition and errors;" referring to the same Confessions. On the third: "Hereunto do the Churches of God subscribe;" referring to the same Confessions. On the fourth: "A truth also approved by the Churches;" referring to the same Confessions. On the fifth: "So testify with us the true Churches elsewhere in the world;" referring to the same Confessions. On the sixth: "And this do the Churches Protestant by their Confessions approve;" referring to the same Confessions.*

And this is not only a testimony as to the meaning of the Article, but as to the light in which the Foreign Non-Episcopal Churches were then regarded by the authorities of our Church, even by so high a Churchman (to use the common phrase) as Archbishop Bancroft.

Proceeding to a later period, we find Bishop Burnet thus commenting on this Article :—

"If a company of Christians find the public worship where they live to be so defiled that they cannot with a good conscience join in it, and if they do not know of any place to which they can conveniently go, where they may worship God purely and in a regular way; if, I say, such a body, finding some that have been ordained, though to the lower functions, should submit itself entirely to their conduct, or finding none of those, should by a common consent desire some of their own number to minister to them in holy things, and should upon that beginning grow up to a regulated constitution, though we are very sure that this is quite out of all rule, and could not be done

* "The Faith, Doctrine, and Religion, &c., expressed in 39 Articles, &c.; the said Articles analyzed into propositions, and the propositions proved to be agreeable both to the written word of God *and to the extant Confessions of all the neighbor Churches Christianly reformed.*" 1607. 4to.

without a very great sin, unless the necessity were great and apparent; yet if the necessity is real and not feigned, this is not condemned or annulled by the Article; for when this grows to a constitution, and when it was begun by the consent of a Body, who are supposed to have an authority in such an extraordinary case, *whatever some hotter spirits have thought of this since that time, yet we are very sure, that not only those who penned the Articles, but the Body of this Church for above half an age after, did, notwithstanding those irregularities, acknowledge the Foreign Churches, so constituted, to be true Churches as to all the essentials of a Church, though they had been at first irregularly formed, and continued still to be in an imperfect state. And therefore the general words in which this part of the Article is framed, seem to have been designed on purpose not to exclude them.*" (Burnet's *Exposition of the XXXIX. Articles*, 5th ed. 1746.)

And Professor Hey justly remarks, that the expression, "who have public authority given unto them in the congregation," "seems to leave the *manner* of giving the power of ordaining quite free: it seems as if any religious society might, consistently with this Article, appoint officers, with power of ordination, by election, representation, or lot; as if, therefore, the right to ordain did not depend upon any uninterrupted *succession*." (*Lectures in Divinity*, 2d ed. 1822, vol. iv. p. 166.)

The same view is taken of the meaning of this Article by Bishop Tomline, ordinarily considered a sufficiently high churchman. (*Expos. of Art.* ed. 1799, p. 376.)

It is quite clear that the words of the Article do not maintain the necessity of Episcopal ordination; and consequently, as the object of the Article is to show the doctrine of the Church of England on the subject, it cannot be said that the Church of England maintains it. No one, therefore, has a right to put forth such a doctrine as the doctrine of the Church of England.

This is the only place in which our Church touches the question of ordination in the abstract; and we see that it is carefully worded, so as to be consistent with the constitution of the Foreign Reformed Churches.

The notice of the three orders of the ministry as having existed from the times of the Apostles in the *Preface to the Ordination Service*, is simply the statement of a fact, which does not touch the question of the validity of the Orders of the Foreign Non-Episcopal Churches. The defence of their case rests upon the peculiar circumstances in which they were placed. And the recognition even of the necessity of Episcopal ordination for ministering in the Church of England was not added till the review after the Restoration; so that, as we shall see presently, those who had only Presbyterian ordination, had previously been allowed to minister in our Church. But this irregularity was very properly put an end to at the Restoration, both by the *Preface to the Ordination Service*, and also by the Act of Uniformity. (13, 14 Car. II. c. 4.)

We are therefore unable to understand the following remarks in a note in the Bishop of London's *Sermons on the Church.* His lordship says:—

"Our Reformers, in the Book of Consecration, approved in the 36th Article, *insist strongly on the necessity of Episcopal ordination*, a point which, as Bishop Sanderson says, 'has been constantly and uniformly maintained by our best writers, and by all the sober, orderly, and orthodox sons of the Church;' but they do not presume to say that it is impossible, under any circumstances, for a Church to exist without it. We may, however, set their formal approval of the Consecration Book against the private opinions of Archbishop Cranmer, in his answers to the ninth question concerning church government." (P. 62.)

Now the simple fact is, that there is not one word about "the necessity of Episcopal ordination" in that book, as drawn up by the Reformers, and sanctioned by the Article. The words that relate to that point were not inserted in the book until the review in the time of Charles II., and then refer only to the ministry of the Church of England. They do not declare the necessity of Episcopal ordination to any valid ministry; nor (we think) does Bishop Sanderson. Consequently, the last observation falls to the ground; and we may observe, that "the private opinions of Archbishop Cranmer" on the point, as shown in his Answers (not to the ninth, but) to the tenth and eleventh Questions on Church Government, were (as we have shown) shared with him, *sufficiently for our present purpose*, by many others of the leading divines of his day.

But still farther; by the 55th Canon of 1604, all our clergy are required, in the bidding prayer before, or rather in the commencement of the sermon, to pray for "the Church of Scotland." Now the Church of Scotland, at the time this canon was passed, was Presbyterian, as it now is. And, consequently, the very men who are now protesting against the recognition of any ordinations as valid but Episcopal, and contending that it is the doctrine of our Church that there is no such thing as a valid ministry but through an apostolically descended episcopate, are by canon bound solemnly to recognize in their prayers every Sunday the existence of a valid ministry without any such ordination. For a prayer for the Presbyterian "Church of Scotland" clearly involves such a recognition.

Some of her majesty's predecessors have occasionally ordered this canon to be observed. It would be but a fair return (though we are far from desiring it) for the remarks in which certain parties are often indulging themselves, that they should be favored with a similar order. They are very fond of appealing to rubrics and canons, when they suit their purpose; and none, we will venture to say, would be more unwilling, consistently, and impartially, to carry them out into practice.

III. The practice of our Church for many years after the Reformation entirely refutes the notion that she holds the ordinations of the Scotch and Foreign Non-Episcopal Churches to be invalid; for, *until the period of the Restoration, ministers of those*

Churches were admitted to the cure of souls in our Church without any fresh ordination.

In 1582 (April 6) a license was granted by the Vicar-General of the Archbishop of Canterbury (Grindal) to a minister of the name of John Morrison, who had only Scotch orders, in the following terms:—

"Since you, the foresaid John Morrison, about five years past, in the town of Garvet in the county of Lothian of the kingdom of Scotland, were *admitted and ordained to sacred orders and the holy ministry, by the imposition of hands, according to the laudable form and rite of the Reformed Church of Scotland;* and since the congregation of that county of Lothian is conformable to the orthodox faith and sincere religion now received in this realm of England, and established by public authority; we therefore, as much as lies in us, and as by right we may, *approving and ratifying the form of your ordination and preferment* (*præfectionis*) done in such manner aforesaid, grant to you a license and faculty, *with the consent and express command* of the most reverend Father in Christ the Lord Edmund, by the Divine providence Archbishop of Canterbury, to us signified, that *in such orders by you taken* you may, and have power, in any convenient places in and throughout the whole province of Canterbury, *to celebrate divine offices, to minister the sacraments, &c.*, as much as in us lies, and we may *de jure*, and as far as the laws of the kingdom do allow, &c." (*Strype's Life of Grindal*, Bk. 2, c. xiii. p. 271; or Oxf. ed. p. 402.)

To this we need only add the testimony of Bishop Cosin, confessedly (as the phrase goes) a High Churchman. He says, in an admirable letter on this subject, written from Paris, Feb. 7, 1650, from which we shall presently give a large extract:—

"Therefore, if at any time a minister so ordained in these French Churches came to incorporate himself in ours, and to receive a public charge or cure of souls among us in the Church of England (as I have known some of them to have so done of late, and can instance in *many other* before my time), *our bishops did not reordain him before they admitted him to his charge, as they must have done, if his former ordination here in France had been void.* NOR DID OUR LAWS REQUIRE MORE OF HIM THAN TO DECLARE HIS PUBLIC CONSENT TO THE RELIGION RECEIVED AMONGST US, AND TO SUBSCRIBE THE ARTICLES ESTABLISHED."—(Letter to Mr. Cordel, in Basire's "Account of Bishop Cosin," annexed to his "Funeral Sermon;" and also in Bishop Fleetwood's *Judgment of the Church of England in the case of Lay Baptism*, 2d. ed. Lond. 1712, p. 52.)

And the same testimony is borne by Bishop Fleetwood, who says that this was "certainly her practice [*i. e.* of our Church] during the reigns of King James and King Charles I. and to the year 1661. We had many ministers from Scotland, from France, and the Low Countries, who were ordained by presbyters only, and not bishops, and they were instituted into benefices with cure. . . . and yet were never reordained, but only subscribed the Articles." (*Judgm. of Church of Engl. in case of Lay Baptism*, 1712. 8vo. pt. ii. *Works*, p. 552.)

If these cases do not prove, that at least our Church has never disowned the validity of the ordinations of the Scotch and Foreign Non-Episcopal Churches, and that her *practice* till the Restoration was to recognize their validity, nothing would do so. For Dr.

Cosin, who must have been well acquainted with the matter (having filled important posts in the Church since the year 1616, and been librarian to Bishop Overal, and domestic chaplain to Bishop Neale), speaks of it, not as a custom with *some* only, but as the practice of "the bishops" generally, and sanctioned by the law.

The last sentence in the extract from Dr. Cosin, no doubt refers to the Act 13 Eliz. c. 12, in which it was enacted, that any professing to be a priest or minister of God's word and sacraments, who had been ordained by any other form than that authorized by Edw. VI. and Queen Elizabeth, should be called upon to declare his assent and subscribe to the Articles of religion. The parties more particularly in the eye of the framers of the Act were probably those ordained by the Romish form, but the application of the clause was of course general.

True, as we have already observed, after the Restoration this was altered. The Act of Uniformity 13, 14 Car. II. c. 4, §§ 13, 14, requires that all admitted to any "ecclesiastical promotion or dignity whatsoever" in our Church, or to administer the Lord's Supper, should have had "Episcopal ordination." And a clause of a similar kind was added in the Preface to the Ordination Services; the words, "or hath had formerly Episcopal consecration or ordination," being inserted at that time.

But this could not affect the doctrine of our Church as previously laid down in the Articles. The Article declaring the doctrine of our Church on the subject of admission to the ministerial office remained the same as it was when ministers of the Foreign Non-Episcopal Churches were freely permitted to minister in our churches. But the Episcopal form of church government being established in our Church, it was very reasonably required by the Act, that all who held any "promotion" in it should have received Episcopal ordination, and this especially at a time when the benefices of the Church had been filled by men attached to the Presbyterian form of church government, and the Episcopalian ministers ejected from them. The state of things at the time shows the object which the Act had in view, as no attempt had been made previously to get such a law passed against the admission of ministers of Non-Episcopal Churches. And in the very next section of the Act (§ 15) we find a recognition of those communities as "the Foreign Reformed Churches." The fact that our Church requires all who hold office in her communion to be ordained according to that form of church government which she has chosen to follow, proves nothing as to her doctrine on the abstract question of the validity of the Orders of Non-Episcopal Churches.

Once more; if it were the case that our Church held all but Episcopal ordinations to be invalid, and that only those who have been ordained by bishops are entitled to preach the word and administer both the sacraments, the whole Bench of Bishops have been for more than a century, if not at the present moment, involved in the guilt of acting directly contrary to the doctrine of the Church; for the missionaries sent out as ordained ministers by the Society for the propagation of the Gospel, which is under the especial direction of the Bench of Bishops, used to be for the most part only in Lutheran orders; and if the practice has been given up, its discontinuance must be of very recent date.

We ought not to omit to add, that in former times collections for the relief of the *ministers* of some of the Foreign Non-Episcopal Churches were made in our churches by public authority. A Royal Brief was issued by Charles I. during the archiepiscopate of Archbishop Laud himself, ordering a collection to be thus made for "*the ministers* in the Palatinate," which was forwarded to the bishops by Laud, in a letter, concluding, "not doubting of your best assistance and furtherance in a work so pious and full of charity, &c." (*Wilk. Conc.* iv. 516.) Several instances of such collections might be adduced.

On these grounds, then, namely, the witness of our early divines, the statements of our Formularies, and the practice of our Church, we maintain, without hesitation, that our Church does not hold the doctrine of the exclusive validity of Episcopal Orders.

We admit that, in that great alteration that gradually took place subsequently to the reign of Elizabeth, in the tone of the doctrine practically held in our Church by many of her divines, there was a great change on this point as well as others.

We find Lord Bacon complaining, just at the close of the reign of Elizabeth, that some of the clergy denied the validity of the Orders conferred in the Foreign Non-Episcopal Churches. He says: "Some indiscreet persons have been bold in open preaching to use dishonorable and derogatory speech and censure of the Churches abroad; and that so far, as some of our men, as I have heard, ordained in foreign parts, have been pronounced to be no lawful ministers." (*Advertisement touch. the Controv. of the Church of Engl.; Works*, ii. 514. ed. 1819.)

This is another proof that men so ordained were allowed by public authority to minister in our Church; and also, no doubt, a proof that there had then arisen a school of divines among us that denied the validity of their Orders. But whatever might be the case with some hot-headed men in our Church, we do not find the *more eminent* divines even of that new school taking such ground. The utmost length to which they go, is to leave the question of the validity of such ordinations doubtful, and decline the determination of it; always, as far as we can recollect, protesting against their having any notion of denying to the Foreign Non-Episcopal Churches the character and essential privileges of Churches of Christ, however imperfectly constituted they might consider them to be. They left it to the superior learning and wisdom of such men as D. C. L., and the young blood of the Bristol Church Union, to declare it to be "the fundamental law of the Church Catholic," and "its teaching in all ages," "that the imposition of Episcopal hands is essential to all valid ordination; and that, without such ordination, none have authority to minister the word and sacraments."

Bishop Andrews, for instance, might perhaps have felt a difficulty with respect to much that our earlier divines had written upon the subject; but, nevertheless, he says, when speaking on the subject of the proper form of government for the Church, in his Letters, in 1618, to Du Moulin :—

"And yet, though our government be by Divine right, it follows not, either that there is 'no salvation,' or that 'a Church cannot stand without it.' He must needs be stone blind, that sees not Churches standing without it: he must needs be made of iron, and hard-hearted, that denies them salvation. We are not made of that metal, we are none of those ironsides; we put a wide difference betwixt them. Somewhat may be wanting that is of Divine right (at least in the external government), and yet salvation may be had. . . . This is not to damn anything, to *prefer a better thing before it:* this is not to damn your Church, to recall it to another form, that all antiquity was better pleased with, *i. e.* to ours: and this, when God shall grant the opportunity, and your estate may bear it." (*Second Lett. to Du Moulin.* See *Wordsw. Christ. Instit.* vol. iii. p. 239.)

After him, Archbishop Bramhall took the highest ground among the eminent divines of that day in favor of Episcopacy; but, nevertheless, was far from pronouncing all but Episcopal Orders invalid. Writing, in 1643, against the Separatists (as the Dissenters were then called), he says :—

"In a difference of ways, every pious and peaceable Christian, out of his discretion and care of his own salvation, will inquire which is '*via tutissima*'—'the safest way.' . . . . . And seeing there is required to the essence of a Church—first, a pastor; secondly, a flock; thirdly, a subordination of this flock to this pastor—where we are not sure that there is right ordination, what assurance have we that there is a Church? [But then he immediately adds] *I write not this to prejudge our neighbor Churches.* I dare not limit the extraordinary operation of God's Spirit, where ordinary means are wanting without the default of the persons. He gave His people manna for food whilst they were in the wilderness. Necessity is a strong plea. Many Protestant Churches lived under kings and bishops of another communion; others had particular reasons why they could not continue or introduce bishops; but *it is not so with us.* . . . . But the chief reason is, because I DO NOT MAKE THIS WAY TO BE SIMPLY NECESSARY, BUT ONLY SHOW WHAT IS SAFEST, where so many Christians are of another mind. I know that there is *great difference between a* VALID *and a* REGULAR *ordination;* and what some choice divines do write of case of necessity; and for my part am apt to believe that God looks upon His people in mercy, with all their prejudices; and that there is *a great latitude left* to particular Churches in the constitution of their ecclesiastical regiment, according to the exigence of time, and place, and persons, so as order and his own institution be observed." (*Serpent-Salve,* § 25. *Works,* Oxf. ed. vol. iii. pp. 475, 476.)

Again, in another subsequent work (written about 1659), he writes :—

"I cannot assent to his minor proposition, that either all or any considerable part of the Episcopal divines in England do unchurch either all or the most part of the Protestant Churches. No man is hurt but by himself. They unchurch none at all, but leave them to stand or fall to their own Master. They do not unchurch the Swedish, Danish, Bohemian Churches, and many other Churches in Polonia, Hungaria, and those parts of the world which have an ordinary uninterrupted succession of pastors, some by the names of Bishops, others under the name of Seniors, unto this day. (I meddle not with the Socinians.) They unchurch not the Lutheran Churches in Germany, who both assert Episcopacy in their confessions, and have actual superintendents in their practice, and would have bishops, name and thing, if it were in their power. Let him not mistake himself; those Churches which he is so tender of, though they be better known to us by reason of their vicinity, are so far from being 'all or the most part of the Protestant Churches,' that, being all put together, they amount not to so great a proportion as the Britannic Churches alone. And if one secluded out of them all those who want an ordinary succession without their own faults, out of invincible ignorance or necessity, and all those who desire to have an ordinary succession, either explicitly or implicitly, they will be reduced to a little flock indeed. But let him set his heart at rest. I will remove this scruple out of his mind, that he may sleep securely upon both ears. *Episcopal divines do not deny* THOSE CHURCHES *to be true Churches wherein salvation may be had.* We advise them, as it is our duty, to be circumspect for themselves, and not to put it to more question, whether they have Ordination or not, or desert the general practice of the Universal Church for nothing, when they may clear it if they please. Their case is not the same with those who labor under invincible necessity . . . Episcopal divines will readily subscribe to the determination of the learned Bishop of Winchester [Andrews] in his *Answer to the Second Epistle of Molinæus* [quoting the passage we have given above]. This mistake proceedeth from not distinguishing between the true nature and essence of a Church, *which we do readily grant them*, and the integrity and perfection of a Church, which we cannot grant them without swerving from the judgment of the Catholic Church." (*Vindic. of himself and the Episcopal Clergy*, c. 3 ; *Works*, vol. iii. pp. 517, 518. See also his *Replication to the Bishop of Chalcedon, Answ. to Pref.* § 1 ; *Works*, iii. 25, 26; and c. 1, § 2. *Ib.* 69, 70.)

And here we must not omit to notice, in passing (what this last extract indicates, and is fully confirmed elsewhere in his *Works*), that there is another material difference in his views from those of our modern Tractarians, namely, that what he *specially* contends for, is, a succession of pastors, not necessarily *bishops consecrated by bishops*, and that out of these pastors one should be appointed as president over the rest; and, therefore, he speaks favorably of the Lutheran Churches. He says, elsewhere, expressly, of "most" of the Protestant Churches "in High Germany," "all these have their bishops, or superintendents, *which is all one;*" . . "three parts of four of the Protestant Churches have either bishops or superintendents, *which is all one.*" (*Serpent-Salve; Works*, iii. 480, 485.) He does not, therefore, insist so much upon a succession of bishops consecrated by bishops, as upon the adoption of the Episcopal form of government. But this by the way.

We may judge, then, from these passages of Bishop Andrews and Archbishop Bramhall, what would have been the feelings of the most eminent even of our High Church divines respecting the language adopted on this subject by the Tractarian school.

We will now add a few of the numerous testimonies that could be given from the writings of our most celebrated divines, since the close of Queen Elizabeth's reign to the present day, showing the light in which they regarded the Orders of the Scotch and Foreign Non-Episcopal Churches.

Of Archbishop Bancroft's opinion we may form some judgment from the countenance he gave to the work of his chaplain, Rogers, on the XXXIX. Articles, already quoted. But, indirectly, we have a still more express testimony of his judgment on the subject, as well as of several of his brother bishops, in the following passage in Archbishop Spotiswood's *History of Scotland.* The Archbishop relates that when, in 1610, a regular episcopate was about to be conferred upon the Church of Scotland, by the consecration of three Scottish clergyman (of whom Spotiswood himself was one) as bishops of that Church, by the Bishops of London, Ely, and Bath, at the chapel of London-House—

"A question in the mean time was moved by Dr. Andrews, Bishop of Ely, touching the consecration of the Scottish bishops, who, as he said, 'must first be ordained presbyters as having received no ordination from a bishop.' The Archbishop of Canterbury, Dr. Bancroft, who was by, maintained, 'that thereof there was no necessity, seeing where bishops could not be had, the ordination given by the presbyters must be esteemed lawful; otherwise, that it might be doubted if there were any lawful vocation in most of the Reformed Churches.' This applauded to by the other bishops, Ely acquiesced; and at the day and in the place appointed the three Scottish bishops were consecrated." (*Spotiswood's Hist. of Church and State of Scotland,* 4th ed. 1677, fol., p. 514.)

Next, let us hear Archbishop Usher's judgment, given at the latter end of his life: —

"I have ever declared my opinion to be, that *episcopus et presbyter gradu tantum differunt non ordine,* and consequently that in places where bishops cannot be had, *the ordination by presbyters standeth valid;* yet, on the other side, holding as I do that a bishop hath superiority in degree above a presbyter, you may easily judge that the ordination made by such presbyters as have severed themselves from those bishops unto whom they had sworn canonical obedience, cannot possibly, by me, be excused from being schismatical. And howsoever I must needs think that the Churches which have no bishops are thereby become very much defective in their government, and that the Churches in France, who, living under a Popish power, cannot do what they would, are more excusable in this defect than the Low Countries, that live under a free State; yet, for the testifying my communion with these Churches (which I do love and honor as true members of the Church universal), I do profess that, with like affection, I should receive the blessed sacrament at the hands of the Dutch ministers, if I were in Holland, as I should do at the hands of the French ministers if I were in Charentone." (*Judgment of the late Archbishop of Armagh,* &c. By N. Bernard. Lond. 1657, 8vo. pp. 125–127.)

No one probably will question the high value which Bishop Hall had for Episcopacy, manifested in his Treatise on the subject. Yet, in a Discourse addressed to the Clergy of his Diocese as Bishop of Norwich, when speaking of the differences between the Church of England and the Non-Episcopal Churches abroad, he writes thus:—

"Blessed be God, there is no difference in any essential matter betwixt the Church of England and her sisters of the Reformation. We accord in every point of Christian doctrine without the least variation; their public Confessions and ours are sufficient convictions to the world of our full and absolute agreement. The only difference is, in the form of outward administration; wherein also we are so far agreed, as that *we all profess this form not to be essential to the being of a Church*, though much importing the well or better being of it, according to our several apprehensions thereof; and that we do all retain a reverence and loving opinion of each other in our own several ways; not seeing any reason why *so poor a diversity* should work any alienation of affection in us one towards another." (*The Peacemaker*, § 6, published in 1647. *Works*, by Pratt, vol. viii. p. 56.)

So also our learned Bishop Davenant:—

"In a disordered Church, where all the bishops have fallen into heresy or idolatry, where they have refused to ordain orthodox ministers, where they have considered those only who are associates of their faction and error to be worthy of holy orders, if orthodox presbyters (for the preservation of the Church) are compelled to ordain other presbyters, I could not venture to pronounce such ordinations useless and invalid." And this he proceeds to apply to the case of certain Protestant Churches. (*Determ. quæst.*, &c. Cant. 1634, fol., q. 42, p. 191.)

And in his Letter to Mr. Dury, on promoting peace among the Protestant Churches, he says:—

"Moreover, I doubt not at all but that the Saxon and Helvetian Churches, and others which either consent with these, or those, acknowledge themselves to have, and to desire to retain, brotherly communion with the English, Scottish, Irish, and other Foreign Reformed Churches. Surely, as concerning us, although we consent not with them in all points and titles of controversial divinity, yet we acknowledge them brethren in Christ, and protest ourselves to have a brotherly and holy communion with them." (Prefixed to his *Exhort. to broth. comm. betwixt the Protestant Churches.* Lond. 1641. 12mo. p. 33. See also the *Treatise* following it.)

One of the most eminent and able divines of our Church was Bishop Morton, of the 17th century, bishop successively of Chester, Lichfield, and Durham. And thus he speaks:—

"Where the bishops degenerate into wolves, there the presbyters regain their ancient right of ordaining (*consecrandi*). I call it ancient, because that the Episcopate and the Presbyterate are, *jure divino*, the same, is laid down by Marsilius, Gratian, &c." (*Apol. Cathol.* pt. 1, lib. 1, c. 21. Ed. 2d. Lond. 1606, 8vo. p. 74.)

Another able prelate of our Church at this period, and a strenuous defender of Episcopacy, was Dr. George Downham. But in a sermon on this subject, after having undertaken to show the *jus divinum* of Episcopacy in the sense of being an apostolical institution, he guards himself against being supposed to take the ground which the Puritans took in behalf of their platform of church government, namely, that because it was to be found in the Scriptures, therefore it was "perpetually and unchangeably necessary in all Churches," remarking:—

"Although we be well assured that the form of government by bishops is the best, as having not only the warrant of Scripture for the first institution, but also the perpetual practice of the Church from the apostles' time to our age for the continuance of it; notwithstanding we doubt not, but where this may not be had, others may be admitted; neither do we deny but that silver is good, though gold be better." (*Serm. at Consecr. of Bp. of Bath and Wells.* 1608, 4to. p. 95.)

And in his *Defence* of this sermon, referring to this passage, he says :—

"Which objection and answer I inserted of purpose into the sermon, to preserve the credit of those Reformed Churches where the Presbyterian discipline is established, and that they might not be exposed or left naked to the obloquies of the Papists." (*Def. of Serm. &c.*, 1611, 4to. lib. 4, c. 7, pp. 145, 146.)

And expressly, on the point of ordination, he says :—

"Thus have I reported the judgment of the ancient Church ascribing the ordinary right of ordination to bishops, but yet, not so appropriating it unto them as that extraordinarily and in case of necessity it might not be lawful for presbyters to ordain; and much less teaching (as the Papists imagine) absolutely a nullity in the ordination which is not performed by a bishop. For suppose a Church (the state of some Reformed Churches) either altogether destitute of a bishop, or pestered with such as the Popish prelates are, heretical and idolatrous, by whom no orthodoxal ministers might hope to be ordained, we need not doubt but that the ancient Fathers would, in such a case of necessity, have allowed ordination without a bishop, though not as regular, according to the rules of ordinary church government, yet as effectual and as justifiable in the want of a bishop." (*Serm.* pp. 42, 43.)

Lord Bacon, though a layman, may fairly claim a place among our witnesses. We have already noticed his rebuke of some of the hot spirits of his day for their language on the subject; but let us hear the impartial testimony of such a mind as his on the general question :—

"For the second point, that there should be but one form of discipline in all Churches, and that imposed by necessity of a commandment and prescript out of the word of God; it is a matter volumes have been compiled of, and therefore cannot receive a brief redargution. I for my part do confess, that in revolving the Scriptures, I could never find any such thing: but that God had left the like liberty to the church government, as he had done to the civil government; to be varied according to time, and place, and accidents, which nevertheless his high and divine providence doth order and dispose. For all civil governments are restrained from God unto the general grounds of justice and manners; but the policies and forms of them are left free: so that monarchies and kingdoms, senates and seignories, popular states and communalties, are lawful, and where they are planted ought to be maintained inviolate. So likewise in church matters, the substance of doctrine is immutable; and so are the general rules of government; but for rites and ceremonies, and for the particular hierarchies, policies, and disciplines of churches, they be left at large." (*Cert. Consid. touching Pacif. of Church; Works*, ed. 1819. vol. ii. pp. 529, 530.)

Our next witness shall be one who was confessedly one of the most able divines of his time, and ranks high, we believe, with our opponents; we mean, Dean Field.

Discussing the question, "whether the power of ordination be so essentially annexed to the order of bishops, that none but bishops may in any case ordain," he points out what is "implied in the calling of ecclesiastical ministers," and that the bishop of a church is only that presbyter that is appointed to be "specially pastor of the place, who for distinction sake is named a bishop, to whom an eminent and peerless power is given for the avoiding of schisms and factions;" and maintains that "the power of ecclesiastical or sacred order" "is equal and the same in all those whom we call presbyters, that is, fatherly guides of God's Church and people; and that only for order's sake, and the preservation of peace, there is a limitation of the use and exercise of the same;" adding:—

"Hereunto agree all the best learned amongst the Romanists themselves, freely confessing that that wherein a bishop excelleth a presbyter is *not a distinct and higher order or power of order, but a kind of dignity and office or employment only.*" "Hence it followeth, that many things which in some cases presbyters may lawfully do, are peculiarly reserved unto bishops, as Hierome noteth, *rather for the honor of their ministry than the necessity of any law.* And therefore we read, that presbyters, in some places, and at some times, did impose hands and confirm such as were baptized, which, when Gregory, bishop of Rome, would wholly have forbidden, there was so great exception taken to him for it, that he left it free again. And who knoweth not, that all presbyters, in cases of necessity, may absolve and reconcile penitents, a thing in ordinary course appropriated unto bishops? *And why not, by the same reason, ordain presbyters and deacons in cases of like necessity?* For seeing the cause why they are forbidden to do these acts, is, because to bishops ordinarily the care of all churches is committed, and to them in all reason the ordination of such as must serve in the Church pertaineth that have the chief care of the Church, and have churches wherein to employ them; which only bishops have as long as they retain their standing, and not presbyters, being but assistants to bishops in their churches; if they become enemies to God and true religion, in case of such necessity, as the care and government of the Church is devolved to the presbyters remaining Catholic and being of a better spirit, so *the duty of ordaining such as are to assist or succeed them in the work of the ministry pertains to them likewise.*" . . . . . . "Surely, the best learned in the Church of Rome in former times durst not pronounce all ordinations of this nature to be void. For not only Armachanus, a very learned and worthy bishop, but as it appeareth by Alexander of Hales, many learned men in his time, and before, were of opinion that, in some cases, and at some times, presbyters may give orders, and that their ordinations are of force; though to do so, not being urged by extreme necessity, cannot be excused from over great boldness and presumption." (*Of the Church*, ed. 1628; lib. 3, c. 39, pp. 155–157. See also ib. lib. 5, c. 27, p. 500.)

Another most important witness on this subject is Archdeacon Francis Mason, the eminent defender of the Episcopate of the English Church against the Romanists. In 1641, a tract written by him was published, vindicating "*the validity of the ordination of the ministers of the Reformed Churches beyond the seas;*" being some papers originally intended by him to form part of his celebrated *Vindication of the Church of England*, but for some reason omitted. Its publication in this way has caused some (especially Mason's translator, Lindsay) to cast a suspicion upon its genuineness; but not only is it spoken of as his by his contemporary Dr. Bernard, Usher's chaplain (*Judgment of the late Archbishop of Armagh*, 1657, p. 133), and first appeared in a Collection of Tracts of which Usher was partly the author, but in a letter of Dr. Ward (then Master of Sidney College, Cambridge) to Usher, written shortly after the publication of the first edition of Mason's work in 1613, we find the following passages: "I pray you inform me, what the specialties are which are omitted in Mr. Mason's book. I would only know the heads." And then returning to the subject at the close of the letter, he says: "I had no leisure when I was with you to inquire how Mr. Mason doth warrant the vocation and ordination of the ministers of the Reformed Churches in Foreign parts." (*Parr's Life and Letters of Usher*, 1686, fol., p. 34.)

Now in this tract Mason says:—

The bishop "in his consecration receiveth a sacred office, an eminency, a jurisdiction, a dignity, a degree of Ecclesiastical pre-eminence." "He hath no higher degree in respect of intension or extension of the character; but he hath a higher degree, that is, a more excellent place in respect of authority and jurisdiction in spiritual regiment. *Wherefore seeing a presbyter is equal to a bishop in the power of order, he hath equally intrinsical power to give orders.*" (Pp. 160, 161.)

The speaker for the Romanist (for it is written in the form of a dialogue), making the precise objection of the Tractarians, observes, "the pre-eminence of bishops is *jure divino;*" to which Orthodox answers thus:—

"First, if you mean by *jure divino*, that which is according to the Scripture, then the pre-eminence of bishops is *jure divino;* for it hath been already proved to be according to the Scripture. Secondly, if by *jure divino* you mean the ordinance of God, in this sense also it may be said to be *jure divino*. For it is an ordinance of the apostles, whereunto they were directed by God's Spirit, even by the spirit of prophecy, and consequently the ordinance of God. But if by *jure divino* you understand a law and commandment of God, binding all Christian Churches, universally, perpetually, unchangeably, and with such absolute necessity that no other form of regiment may in any case be admitted; in this sense neither may we grant it, nor yet can you prove it, to be *jure divino*." "The apostles, in their lifetime, ordained many bishops, and left a fair pattern to posterity. The Church, following the commodiousness thereof, embraced it in all ages through the Christian world." (*Ib.* p. 163.)

The Archdeacon then proceeds to defend the validity of the ordinations in the Foreign Reformed Churches, first on the ground of *necessity;* to which the objector, after some discussion, ultimately replies: "Suppose that ordination might be devolved to presbyters in case of necessity; yet the necessity ceasing, such extraordinary courses should likewise cease. Why, then, do they continue their former practice? Why do they not now seek to receive their orders from Protestant bishops?" To which Orthodox replies: "*The Churches of Germany need not to seek to foreign bishops, because they have superintendents or bishops among themselves. And as for other places which embrace the discipline of Geneva, they also have bishops in effect;*" which he proceeds to prove by showing that they have among them those who have "the substance of the office." And he concludes: "Thus much concerning the ministers of other Reformed Churches, wherein, if you will not believe us disputing for *the lawfulness of their calling*, yet you must give us leave to believe

God himself from heaven approving their ministry by pouring down a blessing upon their labors." (*Ib.* pp. 173–176.)

Another eminent divine of our Church was Dr. Crakanthorp; and he likewise justifies the Foreign Non-Episcopal Churches in this matter on the ground of necessity; and as it respects their not taking the first opportunity of restoring the Episcopal form of government, only remarks:—

"Optamus quidem ex animo, ut cum lex illa necessitatis jam ablata sit, velint et omnes Ecclesiæ ad priscum et ab universali Ecclesia constantissime observatum ordinem, et ordinandi modum redire; clavesque suas Episcopis restituant: *sed optamus, non cogimus. Jus et imperium in eorum Ecclesias nec habemus nos, nec desideramus.*" (*Defens. Eccles. Anglic.* Lond. 1625, 4to. c. 41, § 12, pp. 246, 247.)

We must not forget also to notice the similar testimony of the learned Dr. Willet, in his *Synopsis Papismi*, of which the fifth edition was published in 1634, under the authority of the king's letters patent; but we must content ourselves with referring our readers to the work. (See *5th Controv.* q. 3, p. 276.)

But one of the most important testimonies as to the doctrine of our Church and her most able divines on this subject, is that of Bishop Cosin, to which we have already referred. It occurs in a letter written from Paris in 1650 to a Mr. Cordel, who scrupled to communicate with the French Protestants. To the objection of Mr. Cordel, that "they have no priests," Dr. Cosin thus replies:—

"Though we may safely say and maintain it, that their ministers are not so duly and rightly ordained as they should be by those prelates and bishops of the Church who since the apostles' time have only had the ordinary power and authority to make and constitute a priest, yet that, by reason of this defect, there is *a total nullity in their ordination, or that they be therefore no priest or ministers of the Church at all, because they are ordained by those only who are no more but priests and ministers among them; for my part, I would be loath to affirm and determine it against them.* And these are my reasons. First: I conceive that the power of ordination was restrained to bishops rather by apostolical practice and the perpetual custom and canons of the Church, than by any absolute precept that either Christ or his apostles gave about it. Nor can I yet meet with any convincing argument to set it upon a more high and divine institution. From which customs and laws of the Universal Church (therein following the example of the apostles) though I reckon it to be a great presumption and fault for any particular Church to recede, and may truly say that *fieri non oportuit* (when the college of mere presbyters shall ordain and make a priest), yet I cannot so peremptorily say, that *factum non valet*, and *pronounce the ordination to be utterly void.* For as in the case of baptism, we take just exception against a layman or a woman that presumes to give it, and may as justly punish them by the censures of the Church wherein they live, for taking upon them to do that office, which was never committed unto them; yet, if once they have done it, we make not their act and administration of baptism void; nor *presume we to iterate the sacrament after them*; *so may it well be in the case of ordination, and the ministers of the Reformed Congregations in France;* who are liable to give an account both to God and his Church in general for taking upon them to exercise that power which by the perpetual practice and laws of His Church they were never permitted to exercise, and may justly be faulted for it, both by the verdict of all others who are members of the Catholic Church (as we are that adhere to the laws of it more strictly and peaceably than they do), and by the censures of a lawful meeting or general council in that Church, which at any time shall come to have authority over them. And yet all this while, the act which they do, though it be disorderly done, and the ordinations which they make, though they make them unlawfully, *shall not be altogether null and invalid*, no more than the act of baptizing before mentioned, or the act of consecrating and administering the Eucharist by a priest that is suspended and restrained from exercising his power and office in the Church. Therefore, if at any time a minister so ordained in these French Churches came to incorporate himself in ours, and to receive a public charge or cure of souls among us in the Church of England (as I have known some of them to have so done of late, and can instance in many other before my time), our bishops did not reordain him before they admitted him to his charge, as they must have done, if his former ordination here in France had been void. Nor did our laws require more of him than to declare his public consent to the religion received amongst us, and to subscribe the Articles established. And I love not to be herein more wise or harder than our own Church is, which, because it hath never publicly condemned and pronounced the ordinations of the other Reformed Churches to be void, as it doth not those of the unreformed Churches, neither among the Papists (though I hear that the ministers here in France and Geneva use so to do, who will not admit a Papist priest himself to exercise the office of a minister among them till they have reordained him); for my part, as to that particular, *I dare not take upon me to condemn or determine a nullity of their own ordinations against them;* though in the interim I take it to be utterly a fault among them, and a great presumption, deserving a great censure to be inflicted on them, by such a power of the Church as may, by the grace of God, be at any time duly gathered together hereafter against them, as well for the amendment of many other disorders and defects in their Church as for this particular inorderly ordination and defect of Episcopacy amongst them. Besides that this their boldness, presumption, and novelty (in setting up themselves without any invincible necessity that they had so to do, against the apostolical practice and perpetual order of God's Church till their days) was always faulted, and reserved for farther censure, in due time, which they have justly merited. Secondly.* There have been both learned and eminent men (as well in former ages as in this, and even among the Roman Catholics as well as Protestants), who have held and maintained it for good and passable divinity, that presbyters have the intrinsical power of ordination *in actu primo;* though for the avoiding of schism (as St. Hierom speaks) and preserving order and discipline in the Church, they have been restrained ever since the first times, and still are (but where they take a liberty to themselves that was never duly given them), from exercising their power *in actu secundo;* and therefore that however their act of ordaining of other presbyters shall be void, according to the strictness of the canon (in regard they were universally prohibited from executing that act, and breaking the order and discipline of the Church), yet that the same act shall not be simply void in the nature of the thing, in regard that the intrinsical power remained, when the exercise of it was suspended and taken from them. Of this opinion and judgment in old time were St. Hierom and his followers, alleged by Gratian, dist. 93; and of later times, the Master of the Sentences, lib. iv. dist. 24; Bonavent. *ibid.* 9, 3, art. 2; with other schoolmen, as Aureol. *ibid.* art. 2; and Anton. de Rosellis, *De Potest. Imper. et Papali*, part iv. c. 18; and in this later age, not only Armachanus, in *Sum. ad quæst.* art. 1, 11, c. 2, 3, &c. and c. 7, Alphons. a Castro (verb. Episcopus), Mich. Medina, *De sacr. hom. orig.* lib. 1, c. 5, among the Roman Catholics; but likewise Cassander in *Consult.* art. 14, besides Melancthon, Clementius [? Chemnitius], Gerardus, and Calixtus, amongst the Protestants; and Bishop Jewel (Def. 2, p. c. 3, d. 1, &c. 9, div. 1); Dr. Field, of the *Church*, lib. 3, c. 39; Hooker, *Eccles. Pol.* lib. 3, § 3, ult., and Mason, among the divines of our

* We have taken the liberty of making the second reason commence here (as it evidently does), instead of at the beginning of the previous sentence.

own Church. All which authors are of so great credit with you and me, that though we are not altogether of their mind, yet we would be loath to let the world see that we contradict them all, and condemn their judgment openly; *as needs we must, if we hold the contrary, and say, that the ministers of the Reformed French Churches, for want of Episcopal ordination, have no order at all.*" [Our readers will observe here what the view of Bishop Cosin was as to the sentiments of Jewel, Hooker, Field, and Mason.]

Dr. Cosin adds several other reasons, with which, however, we need not trouble our readers, except the following:—

"If the Church and kingdom of England have acknowledged them (as they did in admitting of them when they fled thither for refuge, and placing them by public authority in divers of the most eminent cities among us, without prohibition to any of our own people to go and communicate with them), why should we, that are but private persons, utterly disclaim their communion in their own country?"

And, therefore, he concludes that:—

"Considering there is no prohibition of our Church against it (*as there is against our communicating with the Papists*, and that well-grounded upon the Scripture and will of God), I do not see but that both you, and others that are with you, may (either in case of necessity, when you cannot have the sacrament among yourselves, or in regard of declaring your unity in professing the same religion, which you and they do) go otherwhiles to communicate reverently with them of the French Church."*

Similar sentiments are expressed by him in a letter published by Dr. R. Watson (Lond. 1684, 8vo.), entitled *Dr. Cosin's Opinion, when Dean of Peterborough, and in exile, for communicating rather with Geneva than Rome;* and also in his last Will, inserted in the Preface to his *Regni Angliæ Relig. et Gubern. Eccles.* Lond. 1729, 4to.

It is almost unnecessary to refer to the *Irenicum* of Bishop Stillingfleet (first published by him in 1659, and a second time in 1662), where he maintains, in a long and elaborate discussion of the question, that no particular form of church government is necessary, and points out that "the stoutest champions for Episcopacy" had acknowledged, "that ordination performed by presbyters in cases of necessity is valid;" "which," he adds, "doth evidently prove that Episcopal government is not founded upon any unalterable Divine right." (Pt. ii. c. 8.)

Thus also speaks Dean Sherlock:—

"I do allow Episcopacy to be an Apostolical institution, and the truly ancient and catholic government of the Church, of which more hereafter; but yet in this very book I prove industriously and at large, that in case of necessity, when bishops cannot be had, a church may be a *truly catholic church*, and such as we may and ought to communicate with, *without bishops*, in vindication of some Foreign Reformed Churches who have none; and therefore I do not make Episcopacy so absolutely necessary to catholic communion as to unchurch all Churches which have it not." "The Church of England does not deny but that, in case of necessity, the ordination of presbyters may be valid." (*Vindic. of some Prot. Principles, &c.*, reprinted in Gibson's *Preserv.*, vol. iii. pp. 410, 432.)

* The whole of this letter is given by Basire and Bp. Fleetwood (as referred to above).

So the excellent Dr. Claget:—

"The Church of England doth not unchurch those parts of Christendom that hold the unity of the faith." (See *Brief Disc. conc. the Notes of the Church*, pp. 166–169.)

Even the nonjuror Archbishop Sancroft, in some Admonitions issued to the clergy of his Province in 1688, speaks in fraternal terms of the Foreign Reformed Churches, exhorting his clergy—

"That they warmly and most affectionately exhort them [*i. e.* "our brethren the Protestant Dissenters"] to join with us in daily fervent prayer to the God of peace for the universal *blessed union of all Reformed Churches both at home and abroad* against our common enemies; that all they, who do confess the holy name of our dear Lord, and do agree in the truth of His holy word, may also meet in one holy communion, and live in perfect unity and godly love." (*D' Oyly's Life of Sancroft*, i. 325; or *Wilk. Conc.* iv. 619.)

For the sentiments of Archbishop Wake, to the same effect, our readers may consult some letters (written in 1719) given in the 4th Append. to *Mosheim's Eccles. Hist.* translated by Maclaine, Cent. xviii. No. xix.–xxii.; one of which is to "the pastors and professors of Geneva," whom he addresses as *fratres charissimi;* and in another (No. xix.) he says:—

"Ecclesias Reformatas etsi in aliquibus a nostra Anglicana dissentientes, libenter amplector. Optarem equidem regimen episcopale. . . . et ab iis omnibus fuisset retentum. . . . Interim absit ut ego tam ferrei pectoris sim, ut ob ejusmodi defectum (sic mihi absque omni invidia appellare liceat) aliquas earum a communione nostra abscindendas credam; aut, cum *quibusdam furiosis inter nos scriptoribus*, eas nulla vera ac valida sacramenta habere, adeoque vix Christianos esse pronuntiem." (*Mosheim*, by Maclaine, vol. vi. p. 184, ed. 1826.) And in a letter to Father Courayer, dated July 9, 1724, he again expresses the same sentiments.—*Mosheim, ib.* p. 30, Cent. xviii. § 23.)

In 1764, we have Archbishop Secker following him in the same strain:—

"Our inclination is to live in friendship with *all the Protestant Churches*. We assist and protect those on the continent of Europe as well as we are able. We show our regard to that of Scotland as often as we have an opportunity." (*Answ. to Mayhew*, p. 68. *Life* prefixed to *Sermons*, ed. 1770. p. lxvi.)

And, defending our Reformation, in one of his sermons against the Romanists, he says:—

"Supposing we had even acted without, and separated from, our Church governors, as our Protestant brethren abroad were forced to do: was there not a cause? When the word of God was hidden from men . . . when Church authority, by supporting such things as these, became inconsistent with the ends for which it was established, *what remedy was there but to throw it off and form new establishments? If in these there were any irregularities, they were the faults of those who forced men into them, and are of no consequence in comparison with the reason that made a change necessary.*" (*Serm.* vol. vi. pp. 400, 401.)

Still more strongly speaks the late Bishop Tomline:—

"I readily acknowledge that there is no precept in the New Testament which commands that every Church should be governed by bishops. No Church can exist without some government; but though there must be rules and orders for the proper discharge of the offices of public worship, though there must be fixed regulations concerning the appointment of ministers; and though a subordination among them is expedient in the highest degree, yet it does not follow that all these things must be precisely the same in every Christian country; they may vary with the other varying circumstances of human society, with the extent of a country, the manners of its inhabitants, the nature of its civil government, and many other peculiarities which might be specified. As it has not pleased our Almighty Father to prescribe any particular form of civil government for the security of temporal comforts to His rational creatures, so neither has He prescribed any particular form of ecclesiastical polity as absolutely necessary to the attainment of eternal happiness. . . . As the Scriptures do not prescribe any definite form of church government, so they contain no directions concerning the establishment of a power by which ministers are to be admitted to their sacred office." And therefore, though he advocates Episcopal ordination as "instituted by the apostles," he does not maintain it as necessary. (*Expos. of Art.* 23, ed. 1799, pp. 396, 398.)

We close the list with the testimony of our late respected Primate, Dr. Howley.

In a statement published by his authority in 1841, the Foreign Protestant Non-Episcopal Churches are spoken of as "the less perfectly constituted of the Protestant Churches of Europe." (*Statem. resp. Jerusalem Bishopric*, p. 5.)

And in 1835, a letter was addressed by the same Prelate, in the name of himself and his "*brother bishops*," to "the Moderator of the Company of Pastors at Geneva," expressing their "*high respect for the Protestant Churches on the Continent*," and speaking of the *Genevan Reformation* as a "noble achievement, which brought light out of darkness, and rescued your Church from the shackles of Papal domination and the tyrannical imposition of a corrupt faith, and a superstitious ritual," wrought by "illustrious men, who, under the direction of Almighty God, were the instruments of this happy deliverance," "an event not less glorious to Geneva than conducive to the success of the Reformation." The whole letter has been so recently published in the public Journals, that we need only give these short extracts.

Could it have been supposed, that, sixteen years after, his successor in the Primacy was to be assailed with a storm of vituperation, and even branded by an Archdeacon of his Province as a heretic, for merely saying that the Church of England does not deny the validity of the Orders of such Churches?

But in those sixteen years a new school has sprung up in our Church, chiefly composed of its younger members, who having formed in their own minds, from their perusal of Romish and Tractarian works, a Procrustean standard of ecclesiastical doctrine and polity, are apparently endeavoring, in the total disregard of the manifest tenets of our Church, to force upon it a position and character which its whole history repudiates. The right of private judgment has rarely been exercised with more unbridled arrogance than by those among us who professedly disown it. Under the thin veil of high-sounding phrases, "the Church," "Catholic consent," and such like, the Romish dreams of hot-headed or prejudiced, and often very ill-informed individuals, are urged upon the public as indubitable verities, which it were a sin to suppose that our Church does not hold; and by which all who differ from them, from the highest to the lowest, are to be judged. We say deliberately, even as to the heads of the party, *very ill-informed* individuals; and on this ground, that whatever may be their learning in other respects (and it is too often to be seen principally in the trifles of the Church ceremonial), they seem rather to avoid than examine those sources of information which best show what the doctrine of our Church really is, as was abundantly proved in the Gorham case; and palm upon our Church views and doctrines which they have gathered by their private judgment from antiquity.

But our space warns us that we must restrain our pen. We deeply regret that our Church should be continually suffering from these internal dissensions. But we fear that, if she is still to remain a witness for Protestant truth, a conflict awaits her, both from internal and external foes, more severe than any she has yet encountered. Would that we could see a more lively consciousness of this coming struggle manifested among those, lay and clerical, who, under God, must be the instruments for her preservation. Few, however, seem to realize the true character of the present times.

Meanwhile, no fear need be entertained that the public discussion of Tractarian dogmas will show that our Church has a leaning toward them. Just the contrary will, we are convinced, be the case. And we leave the Archbishop's assailants quietly to weigh the testimonies given above, and judge for themselves how much they are likely to gain by their recent outbreak—an outbreak as unprecedented for its contempt for constituted authorities as it is destitute of even the shadow of an excuse for it.

A REPLY

TO

ARCHDEACON CHURTON

AND

CHANCELLOR HARINGTON,

ON THE

TERM "CHURCH OF SCOTLAND"

IN THE

FIFTY-FIFTH CANON,

AND ON

NON-EPISCOPAL ORDINATIONS.

BY

W. GOODE, M.A., F.S.A.,

Rector of Allhallows the Great and Less, London.

Second Edition.

NEW YORK:

A. D. F. RANDOLPH, 683 BROADWAY.

1853.

CONTENTS.

REPLY TO ARCHDEACON CHURTON AND CHANCELLOR HARINGTON, ON, &c.

I. ON THE TERM "CHURCH OF SCOTLAND" IN THE FIFTY-FIFTH CANON.

THE following Letter appeared in the *Guardian* of Dec. 3, 1851, in reply to one by Archdeacon Churton in the same paper on Nov. 19 (which I give below),* on the meaning of the term "Church of Scotland" in the 55th Canon:—

To the Editor of the Guardian.

SIR: There is an old saying that, *tua res agitur paries cum proximus ardet.* On this principle, even if not on general grounds, you will perhaps allow me to make a few remarks on an article in your last Number, for November 19.

Your correspondent, Archdeacon Churton, finds fault, in terms of positive ridicule, with "Bishop Lee," (as he calls him,) for saying, that in 1604, when our Convocation passed the 55th Canon,

* *To the Editor of the Guardian.*

"On peut licitement employer des termes équivoques, quand quelque cause *raisonnable* y engage."—*Pére Lacroix.*

Sir: In the notices which I have seen in your paper and elsewhere, of Bishop Lee's late doctrinal exposition to the clergy of Lancashire, I have not discovered any allusion to his Lordship's new historical lights on the Church of Scotland. Bishop Lee is reported, in your paper of November 12, to have said that "the Church of England, in the 55th Canon, enjoined the people to pray for the Churches of England, Scotland, and Ireland; although the Church was then, *as now*, Presbyterian, and Episcopacy was not as yet established." His Lordship means, of course, the Church of Scotland; not of England or Ireland.

As it is no special part of my duty to notice what may be said to the clergy on the other side of Blackstone edge, I have waited a few days, hoping that another hand might have corrected this ingenious equivocal statement. But as it seems that no such correction has yet been administered, though no doubt many of the learned clergy of Lancashire must have smiled to themselves at the humor of the passage, I hope you will allow me to offer a brief comment, which may serve to bring it out of its present obscurity.

The Church of Scotland, in 1604, was about as much Presbyterian as the Diocese of Manchester was in 1848, during the interregnum before the consecration of the present learned and moderate Prelate. As early as 1598, if not earlier, an Act of the Scottish Parliament had secured to the Bishops, and other ecclesiastical Prelates to be appointed by the king, their seats and voices in Parliament. Before 1600, there appear to have been Bishops nominated to the Sees of Aberdeen, Argyle, Dunkeld, Brechin, and Dumblane. David Lindsay and George Gladstone were in that year nominated respectively to the Sees of Ross and Caithness. True, these Bishops-Designate were not consecrated till a few years later; but when the law of the land had recognized their estate, and the men were known and appointed, it appears to me a verbal shuffle, and something more (unintentional, of course), to say that the Church of Scotland "was then, *as now*, Presbyterian."

Yours very faithfully,

EDW. CHURTON.

YORK, Nov. 17, 1851.

bidding the people to pray for the Church of Scotland, that Church "was then, as now, Presbyterian, and Episcopacy was not as yet established."

Now having, more than once, publicly made the same statement, I feel not a little implicated in the censure here so confidently put forward by the Archdeacon against the Bishop. And I trust you will permit me briefly to state the grounds on which I have made the remark that has called forth the Archdeacon's ridicule. I say *ridicule;* for so confident is he of the goodness of his cause, and his own thorough acquaintance with the subject, that he jests about "his Lordship's new historical lights," and how "no doubt many of the learned clergy of Lancashire must have smiled to themselves at the humor of the passage;" and he begs "to offer a brief comment" to point out the truth of the case; and his comment is, that in 1598, if not earlier, the Scottish Parliament had given seats and voices in Parliament to the bishops appointed by the king, and before 1600 bishops had been appointed to several places, though they were not consecrated till 1610. The inference, I suppose, is that the Church of Scotland had a true Episcopate in 1604, and consequently was not then under a Presbyterian form of church government. What "the learned clergy of Lancashire" may think of this reply to the Bishop's statement, I will not venture to conjecture; but there are some, I suspect, who will see much more "humor" in it than in the remark which called it forth.

A brief statement of the facts of the case will enable the reader to judge of the correctness of this comment; and I shall take them almost wholly from an author to whom the Archdeacon cannot object, namely, Mr. Lawson.

On the 24th of August, 1560, the jurisdiction of the Pope in Scotland was abolished, and no bishop or other prelate was to use any jurisdiction thereafter by the Bishop of Rome's authority. (*Lawson's Episcopal Church of Scotland*, p. 24.) And the Romish Hierarchy was succeeded by what was called the Superintendent System of church government, the supreme ecclesiastical authority vesting in a General Assembly of the Protestants, including ministers and laymen. (*Ib.* 80, *et seq.*) That is, such was the system practically adopted, for "no form of church government, not even the Superintendent System, was legally acknowledged." (*Ib.* 96.)

But as the bishops and other prelates were considered an essential part of the Parliament of the kingdom, they were allowed to sit and vote, though *deprived of their right to exercise their clerical functions.* And when the Romish bishops were nearly all dead, the Government of King James became anxious lest the extinction of one branch of the Legislature, the Spiritual Estate, might cause the legality of their acts to be questioned; and therefore, in 1571, "certain of the Protestant preachers were allowed to vote in the Parliament as the successors of the defunct prelates, and officially appointed bishops of the vacant sees." (*Ib.* 96, 97.) The first appointed was John Douglas, who was "nominated Archbishop on Saturday, the 18th of August, 1571, and as such he attended the

Parliament, or Convention, held at Stirling, on the 28th of that month," where he voted as Archbishop of St. Andrews. (*Ib.* 98.) "The 'consecration' was performed by the *lay* Bishop of Caithness, Spotiswood, and David Lindsay, of Leith." After a sermon by Knox, and an address by Winram, Douglas "declared that he would be '*obedient to the Kirk, and that he should usurp no power over the same*,' and that he would '*take no more power than the Council and General Assembly of the Kirk should prescribe*.' The lay Bishop of Caithness, Spotiswood, and Lindsay, then 'laid their hands and embraced the said rector, Mr. John Douglas, in token of admission to the bishopric.' Such was the 'consecration' which those three men had the presumption to perpetrate at the commencement of this spurious Episcopacy; one of them, the Bishop of Caithness, let it be recollected, never in holy orders; and even Lindsay's ordination is doubtful—at least it is so considered by Bishop Keith." "Several of the bishoprics were speedily filled by the leading men among the Reformed preachers, and this novel 'Episcopacy,' or form of ecclesiastical polity, even worse than the Superintendent System, and more objectionable than Presbyterianism, because it was the mere shadow without the substance, was soon carried completely into operation." (*Ib.* 108, 110.) "The situation of the titular bishops, and the domination over them by the General Assembly, are evident from sundry resolutions at this meeting [*i. e.* of the General Assemby in 1574]. It was declared that the 'jurisdiction of bishops in their ecclesiastical function shall not exceed that of superintendents, which they previously had, and still have,' and that, like them, the said bishops shall be subject to the discipline of the General Assembly, as members thereof." (*Ib.* 129.)

So that not only was there the absence of anything like consecration to their office, but *the episcopal office itself was not given them;* in fact, scarcely more than the name. What sort of an Episcopate this was, I leave the Archdeacon to determine.

But farther; while this titular Episcopate was called into being by the Court for political purposes, the General Assembly was progressing towards a regular Presbyterian form of church government. In the General Assembly of 1581, "the Presbyterian system, as subsequently known in Scotland, was developed," (*Ib.* 178,) *and in the Parliament of* 1592 *the system of the Presbyterians was ratified as an establishment.* (*Ib.* 239, 240.) But "the king and council, though they were pleased to confer on Presbytery the advantages of an establishment, had not the least intention of relinquishing or repressing the titular Episcopate as one of the three Estates. In 1597 an Act was passed, declaring that 'all ministers provided to prelacies should have votes in Parliament.'" (*Ib.* 241.) But this was to be "*without prejudice of the jurisdiction and discipline of the Kirk establishment by Acts of Parliament.*" (*Ib.* 242.)

So that the state of the case at that time was this. The form of church government was Presbyterian, established by the law of the land; but it being thought necessary that the Spiritual Estate should be represented in Parliament, the king had the power to give certain of the ministers of the Church (to say nothing now of laymen) the revenues of the old Episcopal Sees, call them Bishops, and so entitle them to seats and votes in Parliament. But how far the Episcopal office was given them, the Archdeacon may judge for himself, from the following rules laid down in the conference at Falkland, in 1598 (where commissioners from the various synods met the king to discuss these matters), *and ratified by the General Assembly that met at Montrose in* 1600, *where the king himself was present.*

"5. That he [the bishop appointed by the king] should be bound to attend the congregation faithfully at which he should be appointed minister, in all the points of a pastor, and be *subject* to the trial and censure of his own Presbytery or Provincial Assembly, as any other of the ministers that bear no commission. 6. In the administration of discipline, &c., he should neither usurp nor claim to himself any more power or jurisdiction than any of his brethren, except he be employed, under pain of deprivation, &c. 7. In Presbyteries, Provincial and General Assemblies, he should behave himself in all things as one of the brethren, and be subject to their censure. 8. At his admission to the office of commissionary [so they called these prelates], he should swear and subscribe all these and other points necessary; otherwise he should not be admitted. 9. If it should happen him to be deposed from the ministry, by the Presbytery, Synod, or General Assembly, he should lose his place in Parliament, and the benefice be void *ipso facto.*" (*Spotiswood's Hist.* bk. vi., a. 1598, pp. 453, 454, ed. 1677.

When these rules were ratified by the General Assembly, in 1600, the two following were added: "That he who was admitted should yearly render an account of his commission to the General Assembly, and laying the same down at their foot should be therein continued; or if his Majesty and the Assembly did think fit to employ another, he should give place to him that was appointed;" and "that they who had voice in Parliament should not have place in the General Assembly, unless they were authorized by a commission from the Presbyters [Presbytery] whereof they were members." (*Ib.* 458.)

Such were the "bishops" of the Church of Scotland in 1600, and such only they remained in 1604. Will the Archdeacon deny that the Church of Scotland, under such circumstances, was under a Presbyterian form of government? That some of the stiffer sort of Presbyterians, both then and since, found fault with it, is no proof of its not being a species of Presbyterian form of government. And it was a form which the "bishops" adhered to. So that if the Church to which the 55th Canon refers was the Church to which these "bishops" belonged (which I suppose will not be denied), it was a Church under a Presbyterian form of government.

It is worth observing, that when, in 1610, three of these "bishops" presented themselves, by King James's direction, to the English prelates for consecration, Bishop Andrews suggested a doubt whether they ought to be recognized as having any orders at all, even those of deacon and priest, but was overruled by Archbishop

Bancroft, who said that "where bishops could not be had, the ordination given by the presbyters must be esteemed lawful; otherwise, that it might be doubted if there were any lawful vocation in most of the Reformed Churches." This we have on the authority of Archbishop Spotiswood (*Hist.* 514), who was himself one of the three then consecrated. And this fact, I may observe, completely answers the objections raised against the possibility of the 55th Canon applying to a Presbyterian community from the supposed views of Bancroft and others.

Most justly, therefore, upon the Archdeacon's own principles, does Mr. Lawson make the following remarks upon this titular Episcopate:—

"The objection to it which must occur to the sound Churchman is, that it was altogether a vain and futile system; that it was no Episcopacy at all, or so only in name; that the 'consecration' of Douglas and others by unauthorized men, one of whom was a layman, was disgraceful, outrageous, and most sinful; and that the whole was a political arrangement to serve particular purposes, and introduce a set of men into the Parliaments to represent the defunct and absent prelates of the fallen hierarchy, assuming their ecclesiastical titles, and pretending to be invested with functions which it was impossible to obtain without consecration from bishops regularly and canonically consecrated. . . . . . Even the people ridiculed the persons 'inaugurated' by such men as the lay bishops of Caithness, Winram, and Lindsay. They were long known by the very appropriate and significant *sobriquet* of *Tulchan Bishops,* derived from a practice then prevalent of stuffing a calf's skin with straw, and placing it before a cow, to induce the animal to give milk, which figure was called a *tulchan*—a term derived from a word signifying a model, or a close resemblance. The tulchan hierarchy was *a complete deception,* and was merely one of *titles* connected with personal arrangements and political expediency, to say nothing of its gross perversion of the real Episcopate, and its schismatical profanity. The men who figured in it as titulars or *tulchans* ought never to have been recognized by Keith in his enumeration of the Scottish bishops." (*Ib.* 111, 112.) "The truth is, that in Scotland THE CHURCH CATHOLIC BECAME EXTINCT FROM THE REFORMATION TO 1610; for neither can the ill-digested Superintendent System, with its array of 'ministers, exhorters, and readers,' nor the miserable titular Episcopacy incorporated with it, nor the human inventions introduced by Andrew Melville, under the name of Presbyterianism, nor all three put together, be considered as entitled to any connection with the true and Apostolic Church." (*Ib.* 133.) The titulars "were merely nominal bishops for political or party purposes, unconsecrated, and of no higher authority than their lay preachers." (*Ib.* 144.) "The titular Episcopate was a matter of mere indifference—a worldly arrangement for political purposes, the loss of which involved nothing of importance, and utterly indefensible by any arguments—opposed to scriptural authority, apostolical practice, and primitive antiquity." (*Ib.* 242.)

Such are the statements of Mr. Lawson respecting this titular Episcopate; and whatever difference of opinion there may be between what are called High and Low Churchmen as to some points in these statements, I suppose both will agree that a grant of the name and revenues, and certain privileges of the Episcopate, by the Civil Power for political convenience, can never make a bishop. Such a notion would indeed be Erastianism of the most flagrant kind. These titular Scotch bishops were no more real bishops than the scarecrows in a field of corn are real men, or the Irvingite apostles and angels are real apostles and angels. Even King James himself, in 1610, guarded himself against being supposed to consider them in reality bishops. (*Spotiswood's History*, p. 514.) Archdeacon Churton probably regards me as a Low Churchman; but I can assure him that his reference to these persons as "bishops," and as showing that the Church of Scotland was then in any degree Episcopal, is a depth of Low Churchism into which I should be sorry to fall. It is not the mere fact of their wanting Episcopal consecration that I insist upon, but that it was a mere political appointment *for State purposes*, and also that they *did not enjoy the episcopal office*. The law of the land, though recognizing them for convenience sake as bishops in name, had expressly established a non-Episcopal form of church government.

Mr. Lawson, therefore, justly remarks, when speaking of the views of James I., soon after his accession to the throne of England in 1603: "He was convinced of the collision which might occur by the existence of *two different ecclesiastical establishments* in Britain, in the event of the accomplishment of the union, and knowing too well the turbulence and ungovernable tempers of the supporters of the *Presbyterian system*, it was a wise and prudent resolution to attempt to amalgamate Scotland as a sister Church with the Church of England." (*Ib.* 267, 268.)

Mr. Scott, of Perth, dates the first "overthrow of the Presbyterian Church," in the year 1606 (*Ib.* 264), on account, probably, of the Acts passed in that year in the Scotch Parliament, one declaring the king's supremacy over all estates, persons, and causes, and another entitled, "Anent the Restitution of the Estate of Bishops;" and in this Mr. Lawson agrees with him, on, as it seems to me, good grounds; the latter Act referring to much more than (as stated by *Spotiswood*, p. 496) the temporalities of the bishoprics. (*Ib.* 276.) The Parliament, therefore, may be said to have restored the episcopal form of government, as far as they could do so, in this year. But, so far as the clergy were concerned, it was with some difficulty that the General Assembly of this year was induced even to allow the bishops to be moderators in the Presbyteries where they were resident. (*Spotiswood*, pp. 500, 501.)

If the canon, therefore, had been passed between 1606 and 1610, there might have been something in the Archdeacon's argument; but as it is, the canon was passed when, by the law of the land, as well as the determinations of the ecclesiastics of Scotland, the form of church government was Presbyterian.

The Archdeacon says: "As early as 1598, if not earlier, an Act of the Scottish Parliament had secured to the bishops and other ecclesiastical prelates to be appointed by the king, their seats and voices in Parliament;" and he adds that before 1600 several bishops had been nominated to different Sees. I reply, Perfectly true, so far as *the name* is concerned, but nothing else. For neither had they consecration nor the episcopal office. They were subject to their Presbyteries like all the rest of their brethren (according to rules agreed to by the General Assembly and the king in 1600), and were merely bishops for civil purposes, to give their vote in Parliament, just as (for the sake of political convenience) the Roman Catholic prelates themselves, after they had been forbidden even to exercise their clerical functions at all, were allowed to vote in Parliament.

The Archdeacon adds: "True, these bishops-designate were not consecrated till a few years later; but when the law of the land had recognized their estate, and the men were known and appointed, it appears to me a verbal shuffle, and something more (unintentional, of course), to say that the Church of Scotland 'was then, *as now*, Presbyterian.'" So that the Archdeacon would have us suppose that the law of the land had then authorized the Episcopal form of church government, and that bishops were accordingly appointed, and their consecration only in a state of abeyance. No description could be farther removed from the facts of the case. The State had been in the habit of appointing these titular bishops since 1571, for the very purpose of their voting in Parliament; and, so far from the law of the land recognizing their estate as governors of the Church, it had established Presbyterianism in 1592 as the form of church government to be followed, and had not in 1604 annulled that argument. And so little was the appointment made on the understanding of future consecration, that, when such consecration was proposed by King James in 1610, it was objected to at first by the "bishops" themselves, on the ground that the Church of England might claim some power over them. In fact, it is evident that consecration would never have been thought of, but from the circumstance, which happened subsequently, of King James's accession to the throne of England.

I regret that the Archdeacon should have used the somewhat offensive phrase of a "verbal shuffle, and something more;" and in the present case he is peculiarly unfortunate in his application of it, when his own cause rests solely upon the use of the *name* of Bishop, where the *thing* had no place. The *reality* is precisely what the bishop has described it to be, and the Archdeacon is only able to throw discredit upon the statement by parading before the reader what turns out to be an empty shadow. His *tulchan* bishops are men of straw, that may do very well to frighten young birds, but will not have the slightest effect upon old ones.

The facts of the case lie in a nutshell. There were no bishops in 1604 in the Church of Scotland, having either Episcopal consecration or the Episcopal office, or even any immediate prospect of one or the other.

There were no Orders but Presbyterian Orders. The Church was under the government (subject, of course, to the king) of a General Assembly, consisting of presbyters and laymen, the representatives of the local presbyteries, by which the affairs of the different districts into which the country was divided were directed; to which the "bishops" were subject; these "bishops" not being allowed, previous to 1606, to be, by right, even the moderators of the synods held in their dioceses.

If this is not a Presbyterian form of church government, will the Archdeacon say what he calls it? And, be it observed, whatever name may be given to it, it certainly is a non-Episcopal form and *destitute of Episcopal Orders;* so that the purpose for which the Canon has been adduced, namely, to show that our Church recognizes, as a Church, one which is destitute of Episcopal Orders, is equally answered, whatever *name* be applied.

It has lately been said, in opposition to such a view as that advocated above, that the Canon refers to "that branch of Christ's Holy Catholic and Apostolic Church which had existed in Scotland from the days of St. Ninianus, in the beginning of the fifth century, and which, amidst persecution and spiritual rebellion, had no more ceased to exist than had the Church of Carthage during the absence and persecution of St. Cyprian; which had been represented subsequent to the Reformation by bishops canonically consecrated, and by the Archbishop of Glasgow, who was restored to his See in 1599, and retained it till his death in the year 1603."

Now, it would be interesting to know who formed this Church in 1604, if it was not the Church of which we have been speaking. All the bishops here mentioned were dead, and had never been allowed to act as bishops; for the two who joined the Reformed Church adopted of necessity its discipline, and the Archbishop of Glasgow was not restored to his See, except as to the enjoyment of its temporalities. At any rate, being all dead, none of these were members of it. The king and the titular bishops belonged to the Church of which the governing body under the king was the General Assembly. And what the form of church government agreed to by the king and the General Assembly was in 1604, we have already seen; and therefore, where the supposed Church is to be found, distinct from the Church of which we have been speaking, I am unable to conjecture; and wherever it was, it had no bishops, for none existed; and only presbyterianly ordained pastors, for none others were to be found; and consequently, however well the words sound, I do not see how they advance the cause they are intended to promote. In truth, *ex nihilo nil fit;* there were no bishops and no Episcopal form of church government, and no *verborum ambages* will produce them. And I should have conceived that the claim of the Church to which the king and his titular bishops belonged, would have been too strong for it to have been passed over by those who made the Canon.

In short, if this matter had not been involved in confusion by the prejudiced statements of party historians, no question would have arisen respecting it. But in this case, as in others about which we have accounts written by a number of zealous partisans of different views, nothing is easier than apparently to prove, by the statements of respectable historians, anything we wish. The zealous Episcopalian, anxious to maintain an uninterrupted series of bishops from the Reformation, talks of these titular bishops as if they were realities. The hot Presbyterian, angry at King James's interference with the General Assembly, often speaks as if his favorite Presbyterianism had been abolished when the power of that Assembly to do just what it pleased was curtailed; as, for instance, Calderwood, who tells us that in 1596 "ended the sincere General Assemblies of the Kirk of Scotland." And if such statements are taken as evidence (and as such they have lately been used), we may give almost any description we please of the state of the Church of Scotland at that period. But if we will only separate *the facts* from the prejudiced statements in which they are involved by the various historians of the period, the case will be perfectly clear.

I am, Sir, your obedient servant,

CHARTERHOUSE SQUARE, Nov. 25, 1851. W. GOODE.

The answer of Archdeacon Churton to this letter I place in a note below, as it is the fairest course to let him speak for himself; and also my reply to a point incidentally arising out of his second letter, but not touching the point in question.*

* *To the Editor of the Guardian.*

Sir: If Mr. Goode, as he seems to wish us to know, led Bishop Lee into making that delusive statement about the Church of Scotland, he was bound to offer a public apology for it. This, I suppose, he has now done at as much length as he desired; and your editorial courtesy has not deprived him of any portion of an answer of three columns to a letter of twenty or thirty lines.

I shall merely beg space to remind your readers that in my letter I stated two or three historical *facts*. They were enough for my purpose, though I could easily have stated more. Has Mr. Goode contradicted those facts? He knows he cannot. He has wasted much time and paper in proving that the Scottish bishops, in those years which preceded their consecration, though barons of Parliament, had no spiritual title or power as bishops in the Church. This he is all the time aware I was so far from denying, that I distinctly pointed it out.

But he argues that these bishops of Parliament were appointed without any ulterior design to make them bishops of the Church. Your readers will know how to judge of this argument, who have read King James the First's *Premonition to Christian Monarchs.* They will know how to estimate the value of the assertion, that "things were then progressing towards a regular Presbyterian form of government." Your readers who are familiar with the Memorials of the Hampton Court Conference will remember in what reverent terms King James there spoke of the said "Scottish Presbytery," and will know what to think of the hypothesis, that this monarch's counsellors were favorable to the erection of that most loyal platform.

Mr. Goode has thought it proper to say somewhere in the course of his long letter, "Archdeacon Churton probably regards me as a Low Churchman." As I have never, to my knowledge, given any opinion about Mr. Goode, I beg the reader to observe, that this name is of his own application, and it is a poor artifice of controversy to impute to me the act of a judgment, which his charity to himself has suggested as something due to his own reputation. E. C.

YORK, Dec. 5, 1851.

(*Guardian*, Dec. 10.)

To the Editor of the Guardian.

SIR: I have not the slightest wish to add one word on the controversy between Archdeacon Churton and myself; but as he has chosen to impute to me a wish to have it understood that I led the Bishop of Manchester into making the statement he did as to the 55th Canon, I must request permission to state that I have never had the slightest communication with the Bishop on the subject, and my letter neither stated nor intimated in any way that such was the case.

From which of us "a public apology" for "delusive statements" is most needed, I willingly leave your readers to determine. Your obedient servant,

W. GOODE.

31 CHARTERHOUSE SQUARE, Dec. 11, 1851.

(*Guardian*, Dec. 17.)

While this sheet was passing through the press, a reply from Archdeacon Churton to this letter appears in the *Guardian* for Dec. 24, which is best left to answer itself.

But for the appearance of Chancellor Harington's pamphlet, in which he has republished several of his letters addressed to the public Journals on this and the kindred subject of Non-Episcopal Ordinations,* I should have been contented with the correspondence in the *Guardian*. But, as Mr. Harington has appealed to the public in a more permanent form, and his pamphlet is referred to by the Editor of the *Guardian* (Dec. 10), in connection with my Letter, as one in which its readers "will find the historical facts well and concisely stated, and the argument from the internal evidence resulting from the Canons themselves forcibly put," it has appeared to me desirable to publish the above Letter in the same form, appending a few observations in answer to the Chancellor's statements on the same subject, and also a reply to his letters on Non-Episcopal Ordinations.

On Archdeacon Churton's answer it can scarcely be necessary to offer many remarks. The *tone* and *quality* of his Letters I leave our readers to judge of; and though I deeply regret, for his own sake and that of the position he holds in the Church, to see him taking such a course, yet I must say that they are highly characteristic of his party; and I believe that their manifold productions of this kind have done good service in showing the public the real value of their inflated pretensions.

The Archdeacon says that he only stated facts, and that I cannot contradict them; and that he "distinctly pointed out," that the Scottish bishops, at the period in question, "had no spiritual title or power as bishops in the Church." Now, so far from doing this, he did, in fact (which, in his haste, he has forgotten), directly the contrary, for he asserted that "the law of the land had recognized their estate," which it had not done; but, on the contrary (as I said before), "had expressly established a Non-Episcopal form of church government." In fact, if he had done so, it would have spoiled his whole argument, for his readers would at once have seen the absurdity of his attacking the Bishop of Manchester for saying that the Church of Scotland was under a Presbyterian form of government, *because* there were persons called "bishops" in Scotland; when he was compelled at the same time to admit that these "bishops" "had no spiritual title or power, as bishops, in the Church." And his charge of a "verbal shuffle" would *by his own testimony* have been brought back upon himself.

When he says that I argue "that these bishops of Parliament were appointed without any ulterior design to make them bishops of the Church," he is putting words into my mouth, to suit his purpose, which I never used; and he urges King James's design to make them real bishops when he might have the opportunity as overthrowing my argument. My letter, as given above, will show what I did say. With King James's *secret designs and wishes*,

* Entitled, "A Letter, &c., on the LV. Canon and the Kirk of Scotland; with an Appendix containing the cases of Morrison, &c., the witness of Anglican divines for Episcopacy, &c. Lond. Rivington." pp. 100, 8vo.

whatever they were, we have nothing to do, nor will they do more to prove what the government of the Church of Scotland *really was*, than the Archdeacon's designs and wishes will show what the government of the Church of England now is.

He remarks, that they who have read King James's *Premonition to Christian Monarchs*, "will know how to estimate the value of the assertion, that 'things were then progressing towards a regular Presbyterian form of government.'" I need hardly remind the reader that these words of mine, spoken with reference to the period just preceding the year 1581, state a *notorious fact*, this form of government having been first developed in the General Assembly in 1581, and *established by Act of Parliament* in 1592. The king and his counsellors may have as much wished to introduce a regular Episcopalian Church into Scotland as King James II. and his counsellors wished to introduce Popery into England; but what we have to deal with is *fact*, not the king's *desires*.

To impute to me "the hypothesis that this monarch's counsellors were favorable to the erection of that most loyal platform" of Presbytery, is one of that species of assertion that are best left to the reader to do justice upon.

We have only to deal with what was *done* by them; and so far as this is concerned, it appears that even so late as 1606, when the king proposed to the General Assembly at Linlithgow, that his titular bishops should be the permanent moderators of their synods, and "this overture, seeming to import *a great alteration in the Discipline*, was not well accepted of divers," "his Majesty's Commissioner declared, that it was so far from the king's purpose to make *any change in the present Discipline*, as he did not long for anything more than to have it rightly settled, and all these eye-lists removed, which had given him so just occasion of discontent." (*Spotiswood*, p. 501.)

The last paragraph I must confess myself unable to understand. How it can be an "artifice of controversy" to suppose that Archdeacon Churton thinks me "a Low Churchman," when it is notorious that he must do so, if he is true to his own avowed principles, which I have no doubt he is, passes my poor comprehension.

I would advise the Archdeacon, another time, first to be a little more careful how he launches a bitter and offensive charge against others, of uttering a "verbal shuffle, and something more," when making a statement on a matter on which (to take the most charitable view) he has but a limited stock of information; and, secondly, when the opposition of his statements to undeniable facts is calmly pointed out, to allow his reason (to say nothing of good manners) to have a little more sway, when he sits down to make his reply; otherwise, he will find that his misstatements will rapidly multiply, and be regretted by himself in his calmer moments.

I now proceed to make a few remarks on Chancellor Harington's statements on this subject; the principal of which I have already noticed in my reply to Archdeacon Churton. And I shall limit myself to a few remarks, because it appears to me that *the facts* proved in my Letter show indisputably what the state of things was in the Church of Scotland in 1604; and no amount of extracts giving the *views* of party writers on the subject, can make the case different from what facts prove it to have been. With real respect for Chancellor Harington, I must say that he does not appear to me to have gone the right way to get at the simple *truth*. He may multiply extracts from various writers sufficient to fill an octavo volume, as easily as his pamphlet: he may ask one and another what they think about the matter, and present us with a mountain of testimonies in his favor; but not *prove* a single point. In short, he may heap Pelion upon Ossa, and Olympus upon Pelion, and be practically as far off as ever from the throne of truth. He himself informs us, that he has "sought a solution of this question, so far as the history of the Kirk is involved, by correspondence and conference with several eminent Presbyterian writers in Scotland." (P. 5.) Now, with all respect for these writers, I confess it would have been one of the last ways I should have thought of for eliciting "a solution of the question" at issue. For these writers would naturally feel great disgust at King James's interferences with the General Assembly, and the subtile way in which he endeavored to undermine that Presbyterian form of government which, while he was *compelled to support*, he secretly disliked; and would be inclined therefore to *antedate* the extinction of what they would wish to be considered the true and genuine Presbyterian form of government; just as some high Episcopalian writers are inclined to antedate the establishment of prelacy. It seems to me somewhat similar to the Pope's recent mode of determining the doctrine of the immaculate conception of the Virgin Mary, by writing round to his bishops, and asking each, What do you think? and, What do *you* think? Of course, he got an abundance of answers to his mind.

What we have to deal with is the simple question, What was the form of church government in Scotland in 1604? I have shown, in my Letter, what it was; and I would ask the Chancellor, as I have asked the Archdeacon, what he calls such a form of church government. It matters nothing to us what modern Presbyterians think of it. That does not alter the facts of the case, nor touch the question at issue. *That Church was then under a Presbyterian form of church government, and it is so now.* That is the statement made; and the truth of it is proved by undeniable facts. That the *present mode of carrying out that government may be different* from that which was followed at that time, does not affect the question.

I must beg permission, therefore, to remind the Chancellor, that all his extracts from various authors, as to the non-recognition of the General Assemblies of the Kirk, after 1597, by certain writers or parties, and as to their *opinion* of certain acts of the king being tantamount to the establishment of Episcopacy, &c., prove nothing. It is a question of *fact* with which we are concerned, and such statements only serve to *obscure the truth.*

The Chancellor tells us (p. 12), that when we "examine into the real sentiments of King James," &c. "the idea of the Presbyterian Kirk . . . being recognized by the Canon as a branch of Christ's Holy Catholic Church, is positively absurd." And he proceeds to devote *six pages* to extracts from King James's works and other sources, to show how, "*from an early period,*" he had recognized "Episcopacy as an ordinance of God," &c. &c., and hence to prove the "absurdity" of such a supposition. Now, to these six pages my reply shall be given in about six lines. The very Act of 1597, so much referred to, "sets forth that *his Majesty*, with advice and consent of the Estates, '*decerns and declares that the Kirk within this realm, wherein the same religion is professed, is* THE TRUE AND HOLY KIRK, and that such pastors and ministers *within the same*, as at any time his Majesty shall please to provide to the office, place, title, and dignity of a Bishop, Abbot, or other Prelate, shall at all time hereafter have vote in Parliament, &c.'" (*Lawson's Hist.* p. 241.) The former part of these words is *omitted* by Mr. Stephen. So that it was "the true and holy Kirk," in King James's estimation, previous to the Act of 1597. Was it less so in 1604?

The next *ten pages* nearly are devoted to extracts intended to show the absurdity of supposing Bancroft to have recognized a Presbyterian community as a Church. My reply is simply the account given by Spotiswood, quoted in my Letter, of what took place at the consecration of the Scotch bishops in 1610, *Spotiswood being one of them.* If Chancellor Harington denies its truth, he may as well deny the value of almost all the records of history we possess. If he admits it, there is an end to the question as to Bancroft's views on the point. If, as is asserted (p. 27), Dr. Bancroft "*added* a more convincing solution," *i. e.* more convincing to those who like it better, that *addition* does not affect the matter. If he said what Archbishop Spotiswood tells us he did say, it is a waste of time to discuss the matter any farther.

In the 3d Letter in his Appendix, Mr. Harington takes up this question again, and speaking of a reference to this statement of Spotiswood, he says, "if historical truth had been aimed at, it should have been stated that Heylin and other writers give a very different solution of the difficulty;" namely, that Bancroft said, that consecration as a bishop supplied all defects as to the lower orders. (P. 97.) But does Mr. Harington mean to oppose Heylin's unsupported assertions, or those of "other writers," to the testimony of Archbishop Spotiswood, who was himself one of the three bishops then consecrated? If not, his censure for not referring the reader to those assertions falls to the ground. In fact, there is no *contradiction* between the two, for Bancroft might have given (as some say he did) both solutions. Mr. Harington proceeds to tell us that Neale ascribes the statement to Abbot. It would have been better, if he had *also* told us, that Neale confirms Archbishop Spotiswood's statement as to Bancroft, ascribing to Bancroft the precise remark which the Archbishop attributes to him.

The extract from Malcolm Laing (p. 99) is directly adverse to Mr. Harington's view; for he says, "their ordination even to the priesthood was questioned; but the objection was overruled, *lest their former Presbyterian vocation should appear invalid;* the subordinate order of priesthood was included, or supposed to be included, in the Episcopal; and was supplied, IF DEFECTIVE, by the regular consecration of these Scottish Bishops." So that here were two ways of removing the difficulty, either of which might be adopted by those concerned in the consecration; and perhaps to Bishop Andrews the latter might be the most acceptable; but we have in these words rather a confirmation than otherwise of Archbishop Spotiswood's statement.

When therefore Mr. Harington sums up, "Unless the writer in the *Herald* can throw any new light upon the subject, I shall conclude that the admission of Presbyterian orders by the bishops who consecrated the Scottish prelates is still *to be proved,*" I must reply (leaving the writer in the *Morning Herald* to answer for himself), that unless Mr. Harington can prove that Archbishop Spotiswood's statement, in a matter where he himself was one of the principal parties concerned, is not to be believed, and so all historical records be made valueless, I shall conclude that such admission is *proved.* And the public must judge between us.

The truth is, that when all these persons were recognizing and cherishing as true Churches of Christ the Foreign Reformed Churches that were under a Presbyterian form of government, it is to me incomprehensible (I will not use Chancellor Harington's phrase *absurd,* lest he might dislike the rebound of his own term), how it can be urged as impossible that they should recognize the Presbyterian Church of Scotland as a true Church, and pray for it as such. Will Chancellor Harington tell us, why they should recognize a Genevan ecclesiastical community as a Church (as even Bishop Cosin did, and communicated with it rather than with Rome), and repudiate the Presbyterian Scotch Kirk?

Chancellor Harington next proceeds to quote Canons 7, 8, and 9, of 1604, as declaring that all who spoke of the government of the Church of England as repugnant to the word of God, were *excommunicated ipso facto;* and, with exclamations of triumph, deduces the conclusion, that therefore by the Canons every consistent member of the Church of Scotland was excommunicated *ipso facto.*

Surely he must see in a moment, upon reconsideration, the fallacy of his argument. It is like arguing that, because the law decrees that everybody that denies the sovereignty of the Queen is a traitor, and ought to be put to death, *therefore* every foreigner all over the world ought to be shot.

These Canons of course apply only to England, and excommunication can only be denounced against those who are considered as being legally within the Church. You cannot turn a man out of your house who never was in it.

If Mr. Harington's argument was sound, it would apply as much to some of the Foreign Reformed Churches—whom our Church then looked upon with the most favorable eye, as the great bulwarks of true religion on the Continent—as to the Church of Scotland. Let Mr. Harington read Beza's abuse of the prelatical government of the Church of England, and then see the terms in which Archbishop Whitgift (*when Archbishop of Canterbury*), in 1593, in a letter *noticing his statements*, addresses him. He commences by styling him his "most dear brother in God," and superscribes his letter to him as "his most *dear brother and* COLLEAGUE *in Christ, and faithful pastor of the Genevan Church.*" (*Strype's Life of Whitgift*, ii. pp. 159, 173.)

Such facts (as Chancellor Harington well knows) might be easily multiplied a hundred fold. And yet, strange to say, we are told it is "absurd" to suppose that a Canon of 1604 could recognize a Presbyterian community as a Church!

Seven more pages are then occupied with extracts from the Canons of 1606, laying down the claims of the Episcopal form of church government, and declaring that he who denies them "doth greatly err." But *cui bono?* The question is not whether our greatest divines have spoken in the strongest terms of the Scriptural claims of Episcopacy, and maintained that those who rejected them, and set up another platform of church discipline, did "greatly err." No one who knows anything about the matter can doubt it. But the question is, whether those who, under certain circumstances, have adopted a different form of church government, are to be considered as destitute of any power to minister the word and sacraments, and outcasts from the communion of the Catholic Church of Christ. Let Chancellor Harington ask himself the question whether Archdeacon Mason or Bishop Cosin would not cordially have assented to those Canons, and then let him remember what both of them have said of the ministry of certain Non-Episcopal Churches. Archbishop Whitgift no doubt thought that Beza did "greatly err" when he attacked the prelatical government of the Church of England in such unmeasured terms; but that did not prevent his addressing him as his "most dear brother and *colleague* in Christ." Oh! for a little more of the same charity among ourselves in the present day!

When, therefore, the Chancellor concludes: "Perhaps you had been misled by the seductive charms of Mr. Macaulay, who tells us that, 'in the year 1603, the Province of Canterbury solemnly recognized the Church of Scotland, a Church in which Episcopal control and Episcopal ordination were then unknown, as a branch of the Holy Catholic Church of Christ,'" I must say, that though not always disposed to agree with Mr. Macaulay in his ecclesiastical statements, he has here recorded *a simple fact*, and stated it with an accuracy of language which places even his words entirely beyond the reach of Mr. Harington's criticism. And I can only wish that the "seductive charms of Mr. Macaulay" had for once detached the Chancellor from those "seductive charms" of modern High Church principles which have led him to turn aside out of the high-road of proved facts, to seek truth in the by-ways of prejudiced statements and inferential reasonings from documents which do not meet the point at issue.

Against Mr. Stephen's *assertions* in the Postscript, I shall merely place the *facts* stated in my letter. His offered *proofs* I shall be happy to see, only reminding him and Mr. Harington of what seems to me to have been too much forgotten in this matter, that *the mere statements* of historians are no *proofs* of the real facts of the case. What Collier may say of what took place in 1606 is, *in itself*, worth no more than what Mr. Macaulay or Mr. Stephen may say. And even in the case of contemporary historians, the greatest care is necessary to separate the *facts* brought down to us in their statements, from the colorings with which those facts are clothed. Thus, the statements of Calderwood and Dr. Hetherington, quoted by Chancellor Harington (p. 7), are so far from throwing any light on the subject, that they only tend to *hide* the truth from the reader, because they give a false view of the subject.

The interpretation which Chancellor Harington gives to the Canon, I have already noticed in my Letter to the *Guardian*, given above. (See p. 8.) It may be worth while to add that of Mr. Stephen, as here stated. Both appear to me remarkably to show the desperate shifts to which our modern High Church interpreters of that Canon are driven to make the words square with their notions. Mr. Stephen says, that Bancroft "no doubt had the 55th Canon so framed as to pray for the grace of Reformation for the Church of Scotland as it then defectively stood; and, by anticipation, for that Branch of the holy Catholic and Apostolic Church, when in reality she should be duly organized according to Christ's appointment. Therefore the Canon neither does nor can refer to the Presbyterian Kirk, but to the titular and real Episcopal Church of that country." This, in other words, amounts to saying Bancroft no doubt framed the Canon according to my view; *therefore* the Canon "neither does nor can" mean anything else than my view. But, to let this pass, let us observe what that view is: it is, that the Canon referred, at the time it was made, to the titular Episcopal Church of Scotland, and, after the consecration of the bishops, to the real Episcopal Church of that country. My reply is, that in 1604 there was no Church attached to the titular Episcopate. The titular bishops formed part of the Presbyterian Church, and had *sworn submission* to the Presbyteries, Provincial and General Assemblies of that Church. Mr. Stephen's alleged Church, therefore, is a nonentity—a phantasm of his own imagination.

II.—ON NON-EPISCOPAL ORDINATIONS.

I NOW proceed to notice the Letters which Chancellor Harington has reprinted in his Appendix, from the *Morning Chronicle*, relating to the question of the doctrine of our Church on Non-Episcopal Orders.

The third Letter, which relates to the consecration of the Scotch Bishops in 1610, I have already noticed. There remain, therefore, only the two former.

I must first observe, however, that I have already discussed this subject at some length in a Review in the *Christian Observer* for November, 1851, which, with the Editor's permission, I have since reprinted in a separate form ;* and, therefore, I shall only *add* here what may be necessary to meet Mr. Harington's statements on the subject, referring to the authorities I have there given. The first Letter is occupied with the cases of Morrison and the Church of Alexandria as mentioned by Eutychius. With the reference to Eutychius I have now no concern, because I am considering the doctrine of the Church of England; though quite ready, at a suitable time, to discuss that also with Mr. Harington.

Morrison's case I have given in my pamphlet (p. 29); and it appears that, though he had only Scotch Presbyterian Orders, Archbishop Grindal granted him a license to minister the Sacraments, &c., in "*the whole Province*" (not *diocese*, as Chancellor Harington states) of Canterbury, which was formally issued by his Vicar-General.

What is Mr. Harington's reply to this case?

Oh! Archbishop Grindal—the chaplain of Bishop Ridley, *a compiler of the Prayer-Book of* 1559, the Bishop of London when the 39 Articles were drawn up in 1562, the Archbishop of York when they were finally settled in 1571, and the immediate successor of Parker in 1576 in the See of Canterbury—did not know what the principles of his Church were. He "acted" in this matter, says Mr. Harington, "in direct opposition to the principles of the Church over which he had presided," and "the truth is not affected by the vagaries of Archbishop Grindal." (P. 45.) And he sends him to the Ordinal in the Prayer-Book (which perhaps the Chancellor forgot, at the moment, he had a principal hand in

* Entitled, "The Doctrine of the Church of England on Non-Episcopal Ordinations, &c. Hatchard," 8vo. pp. 44.

preparing) to learn better. I leave Grindal's cause in the hands of the public.

But Mr. Harington thinks that he has found out another reason for rejecting the argument derived from this case. He says: "After all, is it clear how Morrison was ordained? Your contemporary has omitted certain important words which appear in the Archbishop's license, '*per manuum impositionem admissus et ordinatus fueras.*'" And he then proceeds to remark, that "the *First Book of Discipline* which was recognized by the Kirk from 1560 to 1581, did not admit imposition of hands in ordination," and he "leaves the solution" of this difficulty "in the hands of Grindal's admirer."

The solution is not far to seek. It will be found in "certain important words which appear in the Archbishop's license," which Mr. Harington has "omitted," though they form part of the sentence in which the words he has quoted occur. The sentence runs thus: "Tu præfatus Johannes Morrison circiter quinque annos elapsos in oppido de Garvet in comitat. Lothien. regni Scotiæ *per generalem synodum sive congregationem illius comitatus in dicto oppido de Garvet congregatam juxta laudabilem Ecclesiæ Scotiæ reformatæ formam et ritum* ad sacros ordines et sacrosanctum ministerium per manuum impositionem admissus et ordinatus fueras." (*Strype's Grindal*, App. p. 596, Ox. ed.) And Mr. Harington will find, that ordination by imposition of hands was common in the Reformed Church of Scotland at that period. He seems entirely to have forgotten, that the First Book of Discipline *never had the sanction of the law*, and therefore was never enforced. And the words themselves of that Book are not a clear prohibition, for they run thus: "Other ceremonies than the public approbation of the people, and the declaration of the chief minister, that the person there presented is appointed to serve that Church, we cannot approve: for albeit the Apostles used the imposition of hands, yet seeing the miracle is ceased, the using of the ceremony *we judge not to be necessary*." (*Spotiswood*, p. 156.) But whatever sense may be given to these words, the Book had not the sanction of the law, and in this point particularly was not enforced.

Mr. Harington adds (p. 48), in a postscript: "When will members of the Church of England be taught that they can refute the Papists only by adhering to *sound Church principles?* All other attempts have been, and ever will be, failures."

Will he permit me to remind him, that this argument has recently been so irreparably damaged, that it is absolutely unfit for farther service? Has he forgotten, that these were almost the very words of Mr. Newman himself, when he was hastening rapidly towards Rome? And that his "sound Church principles" have led not himself only, but a host of his followers, into the arms of Rome? And how does it happen that if the "sound Church principles" of the *Morning Chronicle* are the only defence against

Popery, they are so different from those by which they who originally came out from Rome among us were actuated?

When Mr. Harington says, that "the eminent anti-Papal controversialists in James II.'s reign were not Dissenters, nor did they argue on dissenting principles," I quite agree with him; but neither did they maintain the "sound Church principles" of those who have assailed the present Archbishop of Canterbury. There is a mean betwixt the two, which it would be greatly for the advantage of the interests of truth and peace in our Church could the "members of the Church of England be taught" to maintain; and which the works of the chief of these "anti-Papal controversialists," Wake, Stillingfleet, Tenison, Tillotson, Sherlock, &c., if carefully read, would greatly tend to promote.

In an appendix to this Letter, Chancellor Harington gives an extract from his pamphlet in reply to Mr. Macaulay,* in which he takes up the case of Whittingham and Travers—cases which I am not concerned to defend, because I have not referred to them; but as it will always, I trust, be my endeavor fairly to meet any facts or arguments that may be adduced against the views I maintain (truth, not party-views, being what I desire to promote), I shall state precisely what bearing these cases seem to me to have upon the point in question. They have been adduced, as Mr. Harington correctly informs us, as instances of persons who have been allowed to minister in our Church with only Non-Episcopal Orders.

Now, as it respects the case of Whittingham, the Chancellor must permit me to ask him to review his account of it, for he has not correctly stated it; and he will find that, when correctly stated, it assumes a very different aspect from what he has given to it. Mr. Harington says: "Whittingham's '*Orders were called in question by Archbishop Whitgift,*' and a commission was issued to report thereon; which, but for his death, would have ended in his being '*deprived* (to quote Whitgift's language) *without special grace and dispensation.*'" (Pp. 50, 51.) Mr. Harington forgets that Whittingham was dead several years before Whitgift became Archbishop; not to say that Whitgift was Archbishop of *Canterbury*, and Whittingham Dean of Durham, in the Province of *York;* and I must suppose that the name *Whitgift*, in the *first* part of this sentence, was not a slip of the pen for *Sandys*, because, if so, Mr. Harington would have referred to Sandys's account of the matter, which mentions the reason for his calling Whittingham's Orders in question. But I cannot wholly account for the statement; as Strype, in one of the very places to which Mr. Harington refers us (*Annals*, II. 2, p. 167, *et seq.*), tells us from Sandys's *own words* what it was. Archbishop Sandys was "represented as blameworthy for calling in question the Dean's

* Entitled, "The Reformers of the English Church and Mr. Macaulay's History of England."

(Whittingham's) ministry;" and in his defence to the Lord Treasurer he writes thus: "The discredit of the Church of Geneva is hotly alleged. Verily, my Lord, *that Church is not touched.* For he hath *not received his ministry in that Church, or by any authority or order from that Church*, so far as yet can appear. Neither was there any English Church in Germany that attempted the like, neither needed they to have done; having among themselves sufficient ministers to supply the room. But if his ministry, without authority of God or man, *without law, order, or example of* ANY CHURCH, may be current, take heed to the sequel." (*Strype*, Ann. II. 2, p. 167, 8, and App. 620.) And the *Memorandum* of Archbishop Sandys's Chancellor, on the result of an investigation into the matter, states: "W. W., now Dean of Durham, hath not proved, that he was orderly made minister at Geneva, according to the order of the Geneva [book or office] by public authority established there." (*Strype, ib.* p. 170.) The objection of Archbishop Sandys therefore was, that he had not been ordained according to the order of *the Genevan* OR ANY *Church*, and had not in fact received any sort of ordination.

Whittingham's case, therefore, is, to say the least, rather against Mr. Harington than in his favor; for it would seem likely, from the account of the matter thus given, that Archbishop Sandys would have been satisfied if he had had regular Genevan Orders.

The case of Travers (who was inhibited by Archbishop Whitgift from preaching on account of his foreign ordination) is *in itself* not very dissimilar, for he had never been regularly ordained in any of the Foreign Reformed Churches; and this is particularly objected to him by Whitgift in his remarks upon *Travers's Reasons;* but I *fully admit* that it appears, from those remarks, that Archbishop Whitgift held, that "the laws of the realm required, that such as are to be allowed as ministers in this Church of England, should be ordained by a Bishop." (See *Strype's Whitgift*, i. 476–80, and iii. 182–6.) In this view he was opposed to his predecessor Grindal, and also to the generality of the Bishops that immediately came after him; as appears from the statement of Bishop Cosin, a High Church divine, quoted by me in my pamphlet on this subject;* who, after stating that "*our Bishops*" did not reordain such persons before admitting them to a charge here, says, *in direct opposition* to Archbishop Whitgift: "*Nor did our laws require more of him than to declare his public consent to the religion received amongst us, and to subscribe the Articles established.*"

Now, I will not (as Mr. Harington has done by Grindal) attack Archbishop Whitgift for "vagaries," but simply say that the weight of testimony is against his view of the subject. I am not surprised, however, that so strict a disciplinarian as Whitgift should have adopted the view he did. And, in the present day,

* Doctr. of Church of England on Non-Episcopal Ordinations, p. 29.

the question is one of very little importance, as the point has been decided by the last Act of Uniformity and the *additions* made to the Preface to the Ordinal. But Mr. Harington will, perhaps, permit me to leave this question for his consideration: How it was that if Archbishop Whitgift was right, the additions came to be made to that Preface, and words touching this matter inserted in the new Act of Uniformity at the Restoration? To what purpose?

But farther; so far as concerns the great question now at issue, Whether the Church of England admits the validity of the Non-Episcopal orders of the Scotch and Foreign Reformed Churches in the abstract, and apart from the consideration of them as legal qualifications for the ministry of our own Church, *such cases as these do not touch it.* Archbishop Whitgift's views on the abstract question, Mr. Harington may see in the extracts I have already given from his works.*

Chancellor Harington, indeed, appears to quote (p. 57) with approbation, a remark of the Bishop of Exeter, that our Church, in not admitting to the exercise of the ministry in her communion persons not episcopally ordained, "seems to imply the absolute necessity of Episcopal ordination to confer the ministerial character; for, by the most universally admitted rule of Christian communion, all who are constituted Christ's ministers in any one portion of his Church, carry with them their character and commission in every other into which they may migrate."

But the Bishop has here just *assumed* what he had to *prove*, namely, that this rule *is* admitted by our Church at the present day. It may have been a "universally admitted rule" at one time in the Church, but circumstances may have occurred to interrupt its universal admission on more than one account, and in more than one way. And such I submit is the case. The bishop's statement is merely an attempt, *more suo*, to make his *assertion* pass as a *proof* of the rule of our Church, and hence enforce the doctrine he wishes to establish.

One word on the extract given by Mr. Harington (pp. 49, 50) from Dr. Bowden's *Letters to Miller* (Letter 15), vol. ii. p. 36. With respect to that part of it which refers to the Act of 1571, and argues that the passage in it, sometimes referred to on this subject, was passed with a view principally to the Romanists, I fully agree with him; but when he goes on to say: "Let it farther be considered, that it was the avowed doctrine of the Church throughout the whole reign of Elizabeth, that Episcopal ordination was of Divine appointment, and then it will be evident that the Act in question could not have been designed to indulge, under the specified condition, those who had received no other Orders but Presbyterian"—he seems to me entirely mistaken.

If this passage refers to the language of the Ordinal, when it

* *Ib.* pp. 19, 20.

speaks of "the avowed doctrine of the Church," then the argument wholly fails. For the utmost that can be deduced from the language of the Ordinal is, that Episcopacy was of Apostolical institution, which may be fully admitted by those who hold the Non-Episcopal Orders of the Foreign Reformed Churches to be valid. And if it refers to the language of the divines of our Church of that day, it is entirely incorrect, as the passages I have already given from their writings* fully show; for they did not *all* even hold that Episcopacy was so far of Divine origin as that it was regularly instituted by the Apostles. And even if they had so held, the conclusion sought to be established would not have followed. Those who did hold that doctrine communicated with the ministers of the Foreign Reformed Churches as men whose ministry was perfectly valid, and their Churches true Churches of Christ.

On this point, therefore, I must dissent from Dr. Bowden; and it is evident, from Bishop Cosin's statement already quoted, that our Bishops (speaking generally) took the same view of the case.† The clause, though it probably had the Romanists particularly in view, was worded so as to include the case of others also.

In fact, Dr. Bowden himself, though speaking of Episcopacy as a *Divine* appointment, only means, as he himself tells us, that it was instituted by the Apostles; and that will not prove its indispensable necessity for all times, places, and circumstances.

Of Dr. Bowden's sentiments on the great question at issue between Mr. Harington and myself, I shall have occasion to speak presently, when noticing Mr. Harington's reference to him as a witness in his favor.

Chancellor Harington's *Second Letter* is entitled, *The Witness of Anglican Divines for Episcopacy.* Now, if the object of the Letter was truly described in these words, I must say, in the language of Mr. Harington himself to his opponent, that his whole Catena is "*nihil ad rem*," that he might have "quadruplicated his authorities, which he might easily have done," and "not have touched the question at issue; for nobody doubts that our Anglican divines have witnessed "for Episcopacy;" and I can well afford to be liberal enough to throw him in the addition *against Presbyterianism.*

Mr. Harington tells us that his opponent "has strung together a Catena of authorities which seem to recognize the validity of Presbyterian Ordination in certain cases of necessity." (P. 55.) I will take this as a true account of the matter, for I have not seen the article, and am not defending it (as I know nothing of it), but what I deem to be the truth in reply to Mr. Harington's own statements in this Letter.

This Catena Mr. Harington thinks useless, because, he says, the question is this: "Whether the Church Catholic has not,

* See "Doctrine, &c." pp. 17–28. † *Ibid.* p. 30.

from the first to the nineteenth century, maintained the *Divine institution of Episcopacy*, recognizing no other system of Church polity? And whether the Church of England, as a portion of the Church Catholic, does not altogether exclude ordination by Presbyters?"

Now, with all respect for Chancellor Harington, I must say, that this statement is calculated for anything rather than to show clearly the real point at issue, and might leave disputants to argue forever to no purpose, each having a different proposition in view in his arguments. I must remind Mr. Harington of the old saying, that *dolus latet in generalibus.* When he says that the question is, whether the Church of England excludes ordination by Presbyters, does he mean that she does this so far as permission to minister in her own communion is concerned, or as it respects all Churches, all over the world? If the former (and a considerable portion of his testimonies and remarks apply only to this), nobody doubts it; the law is now clear; there is no controversy on the subject. And the reference made to such cases as that of Morrison, is only for the purpose of showing that, until the Restoration, some of the highest authorities of our Church held that there was nothing to prevent persons ordained by Presbyters *even ministering in our own Church;* which is an undeniable fact, and greatly strengthens the argument for the point at issue. If Mr. Harington holds that Archbishop Whitgift took a sounder view of the subject than the generality of his brethren did, be it so. The matter is scarcely worth arguing now. And Archbishop Whitgift is wholly with us in the only question now at issue. But if he means the latter, then the Catena which he tells us is *nihil ad rem*, is obviously *multum ad rem.* And the latter *is the question.* He is well aware that the letter of the present Archbishop of Canterbury (out of which this controversy arose) referred not to the validity of Presbyterian Orders for ministering *in our Church*, which our laws forbid, but to the question of their validity in the abstract in the Church of Christ, when given under the circumstances in which certain Foreign Reformed Churches have been placed by the corruptions of the Papacy.

I cannot quite understand, therefore, how the Chancellor could say, after adding a few remarks about Morrison and the Church of Alexandria, "here the discussion might fairly close." If he had closed it there, he would have closed it without touching the point in question. For if even the writer in the *Herald* so mistook his cause as to make it rest upon a supposed right of Presbyterianly ordained persons to minister in our Church, it surely would have been better for the Chancellor to have set him right on this point, and then grappled with the real question at issue.

But he has, in fact, added a long Catena of authorities on the subject from our English divines—authorities which I cannot but think he meant to prove, that our Church not only forbids those in Presbyterian Orders to minister in our Churches, but disallows the validity of such Orders in the abstract, nullifying the ministrations of those who hold them throughout the whole Church of Christ; and as such I proceed to consider them; for in any other view they are *totally irrelevant* to the great question at issue.

One remark more on his definition of the question under discussion. It would surely have been more unambiguous to speak of the *Apostolical* institution of Episcopacy, than to use the epithet *Divine.* I am quite aware that it has been frequently used, and also of the sense in which it may be legitimately applied; but I am also aware, that whenever the matter has been controverted, it has been found necessary to point out two or three senses in which the word "Divine" may be used, and (with *very few* exceptions) to admit that in one only is it applicable to the origin of Episcopacy, namely, as instituted by men divinely inspired; and in a formal definition of this kind, a vague phraseology is surely to be avoided. Now of the Apostolical institution of Episcopacy I make no doubt; but then I have equally little doubt of the Apostolical institution of the practice of anointing the sick with oil. And though I would not place the importance of one on a par with the importance of the other, yet if the mere fact of a thing having been Apostolically instituted, renders its observance indispensably necessary in all ages and all parts of the Church of Christ, the one of these is as indispensably necessary as the other. And if this argument does not hold good, then the argument of Mr. Harington for the indispensable necessity of Episcopacy from this fact falls to the ground.

There is also one other point on which I would offer a word before proceeding to a consideration of Chancellor Harington's authorities, because I know that much stress is often laid upon it, and that is, as to the meaning of the term *necessity* when used by some of our divines as alone justifying Presbyterian ordination in a Church. It is often said, that such and such Presbyterian Churches might now, if they pleased, receive Episcopacy from more than one Episcopal Church, and, therefore, that they cannot urge the plea of necessity. But it is clear that the word necessity was not used by them in this strict sense. I refer, in proof of this, to the language of Saravia and Crakanthorp,* both of them men in the highest repute with my opponents; and the latter of whom distinctly says, speaking of his wish that those Churches would avail themselves of the opportunity they then possessed of obtaining Episcopal Orders, "*sed optamus, non cogimus: jus et imperium in eorum Ecclesias nec habemus nos, nec desideramus.*" And this opportunity they have had for more than two centuries just as much as at the present day; so that all the testimonies of our divines since that period, such as Mason, Cosin, &c. &c., were written under similar circumstances to those which now exist.

It is clear, also, that when Saravia spoke of necessity, he was alluding to a necessity arising from the corruption of the Bishops

* See "Doctrine, &c." pp. 22, 39.

in any particular Church for the sound presbyters of that Church to perpetuate their order by admitting others to it themselves, though under ordinary circumstances they would have had no right to do so.* He was contemplating each Church as an independent community that had a right to order its own affairs.

And when it is urged, that no necessity exists now for the Foreign Reformed Churches lacking Episcopacy, because certain Episcopal Churches would give them Bishops, I am much inclined to doubt whether even this could be proved, for there may be still many impediments, some arising out of their relations to the different States in which they are found, to their *reception* of Episcopacy, whatever may be the willingness of other Churches to *give* it to them.

Mr. Harington's first quotations are taken from the Ordinal as it stood previous to 1662. Against the interpretation which it is sought to affix to these, we have first the practice of the Bishops of that day, as reported by Bishop Cosin,† the 23d Article;‡ and the fact that when, at the Restoration, it was wished to exclude those in Presbyterian Orders from ministering in our Church, words were added for that purpose.

He then proceeds to his Catena, which is formed from the works of Cranmer, Whitgift, Jewel, Rollock, Bancroft, Morton, Bilson, Andrews, Hall, Hammond, Hooker, Bramhall, Heylin, Mason, Cosin, Potter, Sanderson, Downame, Beveridge, Taylor, Barrow, Sage, Stillingfleet, Brett, Madox, Leslie, Dodwell, Hickes, Burscough, Milbourn, Bowden, Daubeney, Laud, the author of Εικων Βασιλικη, the author of *The Beauty of the Church of England*, Peter Du Moulin, and Thomas's *Answer to Owen.*

Now I suppose it will strike the most cursory reader that several of these authors were *Non-jurors.* Under this description come Brett, Leslie, Dodwell, Hickes; a school of writers whose remarks *on the very point we are now considering*, obtained for them, from one of the most eminent of "the eminent anti-Papal controversialists in James II.'s reign," to whom Mr. Harington has referred us, the appellation of "furiosi scriptores." § I will, therefore, willingly make Mr. Harington a present of them.

Of the others, it can hardly be worth while to spend our time upon the opinions of such very small personages as Robert Burscough, Luke Milbourn, the author of *The Beauty of the Church of England* (from whom Mr. Harington has given us *five* pages), and John Thomas, whose work we are told is "strongly recommended by Dr. Hickes" the Non-juror. Moreover, Bishop Sage and Dr. Robert Rollock belong to Scotland, not England. And of the latter of these I would ask Mr. Harington himself, whether he is prepared to maintain that Dr. Rollock, who acted in the

* See the extracts from him in my former pamphlet, pp. 21, 22.
† See the pamphlet already referred to, p. 29.
‡ *Ib.* pp. 26, 27.
§ See former pamphlet, p. 42.

General Assemblies of the Presbyterian Kirk of Scotland, and was in the communion of that Church till his death in 1599, believed the ministrations of the pastors of that Church to be invalid.

With the rest I will now proceed to deal.

I will take the case of Dr. Bowden, the American, first; because it remarkably illustrates the real nature of the whole Catena. Chancellor Harington has made great use of Dr. Bowden, taking some of his authorities from him. And though I cannot think all Dr. Bowden's arguments valid, or his authorities rightly applied, his work bearing, to my mind, marks of haste and inaccuracy, yet I quite admit it to be, as a whole, a valuable defence of Episcopacy. It will be well, then, to ascertain what the object of Dr. Bowden was; it was, to prove against the assertion of the Presbyterian Dr. Miller that Episcopacy was a mere *human* institution, that, on the contrary, it was "of Divine institution;" meaning by these terms, not that it was ordained by any "express command" of God or our Lord Jesus Christ, which he repudiates, but that it was instituted by the Apostles, "men divinely inspired," and therefore, at the least, had "a Divine sanction." (Lett. 17.) And all his arguments and authorities are directed to the establishment of this point. Consequently, they do not touch the question now at issue, which is—not whether Episcopacy was or was not instituted by the Apostles, but—whether Orders derived from an uninterrupted succession of duly consecrated Bishops from the time of the Apostles, are so necessary to the existence of a Church and a valid ministry that neither can exist without them. And unfortunately for Mr. Harington, Dr. Bowden explicitly and expressly repudiates such a notion. He says: "*Every Episcopal writer that I have ever met with* maintains, that this government is *not absolutely necessary to the very salvation of the Church*, but that it is so necessary, that the Church cannot be in a sound and perfect state without it." The latter, of course, every Episcopalian must think. Again: "I am not endeavoring to unchurch other denominations. This is not the question in this discussion." But this *is* the question between the Archbishop and his assailants. And Dr. Bowden goes on to say: "What the essence of a Church is, neither Presbyterians nor Episcopalians have as yet determined. Upon the question, What defect unchurches, unanimity is not to be looked for. . . . . When you shall have the good fortune to agree among yourselves, what is the precise point at which a Church loses that character, perhaps your discoveries will lead Episcopalians to unanimity; till then, I fear, we shall not be agreed, *whether the Divine right of Episcopacy necessarily involves the consequence, that denominations which have not Bishops, when it proceeds from necessity, want a valid ministry;* and whether, again, the want of such a ministry completely unchurches." He does not therefore suppose, that all true Episcopalians must hold that such denominations "*want a valid ministry*," and he did not apparently think so himself. He adds: "Wake, Bingham, Pretyman, and Gisborne, assert the Apostolic institution of Episcopacy. . . Bingham and Wake, particularly the former, are among its ablest advocates. Yet these four divines do *not consider it as essential to the very being of a Church.* When Christians can have it, they ought to have it; but when they cannot, *necessity frees them from all blame. This appears to be the more common opinion of Episcopalians.*" "I acknowledge that they [the Reformers of the Church of England] do *not consider it as essential to the very being of a Church;* but after making this concession, they insist upon it as necessary to a well organized, sound, and perfectly Apostolical Church; and that a departure from it where it is, is an unjustifiable schism; except when a Church imposes upon its members sinful terms of communion." (Lett. 17.) I give the context, that I may not be supposed anxious to keep back any part of Dr. Bowden's views.

Notwithstanding, therefore, Dr. Bowden's opinion of the Apostolical institution of Episcopacy, he admits, that it may reasonably be maintained, and is "the more common opinion of Episcopalians," that it "is not essential to the very being of a Church," and that there may be "a valid ministry" without it. Consequently Dr. Bowden's testimony is worse than useless to Mr. Harington. It is opposed to him. And his whole Catena, with the exception of his Non-juror witnesses, and perhaps one or two others of a similar school, are at best in the same predicament, and some of them still more strongly opposed to his views.

Dr. Bowden has justly drawn a distinction between the views of Episcopalians on the subject, admitting that some of them maintain the higher ground that a regular Episcopal succession is *essential* to the very being of a Church, and that there cannot be a valid ministry without it; and I am quite ready to concede to Mr. Harington that such Episcopalians there have been, and now are, in our Church. But then he must allow me to request him to confine his Catena to such as do hold this; and I can assure him that I will then leave him in quiet possession of it, and not contend with him for a moment as one who has any right in those "*furiosi scriptores,*" as Archbishop Wake called them, who take such a view. But when he lays claim to the support of those who have distinctly repudiated such a notion, and the whole glory of his Catena is derived from names so used, he must excuse my protest against such an (unintentional) misrepresentation of their views. It is obvious, on the first glance at his Catena, that he has mixed together, without discrimination, divines who notoriously differed in their judgment on the very point under discussion; and has only obtained an appearance of their combined support by an inaccurate representation of the question at issue.

I must again repeat, that that question is not the Apostolical Institution of Episcopacy, which I hold as strongly as Chancellor

Harington can do;* but whether the Foreign Reformed Churches, considering the peculiar circumstances in which they have been placed, do or do not possess a valid ministry.

The first remark, therefore, which I have to make upon all the authorities worth noticing in the Catena is, *that the testimonies quoted do not touch the question.* And the second is, *that many of the best of the authors here quoted, have elsewhere expressly opposed the notion of the absolute necessity of Episcopacy to constitute a valid ministry.* This I shall now proceed to show; and a proof of this will be the best evidence of the truth of the first remark. For if many of the most eminent of the authors so quoted have expressed themselves in the most express and explicit terms in favor of the view of which Chancellor Harington quotes them as the opponents, such language as Mr. Harington has quoted from them, does not prove, in the case of *any* who use it, that they held what he seeks to establish.

Without, therefore, going through the whole Catena (which is quite unnecessary), I shall content myself with showing what many of the best of his witnesses have said elsewhere.

Of *Cranmer* I will merely say, that it shows great courage even to name him in such a matter. I shall only refer, in reply, to the documents I have already quoted in my former pamphlet;† showing his entire repudiation of the notion Mr. Harington seeks to fix upon him.

Of *Whitgift* I say the same, and make the same reference.‡ And I must add that, as Mr. Harington's quotation is from the Archbishop's letter to Beza, it would have been better if he had told us, that the letter is addressed to Beza as his "*most dear brother in Christ,*" and superscribed to him as "*his most dear brother and* COLLEAGUE *in Christ, and faithful pastor of the Genevan Church.*" For I take it for granted, that though the extract is given from Dr. Bowden, Mr. Harington must be familiar with the Letter itself as given by Strype. (*Life of Whitgift*, ii. pp. 159, 173.)

For Bishop *Jewel*, the passages I have given§ from his writings so completely refute the interpretation which Mr. Harington would affix to the passages he has quoted, that nothing need be added here.

Archbishop *Bancroft's* express testimony in favor of the validity of the Orders of the Foreign Reformed Churches, I have given above,|| and in my former pamphlet.¶

Bishop *Morton's* direct recognition of the right of Presbyters to ordain, when the Bishops of a Church have departed from the true faith, I have given in the same place.** In fact, Mr. Harington merely gives a general reference to his work, entitled, "The Episcopacy of the Church of England justified to be Apos-

* I may perhaps be permitted to refer as evidence of this to my defence of this view nearly ten years ago, in my *Divine Rule of Faith and Practice*, vol. ii. pp. 60–72. And in pp. 72–110, I have discussed the question now at issue, and have seen no reason to change the ground I there took on the subject.

† See pp. 13—16. ‡ See pp. 19, 20. § See p. 18.

|| See pp. 7 and 15, 16, above. ¶ See p. 34. ** See p. 36.

tolical," a proof of which does not (to use Mr. Harington's own words) "touch the question at issue."

Bishop *Hall* says, that "there is no difference in any essential matter betwixt the Church of England and her sisters of the Reformation;" and as to the difference in the form of church government, "we all profess this form not to be essential to the being of a Church."*

Hooker tells us, with reference to the case of *Beza*, that "there may be sometimes very just and sufficient reason to allow Ordination made without a Bishop," and that there is no law by which "the Lord hath appointed Presbyters for ever to be under the regiment of Bishops,"† &c.

Of Archdeacon *Mason* we have a work the very object of which is to vindicate "the validity of the Ordination of the ministers of the Reformed Churches beyond the seas;" a work originally forming part of the very book to which Chancellor Harington refers, to prove Mason an advocate of his own views.‡

Bishop *Cosin* has treated expressly of the same subject, and taken the same ground; and acted upon it when in exile, by communicating with those Churches, and exhorting others to do so. His testimony is very full and distinct.§

Bishop *Downham*, in the very same work that Chancellor Harington quotes, expressly defends the Ordinations of the Foreign Reformed Churches, and formally repudiates the notion that because the Episcopal form of church government is to be found in the Scriptures, therefore it is "perpetually and unchangeably necessary in all Churches."||

So that all these authors, the cream of the Catena, have clearly and expressly *advocated* the doctrine which Chancellor Harington seeks to overthrow by their testimony.

His *nominal* thesis of the Apostolical institution of Episcopacy they will no doubt fully support; but his *real* one, of the indispensable necessity of Episcopacy to a valid ministry and a real Church, they distinctly oppose.

And consequently, as to all the remaining authors in his list who have spoken in similar terms, such passages as he has quoted from them prove nothing as to their views on the real question at issue. And the authors to whom I have referred are amply sufficient to show what the views of the great body of our most learned and able divines have been on this subject.¶

My belief is, that even the highest of our High Church divines of former times (excepting of course such men as the Non-jurors, Hickes, Dodwell, &c.) would have declined to take the ground now occupied by the Archbishop's opponents.

For instance, Bishop *Andrews*, whom Mr. Harington has

* See *Ib.* † See *Ib.* pp. 20, 21.

‡ See extracts and a proof of its genuineness given, *Ib.* pp. 38, 39.

§ See it given *Ib.* pp. 39–41.

|| See the extracts given *Ib.* p. 36.

¶ Some farther testimonies will be found in my former pamphlet.

quoted as a witness in favor of his views. High as Bishop Andrews might place the claims of Episcopacy, he distinctly repudiates the notion of unchurching those that are under a different form of church government. (See my former pamphlet, p. 32.)

So again Archbishop *Bramhall* (another of Mr. Harington's witnesses); who reminds us that "*there is great difference between a* VALID *and a* REGULAR *Ordination.*" I have given in my former pamphlet (pp. 32, 33) abundant proof of the nature of his views; but I will here add a remark in reply to Chancellor Harington's argument that because he reordained some who had only received the imposition of the hands of Presbyters, therefore he must have considered their Orders as altogether invalid. I quite grant, that the reference that has been sometimes made to the circumstance here referred to, as if it proved that Bramhall admitted the validity of such Orders because he said he would not discuss the question of their validity, but advised the parties to be ordained in order to obtain a legal title to their tithes, is one which always appeared to me a mistake. The words in the Letters of Orders, "ordines, *si quos habuit,*" appear to me to prove his wish to leave the question of the validity of their Orders wholly undecided. But then on the other hand, Mr. Harington cannot quote him as a witness *against* the validity of such Orders, when he himself carefully abstained from committing himself to that view, and formally and expressly declined to determine the question (nec validitatem aut invaliditatem eorundem determinantes); and as to the act of Ordination, he himself supplies the answer to Mr. Harington's suggestion that he would not have reordained one who in his view had been already ordained, when he says, that in ordaining he was "*solummodo supplentes* quicquid prius defuit *per canones Ecclesiæ Anglicanæ requisitum*, et providentes paci Ecclesiæ ut schismatis tollatur occasio, et conscientiis fidelium satisfiat." And it must also be remembered, that the case of Presbyterians ordained in Ireland during the great rebellion was very different from that of the ministers of the Foreign Reformed Churches, with which alone we are now concerned; and this difference the Archbishop recognizes in the very document from which I am quoting, observing: "*Multo minus* omnes Ordines sacros Ecclesiarum Forinsecarum condemnantes, quos proprio Judici relinquimus."

How far, therefore, Chancellor Harington's Catena will benefit his cause, I leave him and the public to judge. For his *nominal* thesis, he might easily have multiplied his authorities tenfold, and that without going to such extreme authors as Hickes, and Dodwell, and Brett, but he would not have touched the *real* point he wishes to establish. And a large portion of his best witnesses have, in other parts of their writings, expressly and explicitly *advocated* the view he has been laboring to overthrow by their authority.

Dec. 22, 1851.

A REPLY

TO THE

BISHOP OF EXETER'S

SECOND ARRAIGNMENT OF HIS METROPOLITAN

IN HIS

Letter to the Archdeacon of Totnes,

OPPUGNING THE

VALIDITY OF THE ORDERS OF THE FOREIGN NON-EPISCOPAL CHURCHES.

TO WHICH IS ANNEXED

A REJOINDER TO CHANCELLOR HARINGTON,

ON THE SAME SUBJECT.

"Diotrephes, who loveth to have the pre-eminence......Neither doth he himself receive the brethren, and forbiddeth them that would, and casteth them out of the Church."—3 *John*, 9, 10.

BY

W. GOODE, M.A., F.S.A.
Rector of Allhallows the Great and Less, London.

Third Edition.

NEW YORK:
A. D. F. RANDOLPH, 683 BROADWAY.
1853.

CONTENTS.

REPLY TO THE BISHOP OF EXETER.

REPLY TO THE BISHOP OF EXETER.

&c. &c. &c.

Of the many grievous errors which have been lately put forth in our Church under the name of genuine Church principles and Anglo-Catholic doctrine, there is not one, perhaps, more entirely opposed to the truth of the Gospel and the real doctrine of our Church, than that the only legitimate and promised channel through which the grace of God comes to mankind, is a ministry deriving its Orders from an Apostolically-descended Episcopate. This doctrine is the πρῶτον ψεῦδος, the primary false principle, that is at the root of the present controversy among us on the question of Foreign Ordinations. How it is possible for ministers of our Church, in the face of all the testimonies that history sets before us of the close communion maintained by our early Reformers with the Protestant Continental Churches, to maintain such a view as the doctrine of the Church of England, it is difficult to understand. But recent experience seems to show, that there are no bounds to the Romanizing doctrines which some among us can see clearly set forth in our Protestant Formularies.

To the Bishop of Exeter, and certain others among us, it is manifest as the sun at noonday, that the Orders of those who were recognized by our Reformers as esteemed fellow-ministers of Christ, and most dear colleagues in the Christian ministry, are pronounced by the Formularies drawn up by those very Reformers to be altogether invalid and null. But then, it must not be forgotten by the reader, that the same great authority has found his own doctrine of universal regeneration in baptism in the *Calvinistic* Confessions of the Foreign Protestant Churches; and has even, unconsciously, quoted the words of Calvin himself as bearing indubitable testimony to the truth of his view.

Whatever, therefore, be the amount of his Lordship's learning —a question into which I will not enter—it is clear that he has a principle of interpretation ready upon all occasions, by which the writings of any individuals may be shown most manifestly to set forth the doctrine he wishes to defend; even to the extent of making Calvin himself a maintainer of the *opus operatum* efficacy of the Sacraments, and proving those who fraternized with Non-Episcopalian churches and ministers, and considered them the very choicest portions of Christ's Church, and his favored ambassadors to a fallen world, to be men who, in the Formularies they drew up, formally denounced those churches and ministers as uncatholic communities and mere pretenders to powers which they did not possess.

We may reasonably presume to doubt, however, whether this principle of interpretation will be as satisfactory to impartial inquirers as it seems to be to the Bishop of Exeter. But as his Lordship has now publicly come forward with an elaborate defence of his views in this matter, for the purpose of again arraigning his Metropolitan at the bar of public opinion, for false doctrine and teaching opposed to that of his Church,* I venture to offer to the public the following remarks upon his statements. And I may the rather be permitted to do this, as, in the course of his pamphlet, he has, in a way with which we are all now painfully familiar, directly charged me with misrepresentation in my citation of certain authorities on this subject.

His Lordship's Letter has been called forth, he tells us, by the reply of the Archbishop of Canterbury to an Address to him from certain of the Clergy of the Diocese of Exeter, in which they desired "earnestly to record their conviction, in agreement with the judgment of our Church, consentient with that of the Catholic Church, that they only can be deemed validly ordained who have received 'the laying on of hands by those to whom the Apostolic succession has descended.'" In the reply of the Archbishop to this very modest production, in which a few presbyters take upon themselves to lay down the law to the Primate of their Church, and to pronounce *ex cathedrâ* what is "the judgment of our Church," and "that of the Catholic Church," his Grace took the opportunity of "protesting against the unwarranted assumption which it contained." Upon which the Bishop of Exeter thus comments: "Believing, as I do, that *this judgment of* 220 *of my clergy was substantially right*, and apprehending that the censure passed upon it by the Archbishop, if it remain unnoticed, may lead to extensive and pernicious error, I deem it my duty to avow this my belief;" and he proceeds to fulfil "the duty of stating plainly and explicitly the grounds on which he rests it;" and he adds: "These grounds will in the present instance be limited to the authoritative teaching of our own Church, not diverging from it in any way, except to illustrate that teaching: for *the question is, whether it be the judgment of our Church, that they only are truly ordained to the Christian ministry who have received Holy Orders from those to whom the power of conferring them has descended in succession from the Apostles.*" (Pp. 12, 13.)

Such is the position which the Bishop of Exeter has taken upon himself to defend as *the doctrine of our Church*, proved to be so by her "authoritative teaching." The reader will observe that the question to be discussed is not as to the *regularity* of Non-Episcopal Orders, but as to their *validity;* that is, whether persons

* In a letter to the Archdeacon of Totnes, in answer to an Address from the Clergy of that Archdeaconry on the Necessity of Episcopal Ordination. By Henry, Lord Bishop of Exeter. Murray: 8vo. pp. 88.

so set apart have any right to perform anywhere the duties of the ministerial office, or to expect any Divine recognition or blessing in their performance of them. And if such Orders are not *valid*, then the Churches that have not Bishops "descending in succession from the Apostles," have none among them recognized by God as his ministers; they are entirely destitute of any persons holding the ministerial office; and, of course, subject to all the consequences resulting from such a state of things.

But, as I am anxious that the Bishop's views should be fully stated before I proceed to investigate them, I will give him the entire benefit of a species of saving clause which he has thrown in, in one place, when pointing out the answer which he thinks ought to have been given by the Archbishop to Mr. Gawthorn's inquiry. He intimates that his Grace's answer ought to have been, that "he and the Church of England do hold Ordination by Bishops as necessary; *but yet, that we are not forbidden by the Church to hope that, under the peculiar circumstances under which some of these foreigners are placed, their ministrations are not void.*" (P. 7.)

So that the limitation is this: that, while our Church holds that Non-Episcopal Ordinations are altogether invalid, and persons so ordained no ministers at all, yet if a member of it should venture to express a "hope," that the ministrations of "some" such, under some peculiar circumstances, "are not void," our Church has not directed that he should be punished for it. To call them ministers would indeed be a grave offence; but our Church has not (the Bishop thinks) told her clergy: You shall not indulge a *hope* that the ministrations of any such persons can be of any use. Our Church is charitable enough not to *anathematize* those who indulge such a *hope*. Such is the limitation with which the Bishop's position is to be connected. Will the reader expect me to take much farther notice of it?

The judgment of the Archbishop, which it may be well also to state before I proceed farther, is, that our Church does *not* "deny the validity of the Orders" of the Pastors of the Foreign Protestant Churches "solely on account of their wanting the imposition of Episcopal hands," (*Letter to Gawthorn*;) while he at the same time maintains, "that Episcopal government, and therefore that Episcopal Ordination, is most agreeable to Scripture, most in accordance with primitive practice, and is in itself the 'more excellent way.'" (*Letter to Palmer.*)

Which of these two views is most consistent with the doctrine of the Church of England, we are now to inquire.

The Bishop commences his argument with an appeal to the Formularies of our Church, particularly those parts which had been referred to by the Archbishop as expressing doctrine with which his views were "in exact accordance;" namely, the 19th and 23d Articles, and the Preface to the Ordinal; and out of these he constructs, by a long process of argumentation and inferential reasoning, aided by divers additions *ab extra*, a system of church government suited to his views. I must endeavor to follow him in the mazes of the labyrinth he has constructed, and through whose devious and winding paths he has reached his conclusions. His Lordship's mode of argumentation on such occasions strongly reminds one of the ingenious method by which the cuttle-fish is accustomed to elude the grasp of its pursuers; namely, by pouring forth an inky fluid which so darkens the waters through which it takes its course, that their powers of vision are completely unequal to the task of tracking its path. And I doubt much, whether our venerable Reformers would be able to recognize their own Formularies, if presented to them in the state in which they reappear after having been subjected to the action of that potent fluid.

The 19th Article is "Of the Church," and stands thus: "The visible Church of Christ is a congregation of faithful men, in which the pure word of God is preached, and the Sacraments be duly ministered according to God's ordinance, in all things that of necessity be requisite to the same."

From this his Lordship deduces three positions: *First*, that in any body professing to be a Church of Christ, "the pure word of God" is to be preached; a deduction which I shall not dispute. *Secondly*, it must be "*preached*;" "THAT IS," says his Lordship, "publicly set forth for the instruction of the people *by persons duly empowered, or sent, for that purpose;* for we know from St. Paul that the word cannot be 'preached'—that is, not merely recited or taught, but *proclaimed with* assurance and *authority*—except by those who are duly 'sent,' authorized by Him whose word they proclaim, κηρυκες—men unto whom God 'hath committed the word of reconciliation.'" (P. 14.)

Now I beg to ask, where does his Lordship find all this *in the Article?* The Article merely uses the word "preached." Does his Lordship really suppose that any one in search of truth will allow him to raise out of this single word his whole doctrine of the sort of commission necessary to qualify a man for preaching the Gospel? Has he forgotten that even laymen were sometimes allowed to preach in the early Church, and that in the presence of a bishop? Or, still more, has he forgotten that "they which were scattered abroad, upon the persecution that arose about Stephen, travelled as far as Phenice, and Cyprus, and Antioch, *preaching the word*, &c. . . . . And the hand of the Lord was with them, and a great number believed and turned unto the Lord?" (Acts xi. 19–21.) Or (to mention no more) has he forgotten Apollos, who, when "knowing only the baptism of John," and therefore certainly not *ordained* by any apostle or Christian bishop, "spake and taught diligently the things of the Lord," which I suppose amounts to *preaching;* and after receiving farther instruction from Aquila and Priscilla, "helped them much which had believed through grace; for he mightily convinced the Jews, and that *publicly*, showing by the Scriptures that Jesus was

Christ?" (Acts xviii. 24, &c.) All these, it seems, knew nothing of the Bishop of Exeter's doctrine, that nobody might, or even *could*, "preach," but one specially ordained and publicly set apart by Divine commission for the purpose.

Of course I am not here touching the question of the necessity of an inward Divine call and qualification for being am ambassador of Christ, or of what Apostolical practice teaches us to be proper for the due appointment of a preacher of the Gospel in a regularly constituted Church. All I wish now to point attention to is the absurdity (for I can use no milder term) of attempting to raise a whole system of church government out of the single word "preach."

His Lordship's *third* deduction is that, as the Article requires, that in a Church "the Sacraments be duly ministered in all those things that of necessity are requisite to the same," and the 25th Article says, that sacraments are "effectual signs of grace, &c., by which God doth work invisibly in us," &c.; and a Homily says, that "in them God embraceth us," &c.; "manifestly, therefore, among 'those things that of necessity are requisite to the duly ministering the same' must be *authority from God*, given to those who minister them;" and it is added, that "our Church has not left the point to be deduced by our sense of what is right: it is expressly declared in the 26th Article that they who minister the Sacraments 'do not the same in their own name, but in Christ's, and do minister by *his commission and authority*;" and hence the consequence is deduced, that the Sacraments can only be "duly ministered" "by those who have *commission* and authority *from God* given to them for that purpose;" in other words, individuals divinely commissioned "for that purpose." Now, one single consideration annihilates the whole of this argumentation; for if it were correct, lay-baptism would be wholly invalid, which the Bishop well knows is not the doctrine of our Church; and therefore his third deduction is as groundless as his second. The question whether non-episcopally ordained ministers may not be said to minister by Christ's commission and authority, is one that will more properly come under consideration in reviewing the meaning of the 23d Article; to which the Bishop next directs our attention.

This Article is entitled, "Of ministering in the Congregation," and runs thus: "It is not lawful for any man to take upon him the office of public preaching or ministering the Sacraments in the congregation, before he be lawfully called and sent to execute the same. And those we ought to judge lawfully called and sent, which be chosen and called to this work by men who have public authority given unto them in the congregation to call and send ministers into the Lord's vineyard."

It is difficult to understand how any one can read this Article, and not see how carefully it is worded so as not to exclude from "lawful calling" the ministers of the Foreign Protestant Churches.

As Professor Hey says, in his *Commentary* on the *Articles*, the expression "who have public authority given unto them in the congregation," "seems to leave the *manner* of giving the power of ordaining quite free; it seems as if any religious society might, consistently with this Article, appoint officers, with power of Ordination, by election, representation, or lot; as if, therefore, the right to ordain did not depend upon any uninterrupted *succession.*" (*Lect. in Div.* vol. iv. p. 166.) And when we recollect the nature of the intercourse and communion that took place between our Reformers and those Churches and their ministers, both at the time when these Articles were first drawn up, in the reign of Edward VI., and at their re-establishment in the reign of Elizabeth, there is but one way of accounting for a long argumentation, an effusion of ink covering EIGHTEEN pages, to prove that by "men to whom public authority is given," &c., the Article "*must mean Bishops*"(!) and that "*our Church holds that the power of Ordination is in Bishops only.*" (!!) (P. 33.) Painful as the task is of taking to pieces such a web of sophistry, such a tissue of false reasoning and perversion of plain statements, the position of the writer makes it necessary to guard the public mind against such a representation of the doctrine of our Church.

His Lordship commences by observing, that by the Article it is "not lawful" to "execute the ministry in the Church" without "a lawful call and mission." His Lordship is quite aware, as he afterwards informs us, that this is held by his opponents as much as by himself (p. 20), and therefore it might have been supposed that he would at once have passed on to something relevant to the question in hand. But it appears, that by some obliquity of vision, of a very unenviable kind, he saw in it an opportunity of flinging against the Primate a charge of fraternizing with Socinians in the matter. He is "aware" that "Hammond had to defend the Apostle's precept" as to "mission" being "requisite for teaching in the Church;" and "against whom?"—"against Volkelius and other disciples of *Socinus*, whom he asserts 'to be certainly the first that from the beginning of Christianity have in this controversy appeared against us.'" To which his Lordship thinks himself justified in appending the following remark: "This is a sad pedigree; and it behooves those who are unconsciously using the words and arguments of Socinus and his followers, to ponder their founder's purpose in using them—which was no other than to assail the faith, by disparaging the Divine mission of its heralds and guardians." (P. 17.)

Hoping, I suppose, that the reader would be so mystified by his statements as to identify *all* "mission" with that which the Bishop considers *proper* "mission;" and that he would overlook the fact that the Bishop's own quotation from Hammond condemns him—for its terms virtually except the Foreign Protestant Churches from the charge of not thinking any mission requisite—he hurls against the Primate a reproach, which his own statements prove to be groundless. Considering the quarter from which it comes, I content myself with thus pointing it out.

Into his Lordship's theological lucubrations, occupying the next two pages, I shall not enter. What we are inquiring about is the doctrine laid down in the Article. But he concludes thus: "But is all mission now unnecessary? Mission from God himself? The Catholic Church hath from the beginning held the contrary; and our own Church, as a faithful part of it, has in the 23d Article proclaimed the same truth—the necessity of lawful mission generally in the former of its two propositions—in the latter, THE NECESSITY *that this mission be mediately from God*, TRANSMITTED BY SUCCESSION FROM THOSE WHO, AT THE FIRST, RECEIVED THE POWER OF THUS GIVING IT IMMEDIATELY FROM OUR LORD HIMSELF." (Pp. 19, 20.) Such is the doctrine which his Lordship has the courage to assert is *laid down in the latter part of the Article!* He admits, indeed, that it is "not so plainly expressed;" and as the Primate has called it an "unwarranted assumption," he proceeds "to defend it publicly in the face of the Church."

His Lordship says: "There are three several members of the proposition which we are considering: I. That lawful mission to the Christian ministry must be from God by an outward call. II. That we must not look for any outward call from God except mediately through men. III. That it must be given through men who have themselves received the power of transmitting it, publicly given to them by those who have themselves publicly received the power of giving that power from others similarly empowered; in other words, in uninterrupted succession from the Apostles themselves." (P. 20.)

Now here it is obvious, that his Lordship has drawn from the Article propositions not contained in it. The Article does not touch the question of the call "*from God*," but only that of the external call by men. To assert, therefore, that the Article says that lawful mission must be "*from God* by an outward call" is a direct and palpable misrepresentation of it.

And the Bishop's own authority, Bishop Pearson, whom he so highly extols (p. 52)—and not without reason—might have shown him, and in the very passage to which he has referred us, his error in introducing these words into the Article. For Bishop Pearson, treating of the mode of Ordination in the Church of England, says: "Ordinaria vocatio fit a Deo et per homines. *Quatenus est a Deo, est interna;* quatenus est per homines, est externa." (*Minor Theol. Wks.* i. 291, 292.)

In defence of the third proposition, the Bishop argues thus: That when the Article says that the persons through whom lawful mission must be given, are "men who have public authority given unto them in the congregation," it clearly means that this power "is so given *by God—publicè in Ecclesia;* that is, in some outward manner by which it shall be publicly known in the Church to be given;" the Divine Being being represented, after the first bestowal of the power, by a succession of representatives of those to whom the power was first given. For, says the Bishop, "as these [*i. e.*, modern Bishops who give power of mission] must in like manner have received their power of mission from others, who had received it in like manner, the series must be carried backwards, until, as we before said, it reaches the Apostles, whom our Lord sent, 'as the Father had sent Him,' *i. e.*, with power to send others." (P. 22.)

This is the foundation on which his whole argumentation rests; and it is clearly derived from his ADDING words to the Article calculated to carry out his own views. The Article clearly implies, that there is power *in a Church* to authorize certain of its members to call and appoint others to the office of the ministry, which exactly meets the case of the Foreign Protestant Churches. The words "authority given unto them *by God* in the Congregation," are very different from what we find in the Article. They would imply, that the Congregation, or Church, had no voice in the matter, and could not authorize any of their body to do any act of the kind. So that the words which the Bishop has thus foisted into the Article completely change the character of its doctrine. They just determine what the Article has studiously left open, and determine it in opposition to the known sentiments of those who drew up the Article. They make it necessary that the mission should be given by some individual or individuals specially, and individually, and publicly commissioned by God himself, apart from the Church, to bestow it; while the terms of the Article imply that God has left sufficient power with the Church to act in such a matter.

The Article is evidently drawn up so as to *comprehend* the Foreign Protestant Churches. It does not pretend to define exactly what our own Church's particular mode of calling and sending ministers is; but it states the limits of what may be considered a lawful calling. Most just and pertinent are the remarks of Bishop Burnet, in his Exposition of this Article :—

"If," he says, "a company of Christians find the public worship where they live to be so defiled that they cannot with a good conscience join in it, and if they do not know of any place to which they can conveniently go, where they may worship God purely and in a regular way; if, I say, such a Body, finding some that have been ordained, though to the lower functions, should submit itself entirely to their conduct; *or, finding none of those, should by a common consent desire some of their own number to minister to them in holy things*, and should, upon that beginning, grow up to a regulated constitution, though we are very sure that this is quite out of all rule, and could not be done without a very great sin, unless the necessity were great and apparent; yet, if the necessity is real and not feigned, *this is not condemned or annulled by the Article;* for when this grows to a constitution, and when it was begun by the consent of a Body who are supposed to have an authority in such an extraordinary case, whatever some hotter spirits have thought of this since that time, *yet we are very sure, that not only those who penned the Articles, but the body of this Church for above half an age after, did, notwithstanding those irregularities, acknowledge the Foreign Churches so constituted to be true Churches as to all the essentials of a Church, though they had been at first irregularly formed, and continued still to be in an imperfect state.* AND THERE-

FORE THE GENERAL WORDS IN WHICH THIS PART OF THE ARTICLE IS FRAMED, SEEM TO HAVE BEEN DESIGNED ON PURPOSE NOT TO EXCLUDE THEM."

In fact, the Article requires nothing more as necessary for lawful calling than what is required in the Confessions of several of the Foreign Protestant Non-Episcopal Churches; as, for instance, the Helvetic (Art. 16), Bohemian (c. 9), and Belgic (Art. 31). And therefore the Bishop might just as well attempt to fasten his doctrine upon the Confessions of these Non-Episcopal Churches as upon that of the Church of England.

I have already pointed out, in a former publication,* that the first Exposition of the Articles—that by Rogers, Chaplain to Archbishop Bancroft, which was published in 1607, as "perused and by the lawful authority of the Church of England allowed to be public," and which the Archbishop (a High-Churchman) ordered all the parishes in his province to supply themselves with—interprets the Article in this way, and points out its *agreement* with the Confessions I have just referred to; and so also does the late High-Churchman, Bishop Tomline.†

Indeed, the only way in which the Bishop of Exeter can force his doctrine out of the Article, is by garbling it by the addition of words which totally alter its obvious meaning. And presuming, I suppose, upon the ignorance of his readers, he ventures even to quote, in support of his view of it, the *Apology* of Bishop Jewel, which he correctly tells us "had the grateful sanction of that very Synod in which our present Articles were compiled." Now, not to mention Bishop Jewel's notorious recognition of certain of the Foreign Protestant Churches and their ministers, which alone would render such a reference deserving of unqualified censure, the fact is, that the Confession of Faith of the English Church (including this question of Orders), inserted by Bishop Jewel in his *Apology*, was placed by the Foreign Reformers in the *Harmony of the Confessions of the Reformed Churches*, published at Geneva, in 1581, as one with which all the rest were in agreement.

And so completely opposed is Hooker to the Bishop's interpretation of the Article, that he distinctly intimates that there is no "heavenly law" whereby it may appear, "that the Lord himself hath appointed presbyters forever to be under the regiment of Bishops," and that "their authority" is "a sword which the *Church hath power to take from them*," (*Eccl. Pol.* vii. 5;) and expressly says that "the whole Church visible" is "the true original subject of all power;" and that though "*it* hath not ordinarily ALLOWED any other than Bishops alone to ordain, howbeit, as the ordinary course is ordinarily in all things to be observed, so it may be, in some cases, not unnecessary that we decline from the ordinary ways;" and that "there may be sometimes very just and sufficient reason to allow Ordination made without a Bishop." (*Ib.* 14).

* *The Doctrines of the Church of England on Non-Episcopal Ordinations.*
† Expos. of Articles, ed. 1799, p. 376.

The Bishop's remarks upon Bishop Burnet's *Commentary* on the *Articles*, which he finds most inconveniently in his way, I leave to their fate.

The quotation from a posthumous work of Bishop Beveridge, which it does not appear that he left for publication, and which was said by some, at the time of its first appearance, to have been a juvenile work of its author, cannot override the plain language of the Article. There is not one word in the Article that even *implies* the necessity of Ordination by an apostolically descended Episcopate.

Before I pass on, I must notice a very remarkable piece of verbal criticism on the part of his Lordship. No one, I suppose, can have perused the various recent publications that have issued from his Lordship's pen, without observing the happy ingenuity with which he occasionally mystifies his admiring readers, by the profound discrimination with which he brings to light some nice turns of expression in the documents he is quoting, proving beyond contradiction how exactly they fall in with his doctrine. So remarkable an illustration of this occurs here, that I must beg permission to present it to the reader: "This, then," says the Bishop, "I scruple not to accept, and to commend to others, as a sound and irrefragable statement of the real import of the Article; inviting, in confirmation of it, attention to the *reverential tone* in which the Article is conceived: 'Atque illos legitime vocatos existimare debemus.' *This is language highly becoming those who recognize God as the author of lawful mission*, but would hardly be used to designate a call from man. In that case we should rather expect a categorical declaration that such persons *are* called." (P. 26.) So that if I was to say, the Bishop of Exeter *ought to consider* such and such persons lawfully called, I should be using a "reverential tone" in the matter, which would show that I recognized God, and not man, as the author of their mission. Alas! my poor brains are too dull for such transcendental discrimination.

His Lordship proceeds to cite the 26th Article in confirmation of his view of the meaning of the 23d. This Article says, that the ministers of the Church minister "in Christ's name," and "by his commission and authority;" from which it is argued: "This recognition of ministers exercising their ministry in Christ's name, and by his commission, negatives all merely human authority in their appointment." (P. 27.) But this does not touch the real question at issue; which, in fact, his Lordship, throughout his argumentation, from whatever cause, altogether ignores. The question is, whether the power of giving the outward call to men to preach and administer the Sacraments, and of conferring that power upon others, was so exclusively given by Christ to the Apostles, and by the Apostles to the Bishops they appointed, that none other of his followers but those having apostolically derived power in this respect can, under any circumstances, exercise or confer it. Now this supposed *exclusive* gift is just what is to be proved, but what his Lordship throughout his argument *assumes.* It does not necessarily follow, that a mission to execute the ministerial office is by mere human authority, because it is not given by a Bishop deriving his authority by regular succession from the Apostles. And, as I have shown before, a host of our best divines do not hold it to be so.* Our learned Dean Field, in his standard work *Of the Church*, elaborately defends the position, that presbyters have, so far as the capabilities given to them in their Ordination extend, power equally with Bishops to do all things necessary for the maintenance of God's service, "and that *only* for order's sake and the preservation of peace, there is a limitation of the USE and EXERCISE of the same," confining it to Bishops.† And, therefore, even supposing that this limitation originated with the Apostles, and still more if it originated with the subsequent Church, as Jerome and many other of the ancients maintained, circumstances might fully justify its being laid aside. And, moreover, it must be recollected, that it is Christ's own act in calling any one by his Spirit, and qualifying him for his service, that more especially constitutes any one *his* minister, not the *mere* outward commission of man, which insures nothing but the bare *validity* of his ministerial acts.

But the 23d Article, says his Lordship, "leaves to a subsequent Article, the 36th, to tell us who they are to whom this power is given;" the 36th Article sanctioning the Ordinal. (P. 27.) And here we find one of those specimens of unfairness, the constant occurrence of which, in his Lordship's latter publications, deprives one of all confidence in his statements. He quotes the Preface to the Ordinal as it was altered at the Review in 1661, as if it was thus put forth by the framers of the Articles, giving not the slightest intimation to the reader of there being any difference between the two, though the difference is of importance in the point under discussion, and was fully noticed in a Tract then lying under his Lordship's eyes, and criticized by him a few pages farther on! Nay, at a subsequent part of his argument (p. 63), it became convenient to notice this fact, and consequently there we find it. It does not, indeed, of course, make the sense of the 23d Article different from what it was before; but it commits our Reformers to a higher view of the importance of Episcopal Ordination than they in reality took.

The Bishop gives the passage thus: "To the intent that these Orders should be continued and reverently used and esteemed in the Church of England," "no man shall be accounted or taken to be a lawful Bishop, Priest, or Deacon in the Church of England, or suffered to execute any of the said functions, except he be called, tried, examined, and admitted thereunto, according to the form hereafter following, *or hath formerly received Episcopal consecration or ordination.*"

* See Doctrine of Church of England on Non-Episcopal Ordinations.

† See the whole passage below, pp. 27–28.

And in his Lordship's observations upon this passage, he lays the greatest stress upon the concluding words, "or hath formerly received Episcopal consecration or ordination." Now these words, as his Lordship well knows, were not inserted till the revision of the Book in 1661, by the Laudian divines, who then had the upper hand. He knows also, upon the testimony of the High Churchman Bishop Cosin, and others,* lying before him when he wrote, that, in the previous period of our Church, persons having only Presbyterian Orders were admitted to minister in our Church, and that it was the general opinion of the Bishops that there was nothing to prevent this. Hence, not only was there evidence, that our Church admitted the validity of the Orders of the Foreign Protestant Churches, so far as those churches themselves were concerned, but persons so ordained were allowed to minister in our own Church. And the insertion of those words in 1661, requiring Episcopal Ordination for *those who minister in our Church*—obviously with a view to the Presbyterians, who, in the civil war, had usurped the places of the Episcopalian clergy—cannot affect the doctrine of our Church on the abstract question, whether the Foreign Protestant Churches are destitute of any validly ordained pastors.

The direction here given, as it stood both before and after the Review in 1661, is strictly limited to what is required "*in the Church of England.*" There is a marked abstinence from any statement of the necessity of Episcopal Orders for a valid ministry, which it is impossible to conceive that our Reformers would have observed, if they had held the Bishop of Exeter's notions. And when we couple this with their known conduct towards the Foreign Protestant Churches, not the smallest doubt can be left upon the mind of any reasonable inquirer after *the truth* that they did not hold them.

But the Bishop supports his view by two arguments. The first is this. He says: "If persons from Berlin and Geneva, calling themselves ministers of Christ's Church, are really such ministers, it would be a direct act of schism for our Church to reject their ministry; for all who are Christ's ministers at all, are his ministers throughout his whole Church." (P. 30.) But what a mere cobweb is this! Has not a Church a right to say to those ministers who come here from a Church under a different form of government, "We have laid down a rule which we consider most in accordance with Apostolical usage, requiring a certain mode of introduction to the ministry among us, and we think it inexpedient to break it by admitting others not so qualified?" Does it follow from this, that our Church holds them to be destitute of all right to exercise the ministerial office anywhere? Where does his Lordship derive his authority for denying to his Church such a prudential mode of action, and shutting her up to the alternative of

* See "Doctrine, &c.," pp. 29, 30.

either admitting to hold office in her communion any minister of a Foreign Church, whatever its form of government may be, or denying that such a one has any right to exercise the ministerial office to any body of Christians on the face of the earth? The fact is, that his Lordship has in this point, as well as in his advocacy of the exclusive admissibility of one form of Ecclesiastical government, been following in the steps of the early Puritans. His own words are almost identical with those of the notorious Puritan Travers to Archbishop Whitgift. Travers, to show that he had a right to be allowed to minister in the Church of England, though having only Presbyterian Orders (and he could hardly be said to have any), urged, that "the universal and perpetual practice of all Christendom, in all places, and in all ages, proveth the ministers lawfully made in any Church of sound profession in faith, ought to be acknowledged such in any other;" he means, so as to be allowed to *minister* in it. To which Archbishop Whitgift (who, as we know from his writings, *admitted the* VALIDITY *of the Orders of the Foreign Protestant Churches*, but held that "*the laws of this realm* require that such as are to be allowed *as ministers in this Church of England* should be *ordered by a Bishop*, and subscribe to the Articles before him,") replies to the argument thus: "Excepting always such Churches as allow of Presbytery, and practise it." He considered that in such a case an Episcopal Church might fairly object to one not ordained as she required, acting as one of *her own* ministers. But he did not deny the validity of Presbyterian Orders in the abstract. In the same paper to which I am now referring, he admits that Whittingham "was ordained minister by those which *had authority* in the Church" in which he was ordained, though he held such Orders not a sufficient qualification for ministering in the Church of England. (See *Strype's Whitgift*, App. bk. 3, n. 30.)

The second argument is this, that if any of the ministers of Non-Episcopal Churches wish to be ministers of the Church of England, "they must, as a preliminary, renounce all claim at present to any ministerial character whatsoever," and "present themselves as lay candidates for holy orders;" "and yet for our Church thus to insist on their submitting to be ordained anew, if they already have Orders, would be, *not merely an act of schism, but a manifest desecration of Christ's ordinance, a most sinful rejection of his commission.*" (Pp. 30, 31.)

High-sounding words these, no doubt, and very characteristic of their author. But the question is, What truth is there in them? None at all. There is no such "renunciation" required. And the whole notion about the "desecration of Christ's ordinance" involved in such a step, is entirely opposed to the views of our best divines of all parties. What does the High Churchman Archbishop Bramhall say in his *Letters of Orders*, when ordaining one who had previously had only Scotch Presbyterian Orders: "*Non annihilantes* priores ordines (si quos habuit), *nec invalidi-*

tatem eorundem determinantes, multo minus omnes ordines sacros Ecclesiarum Forinsecarum condemnantes, quos proprio Judici relinquimus, sed SOLUMMODO SUPPLENTES *quicquid prius defuit per canones Ecclesiæ Anglicanæ requisitum*, et providentes paci Ecclesiæ, ut schismatis tollatur occasio, et conscientiis fidelium satisfiat, nec ulli dubitent de ejus ordinatione, aut actus sous presbyteriales tanquam invalidos aversentur." (*Works*, Oxf. ed. vol. i. p. xxxvii.)

Let his Lordship's friends determine which is the best authority, the Bishop of Exeter or Archbishop Bramhall.

But, as this is an important point, I shall add some farther testimonies.

And, first, let us hear the opinion of Archbishop Leighton, one whose learning as well as piety is unquestionable. When consecrated Bishop, in 1661, by some of the English bishops, he was required by them to submit to be first ordained Deacon and Priest, on the ground partly of the Act of Uniformity, and partly that, though it might be reasonable to allow Presbyterian Orders under some circumstances, yet that his had been received from those who were in a state of schism, and had without reason revolted from their bishops.* And Leighton's view on the subject is thus stated by his intimate friend Bishop Burnet: "Leighton did not stand much upon it. He *did not think Orders given without bishops were null and void.* He thought the forms of government were not settled by such positive laws as were unalterable; but only by Apostolic practices, which, as he thought, authorized Episcopacy as the best form. Yet he did not think it necessary to the being of a Church. *But he thought that every Church might make such rules of Ordination as they pleased, and that they might reordain all that came to them from any other Church; and that the reordaining a priest ordained in another Church imported no more but that they received him into Orders according to their rules, and did not infer the annulling the Orders he had formerly received.*" (*Hist. of his Own Times*, vol. i. p. 140.)

The testimony of Archbishop Leighton, therefore, is directly against the Bishop on *all* the points of the case.

But a still more important testimony perhaps than even these is that of the learned Bingham, the author of the *Antiquities of the Christian Church.* He says, in his *French Church's Apology for the Church of England*:—

> Nor do I see what can be urged farther in this case, unless it be the business of reordination, which some reckon so great a charge against the Act of Uniformity; because it obliges every beneficiary to receive Episcopal ordination, according to the form and rites of the Church of England. *But what harm there is in this, I confess I never yet could see;* and I am sure there is nothing in it contrary to the principles or practice of Geneva, nor perhaps of the whole French Church. For at Geneva it is their common practice, whenever they remove a minister from one Church to another, to give him a new and solemn ordination by imposition of hands and prayer......Now, if it be

* I shall revert presently to their view on this point. See p. 42.

lawful, by the rules of the Church of Geneva, for a minister to receive a new solemn ordination, when he is translated from one Church to another; why cannot men in England consent to receive a new ordination, when the law requires it, in order to settle themselves regularly in any Church? especially when *it is for the sake of peace and union,* and to take off all manner of *doubtfulness and scruples* from the people. *I dispute not now, whether their former ordinations were valid* [this question, we see, he does not consider *to affect the point to be determined, namely, whether they could properly* submit to reordination]; it is certain, they are not more valid than those of Geneva; nor can they themselves think them more valid than the ministers of Geneva think theirs; wherefore, if it be lawful at Geneva for a minister to receive a new ordination, because the laws require it, I do not see what can make it unlawful in England to submit to the same thing, in compliance with the law, when men have no other regular way to settle themselves in any cure; *let their opinion of their former ordination be what it will,* WHICH COMES NOT INTO THE PRESENT DISPUTE. For even supposing *their former ordination* [*i. e.* the Presbyterian *in this country*] *to be valid, I show they may submit to a new ordination without sin;* and if the will be peaceable, they *ought to do it,* after the example of Geneva, rather than set up separate meetings and preach against the will of their superiors, to the disturbance of the peace of the Church." (*Bingham's Works,* vol. ix. ed. 1845, pp. 296, 297.)

I might add other authorities, but after these it is needless to do so.

I am as well aware as the Bishop of Exeter can be of the decisions of the early Church against reordinations, and, in the state of things which then existed, can quite enter into their propriety. But the circumstances of the Church were then different; and those decisions are no more binding upon us than many that are totally disregarded by all parties. And after all, they only laid down the general rule; for we are not without some precedent for such reordinations even in the early Church. For the great Council of Nice directed, that those who had been ordained by Meletius, after he had been deposed by his Metropolitan, were not to be admitted to minister in the Church until they had been qualified to do so by a "*more sacred Ordination,*" (μυστικωτέρᾳ χειροτονίᾳ βεβαιωθέντας.)* The *validity* of the Ordination is not denied, as it could hardly be, but the defects of its *irregularity* are supplied. It could no more be invalid than those of the Donatists, which we know from Augustine were admitted, in those that came over to the Church, as sufficient to enable them to minister in the Church without any fresh Ordination.

"But," adds his Lordship, "we have not yet done with the Preface to the Book of Consecration and Ordination. In truth, its very first words, duly considered, are conclusive of the whole question: 'It is evident unto all men, diligently reading Holy Scripture and ancient authors, that from the Apostles' time there have been three orders of ministers in Christ's Church, bishops, priests, and deacons.' Now, were these orders appointed by man or God? *No one amongst us can hesitate what answer to give—undoubtedly by God.*" And then, having pointed out the offices and powers which our Ordinal attributes to each, his Lordship seems to sup-

* Epist. Synod. ap. Socrat. lib. i. c. 9.

pose that his work is done, and his wished for conclusion made good.

Now I should be abusing the patience of the reader to attempt any elaborate confutation of such an argument as this. The veriest tyro in these matters knows, that there is no ground whatever to attribute the existence of these three Orders to a direct appointment of God. The utmost that can be said is, that they were appointed by the Apostles, who were divinely inspired to deliver the Gospel message to mankind, and therefore, so far as was necessary for this purpose, under Divine guidance; but as to their ecclesiastical arrangements, we have no proof that they had any express Divine direction, still less that the polity they adopted was unalterable. The extracts I have formerly given* from the works of many of our greatest divines render it unnecessary to say a word more on this point.

I have now gone carefully through the whole of the Bishop's proof of his positions derived from the Formularies of our Church; and I willingly leave the reader to form his own opinion upon the two conclusions to which the Bishop would lead him, namely: "1. That the words of our Church's 23d Article, 'by men to whom public authority,' &c., *must mean bishops;* and 2. That our Church holds that the power of Ordination is in bishops *only.*" (P. 33.)

His Lordship having thus concluded his argument upon the Formularies of our Church, proceeds to deal with our Reformers in a similar way. "The doctrine," he observes, "which has been thus severely censured from the highest place, was the doctrine of our earliest Reformers." And to prove it to be so, he proceeds to quote two works notoriously written before they had given up the errors of Popery on various important points; works published during the reign of Henry VIII., and which advocate the seven Sacraments, images and crucifixes in churches, holy water, creeping to the cross, prayer for the dead, *et id genus omne;* namely, the *Institution of a Christian Man*, and the *Necessary Doctrine*. Such references, however, have this great advantage, that they show us the desperate shifts to which his Lordship's cause is reduced, when he can condescend to make so transparent an attempt to mislead his readers. In these two works, his Lordship announces that he found the power of Ordination attributed only to bishops. I congratulate him upon the discovery of so important a help to his cause. Let us hope that his Lordship will not search farther in the mine he has opened, for the next thing perhaps may be the discovery that the Reformers held almost all the doctrines which the world has been in the habit of thinking that they repudiated, and then in what a position shall we be placed! I will grant his Lordship, then, all the benefit which his extracts from those works can bring him, though I

* See my Doctrine of the Church of Eng. on Non-Episc. Ordinations.

might take exception to them as being themselves insufficient for his purpose; and with these remarks I should have left them to their fate, but for a very characteristic attack of his Lordship upon myself; to which, however unwilling to detain the reader with any personal matters, and however indifferent to any such charges from such a quarter, I am bound to offer a few remarks in reply; and shall avail myself of the opportunity of giving farther information on the whole subject.

At the commencement of my argument on this matter in a former Tract,* before giving the proofs we have of our early Reformers holding the doctrine of the validity under some circumstances of Presbyterian Ordinations, I noticed the fact, that even before the Reformation a doctrine was held which opens the door to such a view, namely, that bishops and priests are of one and the same ministerial order. I observed that, "at the very dawn of the Reformation, the bishops and clergy of our Church put forth a document containing the very doctrine on which the validity of Presbyterian Ordinations has been *chiefly* rested, namely, the parity of bishops and presbyters with respect to the ministerial powers essentially and by right belonging to them;" and showed that this view was maintained in the *Institution of a Christian Man*, and the *Necessary Doctrine;* and then remarked, that "this view certainly *goes far* to remove the difficulty as to recognizing the validity of Presbyterian Ordination in the absence of bishops;" carefully (as the reader will see) recognizing the *distinction* between the *two* views; namely, the parity of order in bishops and presbyters, and the validity of Presbyterian Ordinations; and only observing that the former view *went far* to remove the difficulty there is in receiving the latter. And in the remarks immediately following, as to the opinions of certain divines of our Church put on record about the same period, I noticed how *some* thought that bishops and priests were of the same order, and "some were prepared to take *the next step*, and grant to presbyters under some circumstances the power to ordain presbyters;" still keeping the two views perfectly distinct. The object of course was, to show that the prevalence of this view at the very dawn of the Reformation easily *led the way* to the view afterwards adopted by our Reformers, of the validity under some circumstances of Presbyterian Ordinations. And the sole point in attestation of which the two works just referred to were cited, was *the fact*, that the FORMER view *was* there maintained. And so far from concealing the circumstance, that those works spoke of bishops as the persons who were to ordain, I gave, among the *very* few extracts for which I could find room, one which *expressly stated it*, in the following words: "As the Apostles themselves, in the beginning of the Church, did order priests and bishops, so

* Doctrine of the Church of England on Non-Episcopal Ordinations, &c., reprinted from the *Christian Observer;* which of course accounts for its being anonymous, though it was notorious who was the author.

they appointed and willed the other BISHOPS *after them to do the like.*" (P. 14.)

And I carefully *limited* the "parity of bishops and presbyters," maintained in the works I quoted, to "the ministerial powers *essentially and by right* belonging to them," in order not to include in it that "authority and jurisdiction in spiritual regiment," as Archdeacon Mason calls it, in which bishops had "a higher degree" and "more excellent place." (See my former Tract, p. 38.) There may be ministerial powers belonging to priests by right of their ordination, which, on grounds affecting the welfare of the Church, may have been from the first limited, in their "*use* and *exercise*," (as Dean Field says,) to *some* of their number. And many divines, as I shall show presently, have considered the power of conferring Orders to be one of such powers. So that the words I used were carefully selected, so as to *limit* the parity of bishops and presbyters, advocated in the works referred to, in such a way as not to include the *authority* confided to bishops in the matter of Ordination.

In the face of all this the Bishop has not been ashamed to represent me as concealing certain passages in these works, which attribute the power of Ordination to bishops, in order to deceive the reader.

The character of the charge is apparent from what I have already stated, for I have actually given one such passage, though my object did not render it necessary for me to notice them. But the truth is, that the Bishop is, as we shall see more fully presently, utterly unacquainted with the subject on which he is here speaking. The fact that these works attribute the power of Ordination to bishops, does not touch my statement as to their teaching; nor, indeed, prove that their authors would have denied the validity, under *all* circumstances, of Presbyterian Ordinations. The Bishop is evidently unconscious of what an assertion of the parity of order in bishops and priests means, and supposes that because the Office of Ordaining is maintained to be confided to bishops, my position is overthrown, when in fact it is not touched; as I shall presently show.

His Lordship scornfully observes: "I dwell not on these strange omissions, because, being anonymous [the article appeared in the *Christian Observer*, and the author was well known], they are not very likely to mislead any prudent readers." (P. 38.) For once I am happy to follow the Bishop's example, and dwell not on these suicidal outbreaks of a misguided pen—and, though *they* are *not* anonymous, for the same reason.

I now proceed to his Lordship's criticism upon my remark, that "those who are at all acquainted with ecclesiastical history know, that this view had long been advocated by many of the divines of the Church of Rome, especially among the Scholastic divines, including their great founder, Peter Lombard, the Master of the Sentences." (*Doctrine, &c.* p. 14.)

Of course, I need not add a word to show the truth of this remark. And as to its bearing upon the point in question, I was merely following the leading of some of our greatest divines in referring to this as *preparing the way*, to some extent, for the doctrine that Presbyterian Ordination might, under some circumstances, be valid. I need only instance Dean Field, Archdeacon Mason, and Bishop Cosin;* particularly the High Churchman Cosin, who goes *farther than I have done*, and directly refers to the Master of the Sentences, and a number of the Scholastic divines, as holding views from which the validity of the Orders of "the Reformed French Churches" *necessarily follows.*

The remark, however, though it must be a trite one with those who are familiar with the writings of our great divines, seems to have moved his Lordship's choler in no ordinary degree. He believes that "no considerable school among them ever intended to give the slightest countenance to Ordination by any but bishops." (P. 38.) Perhaps so; no more than they intended to give countenance to what happened at the Reformation, by some of their statements that were nevertheless very useful to the Reformers. Moreover, when they spoke thus, they "were much influenced by their desire to exalt the Popedom," in depressing bishops to the same order as priests. Well, perhaps they were. But what then? Why then, the angry but vapid conclusion is: "So much for the advocacy, by many divines of the Church of Rome, of 'the parity of bishops and presbyters,'" &c., which does not seem very profound reasoning. And then as to Peter Lombard and the Scholastic divines, in whose works his Lordship, wonderful to say, does "not pretend to be well read," (which is in truth very evident,) I have most suspiciously abstained from giving "the slightest reference to any part of their works" in which the "HERETICAL *paradox*" (!) with which I charge them is to be found, and his Lordship has looked and cannot find it. And he may certainly look forever, and not find his own misrepresentation of my statement, namely, that they advocate "*the validity of Presbyterian Ordination*, because they [*i. e.* bishops and presbyters] were accounted one order." (P. 40.) But if he had only given a little attention to the statements of even those few of *our own* divines that I have just referred to, he would have saved himself the humiliation of such a remarkable display of ignorance on the whole matter as now follows; and which comes under the guise of a triumphant reply to my passing reference, on a subordinate point, to the Scholastic divines—a reference supported by the testimony of such men as Bishop Cosin, and the others whom I have quoted.

His Lordship observes, that one great inducement with Peter Lombard and others to consider bishops and priests as "one order,"

* See my former Tract, pp. 36–41; where, however, in my extracts from Field and Mason, I have not had room for their references to the Scholastic divines.

(and that they did so, he admits,) was their desire to magnify the Sacrament of the Eucharist, which is true enough; but then, adds the Bishop, as some ancient authors "accounted bishops a distinct order," "a difficulty presented itself" to them, which "St. Thomas thus meets," (3d *Sup.* qu. 40, c. 5:) "Order may be taken in two ways—in one as it is a sacrament; and then, as has been said before, all order is ordained *ad Eucharistiæ Sacramentum;* wherefore, since the bishop has here no superior power to the priest's, *quantum ad hoc*, Episcopate is not an Order. But Order may be considered in another way, that is, as it is a certain *office*, in respect to certain sacred acts; and so, as the bishop has a power in hierarchical acts, in respect to the mystical Body [the Church] superior to the priest, the Episcopate will be an Order: and it is in this way that Dionysius, and even the Master himself [iv. *Dist.* 24, s. i. m. iii.] speaks of it as an Order."* (Pp. 42, 43.)

Now, first, I did not say a word about "St. Thomas" in particular, but only referred to *some* of the Scholastic divines, as Dean Field and Bishop Cosin have done before me; and therefore am not responsible for anything he has said. But the fact is, that whatever may be the opinion of Thomas Aquinas or any of the rest about the validity, under some circumstances, of Presbyterian Ordination (which is a question I have not touched), *here is just the very species of language to which I referred as held by some of the Scholastic divines; attributing the superiority of the Bishop, not to his having superior powers so far as his* ORDERS *were concerned, but only so far as concerned the* OFFICE *bestowed upon him; that is, the official duties he had to perform.* So that the Bishop has quoted against me a passage precisely confirming my statement!

And then, if there is no greater difference between a presbyter and a bishop than this, may not a presbyter, under some circumstances, be authorized by his Church to perform those duties, and such acts be valid? True enough, these very Scholastic divines might (though I do not think *all* did) maintain the negative of this; but that is nothing to the purpose; and does not prove that, in laying down these views, they did not lay a *groundwork* for those who chose to maintain the affirmative. And it is amusing enough, that the Bishop, through his want of acquaintance with the subject, has just blundered upon the very passage of Aquinas which our learned Dean Field quotes as maintaining the very doctrine which the Bishop adduces it as opposing; as will be seen in the extract I shall give almost immediately from the Dean's work *Of the Church.*

* As I cannot suppose that the Bishop would not have given the *exact* words of this passage, if he had seen the original with his own eyes, he will permit me to advise him to tell the party who supplied him with this bit of information to be more accurate in his citations. The whole of the last clause, "and it is in this way," &c., is a substitution of his for the words "et secundum hoc loquuntur auctoritates inductæ;" which were, no doubt, Dionysius and "Liber Sententiarum." And so the words stand in the Commentary of Aquinas upon the "Liber Sententiarum," from which the whole of this Supplement to his *Summ. Theolog.* was compiled.

And this passage of Aquinas serves also to answer the Bishop's argument from the words in the Preface to our Ordinal as to the "three orders of ministers." (See p. 22, above.)

Here, however, is his Lordship's exclamation, consequent upon his quotation. "Such, and only such, is 'the parity of bishops and priests as one Order' in the Church of Rome, on which our learned ultra-Protestant has built his triumphant argument in favor of Presbyterian Ordination—such the statement to which, by THUS ADOPTING THEM, HE HAS MADE HIS OWN;" a sentence founded upon a blunder, and containing two palpable misstatements. For I have neither built my argument in favor of Presbyterian Ordination on such statements, nor adopted them; but simply stated an undeniable fact as to the views maintained by some of the Scholastic divines, and the effect those views had in preparing the way for the doctrine of the validity of Presbyterian Ordinations; and the passage of Aquinas, on which the censure is founded, is itself a proof of the truth of my statement.

The Bishop tells me that my "self-devotion" to my theory "deserves a better fate than that which it is doomed to meet with." I am sorry that I cannot return the compliment. I hold that "self-devotion" to any theory, such as will induce a man to resort to every expedient to make out his case, deserves no "better fate" than his Lordship's special pleading is, he may rest assured, "doomed to meet with."

And after having charged me with "covering my own statement with *the authority of Rome*," as if in his anger he had forgotten all self-respect in the fabrication of his charges, he assures us that it is "absolutely useless;" nay, that "so far as Presbyterian Ordination is concerned," I have "actually raised up a very strong fresh barrier against my views;" for, wonderful to say, he has discovered that Peter Lombard and Thomas Aquinas tell us that to confer Holy Orders appertains to bishops only. The vulgar sarcasms that follow, about "penning statements in Evangelical Magazines," &c., I leave to their fate, only regretting that a Bishop should descend to language so unworthy of his position. I would, however, point out to the reader's notice the way in which Cranmer's name is here paraded by his Lordship (pp. 44, 45) as on his side of the question, in the face of facts as notorious as his existence, and which I have before referred to.*

Now, if all this had been put forth by a hot-headed youth fresh from college, one might have been contented with reminding him that he ought to have made himself a little better acquainted with the subject before he spoke so positively about it. But when it proceeds from one whose *position* invests whatever comes from him with a certain degree of influence, and who has set himself up as the great Instructor of the Church—insulting his Sovereign, reviling and excommunicating his Metropolitan, and hectoring

* See Doctrine of Church of England, &c. pp. 15, 16.

over a large portion of the Church, because they do not adopt his views of orthodoxy—one is bound to treat it in a different way, and very plainly point out to the world the utter incompetency of this self-constituted oracle for the office he would fain assume. And I must add, that the vaunts of superior theological learning made in behalf of a certain party among us are in odd contrast with the stubborn testimony of facts—facts dating from their first rise.

The correctness of my statement as to the views of some of the Scholastic divines, is shown by the statement of the learned Morinus, in his work on *Ordinations.*

He says that there are four views among "Catholics" on this subject; and adds:—

"Prima et antiquis Scholasticis, eorumque Principibus communissima est, Episcopatum characterem non imprimere, non esse Ordinem seu Sacramentum a Sacerdotio distinctum, Episcopatum nihil illi addere ejusmodi; sed tantum per consecrationem aliquid sacramentale: quidquid Ordinis proprie dicti, qua ratione dicuntur septem Ordines; quidquid Sacramenti et characteris habet, illud a Sacerdotio quo necessario ante Episcopatum imbutus esse debet, haurire. Sed Episcopatum per se nihil aliud dicere quam officium, dignitatem, potestatem, autoritatem *Sacerdoti* DATAM multò ampliorem et augustiorem, per consecrationem Episcopalem, ea quam per Sacerdotii characterem nactus feurat." (*De Ordin.* Antw. 1695, pt. 3, p. 26.)

And he remarks: "*Hæc passim Scholasticorum Doctorum principes;*" referring to Hugo a S. Vict., Peter Lombard, Alexander Hal., Bonaventura, &c. &c., and *among the rest Thomas Aquinas, in the very passage which the Bishop has quoted from him.* And in the following chapter, showing that this view was maintained by many of the Fathers, he notices the custom that prevailed for many years at Alexandria: "Presbyteros Alexandrinos mortuo Episcopo suo unum ex Ordine et gremio Ecclesiæ suæ elegisse, thronoque excelsiori collocasse et Episcopum appellasse;" to whom of course, *when placed in that office,* though *without any fresh Ordination or Consecration,* the duty of Ordination belonged. And among other writers, he cites the author of the *Quæstiones Veteris et Novi Testamenti,* who lived before Augustine, who says: "Quid est enim Episcopus, nisi primus presbyter, hoc est summus sacerdos.... In Alexandria et per totam Ægyptum si desit Episcopus, consecrat Presbyter." (*Ib.* pp. 30, 31.)

Consequently, on this view of the matter, a presbyter needs no fresh Ordination to enable him to confer Orders. *His Ordination as presbyter is sufficient to enable him to fulfil all the duties of the ministerial office,* and the difference between a bishop and a presbyter is not as to "the ministerial powers, essentially and by right belonging to them," but as to the *exercise* of those powers, which has been restrained to a certain extent in those presbyters who have not been appointed to the Episcopal *office.*

But the "*validity*" of Presbyterian Orders is a different question. And his Lordship's charge against me, of citing the Scholastic divines as having maintained that doctrine, only shows his want of acquaintance with the subject. The solution of that question depends upon *the degree in which the restraint laid upon presbyters in the exercise of their powers is binding upon the whole Church.* Many of the Scholastic divines who hold the view I have just noticed, would no doubt have maintained that that restraint was *jure divino*, and so *absolutely* binding. A few of them, however, maintain (as Morinus admits, p. 34) that a bishop is above a presbyter only "jure humano, non divino;" and therefore, though even *they* probably would have contended earnestly for the binding nature of this *ecclesiastical* arrangement, there was but a very short step from their doctrine to that of the validity, under many circumstances, of Presbyterian Ordination.

Before I pass on, it may be well to present to the reader the statement of our learned Dean Field, on the whole subject; including his account of the views of those Scholastic divines whom the Bishop charges me with misrepresenting. Not that I am disposed to attribute any great weight to the teaching of the Scholastic divines, and hence I made but a passing allusion to it in the Tract that has called forth the Bishop of Exeter's ire; but the Dean's statement will show what degree of weight is due to his Lordship's account of the matter.

"The Apostles of Christ and their successors, when they planted the Churches, so divided the people of God converted by their ministry into particular Churches, that each city and the places near adjoining did make but one Church. Now because the unity and peace of each particular church of God and flock of his sheep dependeth on the unity of the pastor, and yet the necessities of the many duties that are to be performed in churches of so large extent require more Ecclesiastical ministers than one; therefore, though there be many presbyters, that is, many fatherly guides of one Church, yet there is *one amongst the rest* that is specially Pastor of the place, who, *for distinction sake, is named a Bishop;* to whom an eminent and peerless power is given, for the avoiding of schisms and factions; and the rest are but his assistants and coadjutors, and named by the general name of presbyters. So that in the performance of the acts of Ecclesiastical ministry, when he is present, and will do them himself, they must give place; and in his absence, or when being present he needeth assistance, they may do nothing without his consent and liking. Yea, so far *for order's sake* is he preferred above the rest, that some things are specially reserved to him only, *as the ordaining of such as should assist him in the work of his ministry,* the reconciling of penitents, confirmation of such as were baptized, by imposition of hands, dedication of Churches, and such like. These being the diverse sorts and kinds of Ecclesiastical power, it will easily appear to all them that enter into the due consideration thereof, that the power of ecclesiastical or sacred order, that is, the power and authority to intermeddle with things pertaining to the service of God, and to perform eminent acts of gracious efficacy, tending to the procuring of the eternal good of the sons of men, is *equal and the same in all those whom we call presbyters, that is, fatherly guides of God's Church and people: and that,* ONLY FOR ORDER'S SAKE, *and the preservation of peace, there is a limitation of the use and exercise of the same.* HEREUNTO AGREE ALL THE BEST LEARNED AMONGST THE ROMANISTS THEMSELVES, FREELY CONFESSING THAT THAT WHEREIN A BISHOP EXCELLETH A PRESBYTER, IS NOT A DISTINCT AND HIGHER ORDER, OR POWER OF ORDER, BUT A KIND OF DIGNITY AND OFFICE OR EMPLOYMENT ONLY.* Which they prove, because a presbyter

* To this sentence he attaches the following references; the first being, as the reader will observe, *the very passage in Thomas Aquinas cited by the Bishop for a contrary*

ordained *per saltum*, that never was consecrated or ordained deacon, may notwithstanding do all those acts that pertain to the deacon's order (because the higher order doth always imply in it the lower and inferior in an eminent and excellent sort); but a bishop ordained *per saltum*, that never had the ordination of a presbyter, can neither consecrate and administer the Sacrament of the Lord's body, nor ordain a presbyter, himself being none, nor do any act peculiarly pertaining to presbyters. Whereby it is most evident, that that wherein a bishop excelleth a presbyter, is not a distinct power of order, but an eminency and dignity only, *specially yielded to one above all the rest of the same rank, for order's sake, and to preserve the unity and peace of the Church.* Hence it followeth, that many things which, in some cases, presbyters may lawfully do, are peculiarly reserved unto bishops, as Hierome noteth (*Contra Luciferianos*), *Potius ad honorem sacerdotii, quam ad legis necessitatem; rather for the honor of their ministry than the necessity of any law.* And therefore we read (*Greg. Januario Ep.* l. 3, indict. 12, epist. 26,) that presbyters in some places, and at some times, did impose hands, and confirm such as were baptized; which when Gregory bishop of Rome would wholly have forbidden, there was so great exception taken to him for it, that he left it free again. And who knoweth not, that all presbyters in cases of necessity may absolve and reconcile penitents (Carth. 3, can. 32); a thing in ordinary course appropriated unto bishops? and why not by the same reason ordain presbyters and deacons in cases of like necessity? For seeing the cause why they are forbidden to do these acts, is, because to bishops ordinarily the care of all churches is committed, and to them in all reason the ordination of such as must serve in the Church pertaineth, that have the chief care of the Church, and have churches wherein to employ them; which only bishops have as long as they retain their standing; and not presbyters, being but assistants to bishops in their churches; if they become enemies to God and true religion, in case of such necessity, as the care and government of the Church is devolved to the presbyters remaining Catholic, and being of a better spirit; so the duty of ordaining such as are to assist or succeed them in the work of the ministry pertains to them likewise. For if the power of order, and authority to intermeddle in things pertaining to God's service, be the same in all presbyters, and that they be limited in the execution of it, only for order's sake, so that in case of necessity every of them may baptize, and confirm them whom they have baptized, absolve and reconcile penitents, and do all those other acts which regularly are appropriated unto the bishop alone; there is no reason to be given, but that in case of necessity, wherein all bishops were extinguished by death, or *being fallen into heresy, should refuse to ordain any to serve God in his true worship;* but that presbyters, as they may do all other acts, whatsoever special challenge bishops in ordinary course make unto them, might do this also. *Who then dare condemn all those worthy ministers of God, that were ordained by presbyters in sundry churches of the world, at such times as bishops in those parts where they lived opposed themselves against the truth of God, and persecuted such as professed it?*"

And he then adds some references to show that, even in the Church of Rome, Ordinations of this nature have been held by some to be valid; but into this question it is unnecessary to enter. And as it respects the early Church, he remarks:—

"All that may be alleged out of the Fathers, for proof of the contrary, may be reduced to two heads. For first, whereas they make all such ordinations void, as are made by presbyters, it is to be understood according to the strictness of *the Canons in use in their time, and not absolutely in the nature of*

purpose: Thomas, 3, p. in addit. quæst. 40, art. 5. Bonaven. l. 4, dist. 24, ar. 2, q. 3. Dominicus a Soto, l. 10, de justitia et jure, q. 1, art. 2, and in 4, dist. 24, q. 2, art. 3. Armacanus, l. 11, ostendit nullum prælatum plus habere de potestate sacramentali sive ordinis, quam simplicis sacerdotes. Cameracensis in 4, quæst. 4. Contarenus de Sacramentis, lib. 4.

the thing; which appears, in that they likewise make all ordinations *sine titulo* to be void; all ordinations of bishops ordained by fewer than three bishops with the metropolitan; all ordinations of presbyters by bishops out of their own churches without special leave; whereas, I am well assured, the Romanists will not pronounce any of these to be void, though the parties so doing are not excusable from all fault. Secondly, their sayings are to be understood regularly, not without exception of some special cases that may fall out."*

In a subsequent part of his work he reverts to the same subject, and adds the following remarks:—

"Touching the pre-eminence of bishops above presbyters, there is some difference among the School-divines. For the best learned amongst them are of opinion, that bishops are not greater than presbyters in the power of consecration or order; but only in the exercise of it, and in the power of jurisdiction, seeing presbyters may preach, and minister the greatest of all sacraments, by virtue of their consecration and order, as well as bishops. Touching the power of consecration or order, saith Durandus (in 4 *Sent. dist.* 24, q. 5), it is much doubted of among divines, whether any be greater therein than an ordinary presbyter: for Hierome seemeth to have been of opinion, that the highest power of consecration or order is the power of a priest or elder; so that every priest in respect of his priestly power may minister all sacraments, confirm the baptized, *give all Orders*, all blessings and consecrations; but that for the avoiding of the peril of schism, it was ordained that one should be chosen, who should be named a bishop, whom the rest should obey, and to whom it was reserved to give Orders, and to do some such other things as none but bishops do. And afterwards he saith, that Hierome is clearly of this opinion; not making the distinction of bishops from presbyters a mere human invention, or a thing not necessary, as *Aerius* did; but thinking that, amongst them who are equal in the power of order, and equally enabled to do any sacred act, the Apostles (for the avoiding of schism and confusion, and the preservation of unity, peace, and order) ordained that in each church one should be before and above the rest, without whom the rest should do nothing, and to whom some things should be peculiarly reserved, as the dedicating of churches, reconciling of penitents, confirming of the baptized, and the ordination of such as are to serve in the work of the ministry; of which the three former were reserved to the bishop alone, *potius ad honorem Sacerdotii, quam ad legis necessitatem;* that is, rather to honor his priestly and bishoply place, than for that those things at all may not be done by any other. And therefore we read (*Ambros.* in 4 *ad Ephes.*) that at some times, and in some cases of necessity, presbyters did reconcile penitents, and by imposition of hands confirm the baptized. But the ordaining of men to serve in the work of the ministry is more properly reserved to them. For seeing none are to be ordained at random, but to serve in some church, and none have churches but bishops, all other being but assistants to them in their churches, none may ordain but they only, unless it be in cases of extreme necessity, as when all bishops are extinguished by death, or, fallen into heresy, obstinately refuse to ordain men to preach the Gospel of Christ sincerely. And then as the care and charge of the Church is devolved to the presbyters remaining Catholic, so likewise the ordaining of men to assist them and succeed them in the work of the ministry. But hereof I have spoken at large elsewhere. Wherefore, to conclude this point, we see that the best learned amongst the Schoolmen are of opinion, that *bishops are no greater than presbyters in the power of consecration or order, but only in the exercise of it,* and in the power of jurisdiction, with whom Stapleton (*Relect. Contro.* 2, q. 3, art. 3,) seemeth to agree, saying expressly that *Quoad ordinem sacerdotalem, et ea quæ sunt ordinis,* that is, *in respect of sacerdotal order, and the things that pertain to order,* they are EQUAL; and that therefore in all

* Of the Church, bk. 3, c. 39, 2d ed. 1628, pp. 156–158.

administration of sacraments which depend of order, they are *all equal* POTESTATE, *though not* EXERCITIO; that is, in power, though not in the execution of things to be done by virtue of that power. Whence it will follow, that ordination, being a kind of sacrament, and so depending of the power of order, in the judgment of our adversaries might be ministered by presbyters, but that, for the avoiding of such horrible confusions, scandals, and schisms, as would follow upon such promiscuous ordinations, they are restrained by the decree of the Apostles; and none permitted to do any such thing, except it be in case of extreme necessity, but bishops, who *have the power of order in common together with presbyters*, but yet so, as that they excel them *in the execution of things to be done by virtue of that power*, and in the power of jurisdiction also."

And he then proceeds to animadvert upon Bellarmine's opposite view on the subject. (*Ib.* bk. 5, c. 27, pp. 500, 501.)

I have given these passages *in extenso*, because they will serve to show the reader the grounds upon which the validity of Presbyterian Ordinations is rested in one of the standard works of our Church. And with them he may compare the recent effusions with which our Church has been favored on the same subject.

And I must add, that if I had been anxious to dwell upon this argument, derived from ante-Reformation authorities, for the parity of order of bishops and presbyters, I might have added several others of a more stringent kind.

I might have pointed to early canons of our own Church recognizing this doctrine; as, for instance, to one in the Canons of Ecgbright, Archbishop of York, in 750, Can. 27: "That the bishop in the church sit elevated above the Bench of Presbyters, but in the House let him know himself to be a colleague of the presbyters." (*Wilk. Concil.* vol. i. p. 103.) And again, to the 17th of Elfric's Canons, in 970: "There is no more difference between a bishop and a presbyter, than that the bishop is *appointed* to ordain presbyters, and to confirm children, and to hallow churches, and to take care of God's rights: *since it would be too much, if every presbyter might do this:* FOR THEY HAVE THE SAME ORDER, BUT THE OTHER IS MORE HONORABLE." (*Ib.* p. 252.)

And above all, I might have referred to an authority which I am sure his Lordship would have received with the most profound respect. Indeed, I am astonished beyond measure that his Lordship should venture for a moment to question the truth of the doctrine in the face of the authority I am about to mention. Has his Lordship already forgotten the fourth Council of Carthage?—a Council of which he recently informed his Metropolitan, that he "need not remind" him, that it was "received generally, and one whose canons were adopted by the General Council of Chalcedon," and is "thus seen to have had *the authority of the whole Catholic Church?*"* His Lordship, therefore (to use his own language to his Metropolitan), "will not consider it irrelevant, if I present" him with the 35th Canon of this Council, which runs thus: "Ut Episcopus in Ecclesia et in consessu presbyterorum

* Letter to Archbishop of Canterbury, p. 15.

sublimior sedeat. Intra domum vero *collegam se presbyterorum esse cognoscat.*" (*Concil.* ed. Hardouin. tom. 1, col. 981.) So that, according to his Lordship's own showing, my "*heretical* paradox" has "the authority of the whole Catholic Church" of primitive times in its favor. I need not, indeed, inform him of my own opinion of the authority of this Council, which remains perfectly unaltered by anything which his Lordship's defenders have urged against my remarks upon it; and which certainly is not likely to be changed by the very amusing blunder of his favored advocate Mr. Watson, who actually confounds the Canons of this fourth Council of Carthage with what is called the Code of the African Church; a specimen of the remainder of his pamphlet; which I leave to the fate the public have already assigned to it. I can assure his Lordship, therefore, that *by me* he will not be condemned for rebellion against the doctrine of "the whole Catholic Church" for not accepting its canons; but his Lordship's *self-condemnation* must be complete.

I now go on with my task.

The Bishop next proceeds to deal with the argument derived from the writings and conduct of our divines. And here his Lordship's attempt at evidence of this kind in his favor almost amounts to a confession of failure. With the exception of Cranmer, whose views were notoriously opposed to his doctrine, he quotes none for the reign of Edward VI. He mentions, indeed, the *name* of Ridley (p. 44), but makes no reference to any part of his writings; and therefore, in reply to this vague claim, I shall merely refer the reader to Ridley's Letter to Grindal, then at Frankfort, in which he speaks of his prayers to God "for all *those Churches abroad* through the world, which have forsaken the kingdom of Antichrist, and professed openly *the purity* of the Gospel of Jesus Christ," (*Works*, p. 393;) in which his recognition of those Churches is, I suppose, sufficiently manifest.

And as to other testimonies of this period, they exist in abundance. Thus Archdeacon Philpot, the martyr, says:—

> "I allow the Church of Geneva, and the doctrine of the same; for it is *una, catholica,* et *apostolica,* and doth follow the doctrine that the Apostles did preach; and the doctrine taught and preached in King Edward's days was also according to the same." (*Works*, p. 153.)

Thus also we find Bishop Hooper, and Drs. Cox and Aylmer, both afterwards bishops, addressing the ministers of the Foreign Reformed Churches as dear brethren and ministers of the Church of Christ;* and this before any of our Reformers were indebted to them for an asylum in time of persecution; a circumstance which the Bishop somewhat unfairly adduces as rendering invalid a similar testimony from the divines of Elizabeth's reign.

Many other similar testimonies abound.

* See Letters relative to Engl. Reform. Parker Soc. ed. vol. i. pp. 33, *et s.*, 119, *et s.*, 275, *et s.*

On proceeding to the reign of Elizabeth, the Bishop finds himself, in the early part of that reign, in a state of things so entirely opposed to his views, that he is obliged to shut up all argument in some general remarks as to the gratitude of our Reformers towards the foreign Calvinists for the asylum afforded them in the reign of Mary, producing "a great laxity of practice in our Church" "in the Article of Orders." (P. 45.) "In short," he observes, after noticing a few cases of this kind, "sympathy with the foreign Calvinists, whom so many of the bishops and higher dignitaries in the age of Elizabeth at once loved as their benefactors and *reverenced as their teachers*, continued to influence both *doctrine* and practice in the English Church *during that whole generation*." (P. 46.) And these are the very men, let us observe, by whom our Formularies—the Articles as they now stand, and the Prayer-Book except a few alterations not affecting the doctrine in question—were drawn up. And the only two persons whom the Bishop has ventured to claim as witnessing in his favor, during the whole of Queen Elizabeth's reign, are Hooker and Bishop Bilson.

How far the former of these is a supporter of his Lordship's views, may be judged from the passages I have formerly quoted from him on this subject.* But let us see how the Bishop endeavors to make good his ground in claiming his support. He first criticizes and condemns Hooker's doctrine, "that the whole Church visible is the true original subject of all power;" and also the remark which flows from it, namely, that by the imposition of the bishop's hands "the Church giveth power of Order both unto presbyters and deacons;" which the Bishop sees to be clearly opposed to his statement as to what is required for lawful ordination. On this I offer no remark, as it is not any part of my task to defend Hooker against the Bishop of Exeter. But he proceeds to fix upon a remark of Hooker, that ordinations must ordinarily be by bishops, except in the case of an extraordinary commission by God, or "when *the exigence of necessity* doth constrain to leave the usual ways of the Church—when the Church must needs have some ordained, and neither hath nor can have possibly a bishop to ordain." (Pp. 46, 47.) And he argues that, as this *necessity* cannot now be pleaded for the Foreign Reformed Churches, "Hooker must be cited as a very strong authority against the Orders of the Foreign Protestants, whose case we are considering." (P. 49.)

Now on this argument from "necessity" I have already offered some remarks,† and shown that the term, as used by our early divines in this matter, was not intended to denote such a necessity as the Bishop here supposes, that is, that there should be no bishops in the world who would give them ordination, but only one arising from a failure of orthodox bishops in the Church in

* See Doctr. of Ch. of Engl. on Non-Ep. Ord. pp. 20, 21.

† Reply to Archdeacon Churton and Chancellor Harington, p. 26.

which such ordinations took place. But in truth the Bishop himself has saved me all farther trouble by refuting himself; for he has been at pains to show, that in Hooker's own time the Foreign Protestant Churches might easily have obtained Episcopal Orders. (P. 49.) Consequently, as they did not do so, and yet, nevertheless, Hooker held* that their Orders (instancing in *Beza's*, which had less in their favor than some others) were valid, he "must be cited as a very strong authority," to use the Bishop's own words, *in favor of* the Orders of the Foreign Protestants, whose case we are considering.

The reply to the extracts from Bishop Bilson is, that he is speaking of the ordinary state of things, in which, as established by the custom of the Church, bishops only might ordain. But that he did not mean to tie the Church to bishops, is evident from what he says in another work; that, "to bishops speaking the word of God, princes as well as others must yield obedience; but if bishops pass their commission and speak besides the word of God, what they list, both prince and people may despise them."†

To the extracts from Hooker and Bishop Bilson, the only other testimonies which his Lordship has added in favor of his views, from the Reformation to the present day, are two from Bishops Sanderson and Pearson.

To set before the reader the views of the former, he quotes a passage in which the following sentence occurs: "A man might therefore justly wonder how it should come to pass that the Episcopal power, in *that which is peculiar to bishops above other* their brethren in the ministry, viz., *the ordaining of priests and deacons*, and the managing of the keys, cannot be said to be of God, but it must be forthwith condemned to be highly derogatory to the regal power," &c. (P. 51.) And then, adds the Bishop of Exeter, "having stated various ways in which *divino jure* may be understood, he thus gives his own view, in a Postscript: 'My opinion is, that Episcopal government is not to be derived merely from Apostolic practice or institution; but that it is originally founded in the Person and Office of the Messiah our Lord Jesus Christ, who, being sent by His Heavenly Father to be the great Apostle, Bishop, and Pastor of His Church, &c. . . . did afterwards, before His ascension into Heaven, send and empower His holy Apostles, giving them the Holy Ghost, as His Father had before sent Him to execute the same Apostolical, Episcopal, and Pastoral office for the ordering and governing of His Church even unto the end of the world. This I take to be so clear from those and other texts,' &c." (Pp. 51, 52.)

And hence his Lordship draws the conclusion, that Bishop San-

* Eccl. Pol. vii. 14.

† True Difference between Christian Subjection and Unchristian Rebellion. Oxf. 1585, 4to. pp. 261, 262.

derson "*thus asserted the exclusive power of bishops to ordain divino jure.*" (P. 52.)

Now if the Bishop of Exeter had been put on his trial for holding such a doctrine as is here maintained, it would have been quite fair for him to have referred to these words of Bishop Sanderson in his defence. But when he is arraigning his Metropolitan and others for error and heresy because they do not take such a view, it is anything but fair to refer to Sanderson as he has done.

For, in the first place, Bishop Sanderson points out two different senses of the phrase *jus divinum*, observing:—

"Sometimes it importeth a *Divine precept* (which is indeed the primary and most proper signification) when it appeareth by some clear express and peremptory command of God in his Word, to be the will of God that the thing so commanded should be perpetually and universally observed. Of which sort, setting aside the Articles of the Creed, and the moral duties of the law (which are not much pertinent to the present inquiry), there are, as I take it, very few things that can be said to be of *Divine positive right* under the New Testament. *The preaching of the Gospel and administration of the Sacraments are two; which, when I have named, I think I have named all.* But there is a secondary and more extended signification of that term, which is also of frequent use among divines. In which sense such things as, having no express command in the Word, yet are found to have authority and warrant from the institution, example, and approbation either of Christ himself or his Apostles; and have (in regard of the importance and usefulness of the things themselves) been held, by the consentient judgment of all the Churches of Christ in the primitive and succeeding ages, needful to be continued; such things I say are (though not so properly as the former, yet) usually and *interpretativè* said to be of *Divine right.* Of which sort I take the observation of the Lord's day, the ordering the keys, the distinction of presbyters and deacons, and some other things (not all perhaps of equal consequence) to be. Unto *Jus Divinum* in that former acception, is required a Divine precept; in this latter, it sufficeth thereunto that a thing be of Apostolical institution or practice. Which ambiguity is the more to be heeded, for that the observation thereof is of great use for the avoiding of sundry mistakes, that through the ignorance or neglect thereof daily happen to the engaging of men in endless disputes, and entangling their consciences in unnecessary scruples."

And having thus pointed out these two senses of the term *Jus Divinum*, he proceeds to show in what manner the phrase is to be applied in the matter of Episcopacy. And he says:—

"Now that the government of the Churches of Christ by bishops is of Divine right in that first and stricter sense, is an opinion at least of *great* PROBABILITY, and such as may more easily and upon better grounds be defended *than confuted*.... Yet because it is both inexpedient to maintain a dispute where it needs not, and needless to contend for more, where less will serve the turn; I find that our divines that have travailed most in this argument, where they purposely treat of it, do rather choose to stand to the tenure of Episcopacy *ex Apostolica designatione*, than to hold a contest upon the title of *Jus Divinum*, no necessity requiring the same to be done. They therefore that so speak of this government as established by Divine right, are not all of them necessarily so to be understood, as if they meant it in that first and stricter one. Sufficient it is for the justification of the Church of England in the constitution and government thereof, that it is (as certainly it is) of Divine right in the latter and larger signification: that is to say, of Apostolical institution and approbation; exercised by the Apostles themselves, and by other persons in their times, appointed and enabled thereunto by them, according to the will of our Lord Jesus Christ, and by virtue of the commission they had received from him."

So that all he ventures to say in favor of Episcopacy being *jure divino* in the strict sense of the phrase—which alone would make it of absolute necessity—is that it appears to him to be "an *opinion* at least of great PROBABILITY;" and he admits, that our divines for the most part only contend for the *apostolical* institution of Episcopacy.

He then remarks, that this latter view is "a part of the established doctrine of the Church of England," (in which I entirely agree with him,) and that it "hath been constantly and uniformly maintained by our best writers, and by all the sober, orderly, and orthodox sons of this Church. (*Episcop. not prejud. to Reg. Power*, Lond. 1673, Sec. II. §§ 3–6.)

The latter is a somewhat large assertion, but no doubt true of a great majority of such divines. But then, as I have already abundantly shown,* those among them who held this view maintained *also* the validity under some circumstances of Presbyterian Ordinations.

And now, with respect to the passage quoted by the Bishop of Exeter from the "Postcript" to this work, I shall merely take the liberty of giving the reader the previous context. Bishop Sanderson says:—

"Whereas in my answer to the former of the two objections in the foregoing Treatise, I have not anywhere made any clear discovery what my own particular judgment is concerning the *Jus Divinum* of Episcopacy in the stricter sense, either in the affirmative or negative; and for want of so doing, may perhaps be censured by some to have walked but haltingly, or at leastwise with more caution and mincing than became me to do in a business of that nature; I do hereby declare: 1. That to avoid the starting of more questions than needs must, I then thought it fitter (and am of the same opinion still) to *decline that question, than to determine it either way;* such determination being clearly of no moment at all to my purpose, and for the solving of that objection. 2. That nevertheless (LEAVING OTHER MEN TO THE LIBERTY OF THEIR OWN JUDGMENTS) my opinion is, that Episcopal government is," &c. (as follows in the Bishop of Exeter's extract.)

Now if the Bishop of Exeter will follow Bishop Sanderson's course in "*leaving other men to the liberty of their own judgments*," and not denounce as heretics and unfaithful to the doctrine of their Church, those who take the lower of the two views mentioned by Sanderson, I for one will leave him to follow Sanderson, without molestation, in taking the higher view. But let him not think to avail himself of the authority of Sanderson in his assault upon his Metropolitan and seven-tenths at least of the clergy, by quoting scraps from him which only show *half* his mind.

And I must add, with respect to Bishop Sanderson's own doctrine, that it does not seem to have prevented his recognizing the Foreign Non-Episcopal Churches as true Churches of Christ, and therefore their ministers as true ministers of Christ. For in his brief *Discourse concerning the Church*, he has a chapter entitled, "Concerning Protestant Churches;" and he defines them as "those

* See the authorities quoted in my former Tract, *The Doctrine of the Church of England on Non-Episcopal Ordinations.*

visible particular churches, which, having by an external separation freed themselves from the tyranny and idolatry of Popery, have more or less reformed the doctrine and worship from Popish corruptions, and restored them more or less to the ancient and primitive purity;" and he adds, as instances, "the Church of England, the Church of Denmark, *the Church of Saxony*," &c. (*Disc. conc. the Church*, Lond. 1688. 4to. pp. 19, 20.)

Whatever, therefore, might be Bishop Sanderson's view, he certainly found some way of reconciling it with the notion that the Foreign Non-Episcopal Churches were true Churches of Christ, and therefore their ministers true ministers of Christ.

The Bishop next claims the authority of Pearson in his favor. And he quotes first from some "Theological Determinations,"* designed to be part of a work entitled, *Summa Theologiæ ex Sententia Doctoris in Ecclesia Anglicana tradita;* and which, the Bishop tells us, "is, *therefore*, his deliberate expression of what he deemed *the doctrine of our Church* on the subjects treated therein." I must submit that the words of the title are by no means so *exclusive*, and imply no more than doctrine which may be lawfully maintained in the Church of England. These "Determinations" are in number three, and entitled: "I. Ordo Episcopalis est Apostolicus. II. Ordinandi potestas solis competit Episcopis. III. Ordinatio Anglicana complet totam Essentiam externæ Vocationis ad Ministerium."

Now it is quite possible, that Pearson, like Sanderson, may have taken the highest view of the *Jus Divinum* of Episcopacy; and I am not concerned to disprove it; but I hardly think that the "Determinations" to which the Bishop here refers us will prove it. And for this reason; that they lay down *the general rule*, and do not touch the question, whether there are or are not any *exceptional cases*. And we may find quite as strong passages as occur in these "Determinations," in authors who nevertheless, in other parts of their writings, have distinctly admitted the validity, under some circumstances, of Presbyterian Ordinations; as, for instance, Archdeacon Mason.

The Bishop's remaining citation is from a Letter of Bishop Pearson against the allowance of "promiscuous Ordinations" in the Church of England.† The matter, therefore, against which the Letter is directed, is very different from that now under discussion. For it would no doubt be very undesirable to allow such Ordinations in *one and the same* Church, while yet Non-Episcopal Ordinations might be valid in other Churches.

But his Lordship will say: "Read what he says." Let us do so; and first let us take his Lordship's citation, which is this:—

"That the order of the ministry is necessary to the continuation of the Gospel according to the promises of Christ, as it was to the first plantation of it according to His institution, is a doctrine indubitable. That this ministry is derived by a succession and constant propagation, and that the unity

* Minor Theological Works of Bishop Pearson. Oxf. 1844, vol. i. p. 271, *et seq.*
† Minor Theological Works, vol. ii. p. 231.

and peace of the Church of Christ are to be conserved by a due and legitimate ordination, no man who considereth the practice of the Apostles and Ecclesiastical history can ever doubt." "However, in the peculiar and happy condition of our Church, these promiscuous ordinations, if at all allowed by it, are most destructive to that which is the safety and honor of it. We have the greatest felicity which could happen to a Reformation, as being regular and authoritative," &c. &c.—the Bishop extending his quotation much farther.

But here I paused in reading, for it was impossible not to see that something was *omitted* where the inverted commas indicated a break in the quotation, very germane to the question under discussion. It was tolerably clear, by the words, "*However*, in the peculiar and happy condition of *our* Church," &c., that some concession had been made representing Churches *not* in so "peculiar and happy a condition." And accordingly I found there the following passage:—

"This way of Ordination, having continued so many ages one and the same, could never be considerably altered without some great commotions and dissensions in the Church, and the manifest breach of union and communion in that body; *whomsoever we judge guilty of the breach of that union; which is not necessary now to dispute*. And as the first introduction of *different ordinations* caused a standing and settled opposition, precluding all ways of reconciliation; so they cannot be brought into any *one* Church, but they must make such a division and disparity in the administrations, as will amount to no less than a schism." And then follows the remark contrasting with what is here alluded to, the "peculiar and happy condition of *our* Church," and the "felicity" of our Reformation "as being regular and authoritative."

Now this allusion to the Foreign Protestant Churches is not that of one who entirely disowns them as Churches, but rather of one who considered it as their misfortune that their reformation was not regular, and held that the guilt of the consequent "breach of union and communion" might not rest with them. This remark, which is the only one in the whole Letter directly affecting the point in question, the Bishop has *omitted* in his extracts, though he has cited almost the whole of the rest of the Letter.

His Lordship adds, that he has cited these testimonies as occurring, "not in *obiter dicta*, but in works written on the very subject of Orders," and consequently worth more than "a whole Catena of writers, however eminent, who are treating the matter either incidentally and *aliud agentes*, or under collateral influences, such as a desire to make out as good a case as they can for Foreign Protestants among whom they were living;" and he adds: "This last remark specially applies to the strongest testimony on that side with which I am acquainted, Dr. Cosins's [Cosin's] letter to Mr. Cordel at Blois, dated Paris, Feb. 7, 1650." (P. 56.)

But, in the first place, this is no reply to such testimonies as have been brought from Saravia, from Archbishop Whitgift, from Dean Field, from Archdeacon Mason. And secondly, whatever truth there is in the general proposition, that a testimony derived from a work written expressly on the subject is of more value than an *obiter dictum* respecting it in a work on a subject, this observation does not apply to the case in hand; for what we want to know is the opinion of our divines, *not on the general question* of the Scriptural and Apostolical form of government for the Church, but *on certain exceptional cases*, and whether under some circumstances that form of government may not be lawfully departed from. And we see in the case of Archdeacon Mason, that a work may be published *on the general subject*, from which the views of the author on *exceptional cases* cannot be judged, but, on the contrary, greatly misapprehended.*

To attempt to get rid of the testimony of Bishop Cosin, given in his able and elaborate letter *written expressly on the point under discussion*, is, of course, not worth one word in the way of refutation. It simply shows the utterly impervious character of the mind that indited it to anything that it does not wish to receive.

What follows is still more extraordinary. For the Bishop adds:—

"Yet even he refers the question [*i. e.* of "communicating with them of the French Church"] ultimately to the decision of our own Church; which decision, solemnly given by Convocation in 1661, and afterwards confirmed by the Act of Uniformity, was, we know, against the concession here made; yet it had the full assent, concurrence, and earnest co-operation of Cosins [Cosin]† himself." (P. 56.)

Now, with all due respect, I beg to say, first, that Dr. Cosin did not refer the question to the decision of our own Church, for he merely stated his "protestation" "not to recede in anywise from the doctrine and discipline of the Church of England," which renders his testimony all the stronger; and he added, that there was "no prohibition of our Church against it;" and secondly, as the reader probably well knows, there was *no subsequent decision* of Convocation in 1661, or of the Act of Uniformity, "against the concession here made." And I suspect his Lordship himself would be very sorry to be prosecutor in a suit against one who had chosen, when abroad, to communicate with the Non-Episcopal Churches of the Continent.

And thus, when we contrast the real value of his Lordship's statements with the magisterial and imperious tone in which they are delivered, we seek in vain for any justification of his Lordship's high pretensions.

So ends the Bishop's attempt to support his doctrine from the writings of our divines. And whatever may be the opinion of the reader as to the views of his Lordship's referees, I must again *remind him, that I do not pretend to show that* none of our divines ever held the doctrine of the exclusive lawfulness of Episcopal Ordination. This I am not concerned to prove, and do not profess to do so. And if the Bishop likes to maintain such a view without

* See Doctrine, &c., pp. 37, 38; and Reply to Churton and Harington, p. 31.

† It is somewhat remarkable that the very name of this learned Bishop seems unknown to his Lordship.

arraigning as heretics and unfaithful sons of our Church those who hold a contrary opinion, let him do so. Our Church has not *forbidden* the view, though she clearly has not sanctioned it in her Formularies; and her 23d Article *implies* a contrary doctrine.

But when the Bishop takes the ground he does, he is bound to show, when treating of the testimonies of our divines on the subject, that there is *not* that testimony in favor of the *opposite* view in their writings that raises a good argument for it from that source. And therefore what he had more especially to do was, not to adduce two or three supposed testimonies in favor of *his own* view from those writings; but to show that the host of testimonies cited for the opposite view were incorrectly cited, and that there was in fact no weighty evidence of that kind to be adduced in its behalf. But, instead of this, he has passed them by, with the exception of Hooker and Cosin, in profound silence; though they were brought under his eye in the very Tract he here criticizes. And very remarkable it is, that while his Lordship has thought it worth while to spend several pages upon my few remarks on the Formularies of the time of Henry VIII. and the Scholastic divines—which were introduced as but indirectly bearing on the real question at issue—he has passed over without the slightest notice all but two of the direct testimonies I have cited, showing both the doctrine and practice of the greatest divines of our Church from the Reformation to the present day.

Before I conclude, I shall call the reader's attention to a brief recapitulation of the authorities which the Bishop has thus passed by. But, previous to doing so, there is one more point to be noticed in the Bishop's Letter. His Lordship has, with much reason, conceived it necessary to offer some remarks, before he closed his argument, on the 55th Canon; which had, of course, been quoted as entirely opposed to the doctrine he is attempting to establish. That Canon, passed in 1603, orders the clergy to pray for "the Church of Scotland;" while it is an *undeniable fact*, that the Church of Scotland had then no bishops, in the proper sense of the word, and therefore of course none but Presbyterian Orders at the best. The consequence is obvious, namely, that our Church did not then consider Episcopal Orders necessary under all circumstances to constitute a valid ministry.

The particulars of the case of the Church of Scotland at this period I have so fully stated in a recent publication,* that I do not here repeat them.

To the overthrow of this obvious and necessary conclusion, his Lordship has devoted six pages. With what success may easily be foreseen.

He commences with the following very remarkable observation:—

"What was the exact position of *the Presbyterian* government in Scotland

* Reply to Archdeacon Churton and Chancellor Harington.

according to law in 1603, I confess myself *unable to ascertain without more of labor than the point itself would seem to be worth.* The ecclesiastical history of that country at that period is so full of intricacy as to *baffle ordinary research.* I think it very likely that the English Convocation in 1603 was itself *scarcely better informed on this point than we are,"* &c. (P. 57.)

With this amount of information on the subject, his Lordship thinks himself justified in dogmatically determining—after quoting some passionate exclamations of James I. against Presbyterianism, and such like fruitless evidence—that the notion that the Kirk of Scotland, as it then existed (and which was the only visible Church of Scotland in existence), "should be 'the very Church of Scotland' designated by the Canon as the object of our prayers, is too gross for an ordinary understanding to digest. (P. 58.)

Whether this mode of settling the matter by one who confesses his ignorance of the data upon which any sound conclusion must be grounded, will be satisfactory to his Lordship's adherents, I know not. But certainly with any others it must be utterly worthless.

The Bishop perhaps thinks so himself, for he adds some arguments on the subject; and the first is this:—

"That the Church which is really intended in the Canon," says the Bishop, "*must* be in communion with *that which thus recognizes it in her prayers to be a Church,* I need not say." (Pp. 58, 59.)

So that the Church of England, according to the Bishop, recognizes no Christian community to be a Church but those that are in communion with her! When, therefore, we pray for the Catholic Church, we mean the Church of England and that portion of the Christian world that is in communion with her!

And then follows another still more remarkable specimen of his Lordship's mode of reasoning, addressed to the "soberer portion" of those who differ from him in this matter. His Lordship commences with a formal proof that the "realm of Scotland" is included in the terms used in the 1st, 36th, and 55th Canons to describe the countries over which King James ruled, which might have been readily granted. But in those Canons the king is described (to quote the words of the last) as "supreme governor in these his realms, over all persons, in all causes ecclesiastical as well as temporal." Now for the consequence. "*Therefore,*" writes his Lordship, "Mr. Macaulay, and all who may have availed themselves of the ingenious suggestion, that the 'Church of Scotland was in 1603, as now, Presbyterian,' must be prepared to accept, as a corollary, that the Queen's Majesty is supreme in all causes ecclesiastical or spiritual within the limits of the 'Holy Kirk.'" So that because the Church of England chose to recognize King James, in 1063, as supreme governor in all causes ecclesiastical throughout his dominions; therefore, if the Church of Scotland (which did *not* do so) was then, as now, Presbyterian, the Queen is now *de facto* supreme in all causes ecclesiastical in the present Scotch Presbyterian Church. To state such an argument is to refute it.

I need hardly observe, that the acknowledgment of the Church of England of her own doctrine on the subject (and the Canon of course is nothing more) affords no proof of the estate or views of other communions in the King's dominions. And certainly it could not make a communion Episcopal that had no true bishops belonging to it. In fact, it does not touch the question, whether the Church of Scotland was Presbyterian or Episcopal; for it might have been the latter, and yet not have recognized the Royal Supremacy as our Canons do, as is the case with the present Episcopal Church in Scotland. And the existence of this Church in Scotland, and even of the present Romish hierarchy in England, does *not make it necessary for us to make the slightest alteration in* the Canons.

The Bishop is, in fact, refuted by his own statements. For he contends that our Church is now in communion with the Episcopal Church existing in Scotland, which he calls the "Catholic and Apostolic Church of Scotland." Whether we are or not, I shall not now dispute; but, by his own showing, our acknowledgment of the Royal Supremacy does not prevent our recognizing as "the Catholic and Apostolic Church of Scotland" a Church that does not thus acknowledge it.

But, adds his Lordship (p. 61): Do not accuse me of being so uncharitable as to exclude such communities from the *benefit of my prayers.* I will pray for them as much as you please, but not as "a Branch of the Church of Christ." "To pray for it [the Scotch Presbyterian "community"] as such, would be in truth to pray for the destruction of our own Church, for it is the avowed principle of that Presbyterian body to labor to that end." (P. 61.) "I will pray for them among 'our enemies, persecutors, and slanderers, and that it may please God to turn their hearts;' but I will not pray for them AS A RELIGIOUS BODY—still less as a Church—least of all as the Church of Scotland," &c. (P. 62.)

And is it really so hard a task to his Lordship's Christian charity to recognize as a Church, or even as *a religious body*, those who are attacking our form of church government and endeavoring to propagate their own?—so impossible a matter to own as a Christian brother one who thinks us in error on such a point, and perhaps in the warmth of his feelings gives us some very hard names? I will only say, that I trust there are many among us who do not sympathize with his Lordship in such feelings.

But of one thing the Bishop of Exeter will allow me to remind him; namely, that if such are his views, then *à fortiori* the Romish "community" must not be recognized in our prayers as "a Branch of the Church of Christ;" a consequence which, I suspect, his Lordship has forgotten.

In connection with this subject the Bishop finds it convenient to mention what, in the part where he ought to have specially taken it into account, he altogether passed over in silence; namely, that at the Restoration, in 1661, "this important *addition* was made" in the Preface to the Ordinal: "or hath had formerly

Episcopal consecration or ordination," (p. 63,) which he calls a "decision of our Church" on "the indispensable necessity of Episcopal ordination; but which, I need not remind the reader, applies only to our own Church.

And finally he observes, that "the persons designated for bishops" in Scotland, "though they struggled hard to assert the reality of their Presbyterian Orders, were required, as an indispensable condition before their consecration, to be first ordained deacons and priests, because they were 'mere laymen;' and this notwithstanding the precedent of 1610, when James's bishops elect were consecrated at once," (p. 64:) which is quite true, but which the following account of the matter by Bishop Burnet, the familiar friend of Leighton, who was one of them, will show to be quite insufficient for the Bishop's purpose:—

"When the time fixed for the consecration of the bishops of Scotland came on, the English bishops finding that Sharp and Leighton had not Episcopal ordination, as priests and deacons, the other two having been ordained by bishops before the wars, they stood upon it, that they must be ordained, first deacons and then priests. Sharp was very uneasy at this, and remembered them of what had happened when King James had *set up Episcopacy.* Bishop Andrews moved at that time the ordaining them, as was now proposed; but that was overruled by King James, who thought it went too far towards the unchurching of all those who had no bishops among them. But the late war, and the disputes during that time, had raised these controversies higher, and brought men to stricter notions, and to maintain them with more fierceness. The English bishops did also say, that by the late Act of Uniformity that matter was more positively settled than it had been before; so that they could not legally consecrate any but those who were, according to that constitution, made first priests and deacons. *They also made this difference between the present time and King James's: for then the Scots were only in an imperfect state,* HAVING NEVER HAD BISHOPS AMONG THEM SINCE THE REFORMATION; *so in such a state of things, in which they had been under a real necessity,* IT WAS REASONABLE TO ALLOW OF THEIR ORDERS, *how defective soever;* but that of late they had been in a state of schism, had revolted from their bishops, and had thrown off that order: so that Orders given in such a wilful opposition to the whole constitution of the primitive Church was a thing of another nature." (*Burnet's Hist. of his Own Times,* i. 139, 140.)

From this passage two important conclusions follow: first, that these bishops fully recognized the fact, that the *validity* of the Orders of those consecrated in 1610 was admitted by the bishops who consecrated them; and secondly, that these bishops held that there was good ground for so doing. I commend this to Chancellor Harington's consideration.

To the remarks on the *Address* of "the Devon and Cornwall Church of England Protestant Association" and the Archbishop's *Answer* (pp. 64, 65), I shall merely say, that no such conclusion follows from the Archbishop's answer as the Bishop has deduced from it; namely, that the Archbishop has made "Orders depend on the soundness or unsoundness of the doctrines held by the persons whose Orders are in question." This is so obvious to any impartial reader, that I shall not waste words upon it. And with this charge his very characteristic attack upon the Archbishop for an "ultra-Protestantism" "closely allied to Popery," falls to the ground.

The Bishop is very anxious that His Grace should enter into a discussion with him as to what is "the authority necessary to confer Holy Orders." (Pp. 65, 66.) I suppose His Grace, if he thought any reply necessary, would refer his Lordship to the Articles of our Church, where he will find an answer to his question.

To his Lordship's inquiry, what the ministers of the Foreign Non-Episcopal Churches are to be considered, as he fears they may be "an order unknown to Scripture," I think his anxiety on that head may be at once relieved, by informing him, that they are evidently intended to correspond with the presbyters of whom we read in the Acts of the Apostles.

The Bishop here repeats the inference from the words in the Preface to the Ordinal, to which I have already replied.* But he adds, that "even if, for any special reasons of a local or temporary kind," in the case of foreigners a "prohibition of 'Bishops, Priests, or Deacons,' to execute any of the said [*i. e.* ministerial] functions *within our Church* be in any way justifiable, yet the absolute refusal to recognize them as ministers *in the Church of Christ*, would be an act so grossly schismatical, that no man of Catholic principles would know how to justify his continuing to communicate in the Church which is guilty of it." (P. 67.) I reply, perhaps it would; and I am glad to know, that our own Church does nothing of the kind, but, on the contrary, has clearly in her Articles extended the limits of a valid ministry beyond that which is constituted precisely according to her own rules, and by an overwhelming majority of her divines for a long period after the Reformation has directly recognized the validity of the Orders of various Non-Episcopal Churches. But it seems to me, that a *worse* case than that of *a Church* refusing to recognize such persons as "ministers in the Church of Christ," is that of one who, while bearing office in a Church that does *not* refuse such recognition, not only refuses, but reviles his Metropolitan for taking a different course—not only "himself refuses to receive the brethren, but forbiddeth them that would, and casteth them out of the Church."

Thus ends his Lordship's argument drawn from the Formularies and divines of our Church on the subject before us; the remainder of the pamphlet being devoted to remarks upon the present state of the Protestant Continental Churches, and the individuals who recently came over to this country from them.

I shall here, therefore, take the opportunity of briefly recapitulating the authorities I have before adduced on this subject, making some occasional additions to them as I proceed.

Thus—not to notice the period of Edward VI., for which I have already given sufficient testimonies†—we have for the reign of Elizabeth, when our Articles and Formularies were settled as

* See p. 15 above.

† See p. 31 above.

they now (with few exceptions) stand, Dr. Alley, bishop of Exeter, in 1560, Dr. Pilkington, bishop of Durham in 1563, and the learned Dr. Whitaker, Regius Professor of Divinity at Cambridge, at the close of the century—all testifying to the parity of bishops and presbyters as to their order, and the superiority of bishops in respect of *office* being only due to human appointment;* we have Bishop Jewel taking similar ground, and, moreover, testifying strongly to the necessity of bishops to constitute a Church;† we have Archbishop Whitgift distinctly maintaining that a presbyter and bishop are one "*quoad ministerium*," and that the Scriptures do not "set down any one certain form and kind of government of the Church to be perpetual for all times, persons, and places, without alteration;" and that he does not "condemn any churches" where the Presbyterian form of church government "is lawfully and without danger received:"‡ we have Hooker testifying, as already stated:§ we have the High-Churchman Saravia expressly affirming the validity of the Orders of the Foreign Non-Episcopal Churches, and their right to act independently of other churches in the matter of Orders:‖ and Archbishop Whitgift assured Beza that "the purpose of Dr. Saravia to assert degrees among the ministers of the Gospel was wholly undertaken without the injury or prejudice of any particular Church:"¶ we have Bishop Bridges saying, in 1587, that the form of Ecclesiastical government may be varied, and that "we ought neither to condemn, nor speak, nor think evil of other good churches that use another Ecclesiastical government than we do:"** we have Bishop Cooper, one of the leading defenders of our Church against the Puritans, asserting in 1589 that "one form of church government is not necessary in all times and places of the Church;" and that he "doubted not," that "all those Churches in which the Gospel in those days, after great darkness, was first renewed, and the learned men whom God sent to instruct them," had "been directed by the Spirit of God to retain this liberty, that in external government and other outward orders, they might choose such as they thought in wisdom and godliness to be most convenient for the state of their country and disposition of the people:"†† and we have the learned Dean of the Arches, Dr. Cosin, in 1584, laying it down, in express defence of the Foreign Reformed Churches, that it "cannot be proved, that any set and exact particular form" of church polity "is recommended unto us by the word of God."‡‡

This was the ground they took against the Puritans, who insisted upon the exclusive divine right of the Presbyterian form of church government. And instead of meeting this by a counter-claim of a similar kind, as the Bishop of Exeter would do, they

* See Doct. of Ch. of Engl. &c. pp. 17, 18, 20.
† *Ib.* p. 18.
‡ *Ib.* pp. 19, 20.
§ See pp. 32, 33 above, and *ib.* pp. 20, 21.
‖ *Ib.* pp. 21, 22.
¶ Strype's Whitgift, p. 405.
** Doctrine, &c. p. 22.
†† Doctrine, &c. pp. 23, 24.
‡‡ *Ib.* p. 24. I must refer the reader to my former Tract for the full citation of these passages, from which alone he can see their real force.

protested against such a notion as totally unwarranted by Holy Scripture.

And for their practical treatment of the ministers of the Foreign Non-Episcopal Churches, we find Archbishops Parker, Grindal, and Sandys, Bishops Jewel, Parkhurst, Cox, Horn (to mention no others), writing to the ministers of those Churches as acknowledged and valued ministers of the Church of Christ;* and Archbishop Whitgift writing to Beza as "his most dear brother in Christ," and superscribing his letter to "his most dear brother and *colleague* in Christ, and faithful pastor of the Genevan Church."†

And against all these testimonies, the only shadow of an opposite testimony that can be brought for this period is that from Bishop Bilson, which I have already considered.‡

Then, for the *practice* of our Church we have various testimonies, showing that, by at least the great majority of our bishops, persons having only Presbyterian Orders were admitted to the cure of souls in our Church, until the period of the Restoration, without any fresh ordination.§ I have before mentioned the case of Morrison, who had only Scotch Presbyterian Orders, but was licensed by Archbishop Grindal to minister the word and sacraments throughout the Province of Canterbury without any fresh ordination; and have given the testimonies of Bishop Cosin (who, having been librarian to Overall, and chaplain to Neyle, is a most unexceptionable witness), and of Bishop Fleetwood, showing that it was not the custom of our bishops, previous to the Restoration, to reordain those who had only Presbyterian Orders, when they admitted them to cures in this country.||

The same testimony is borne by Bishop Burnet, who says:—

"Another point was fixed by the Act of Uniformity, which was more at large formerly: *those who came to England from the Foreign Churches had not been required to be ordained among us:* but now all, that had not Episcopal ordination, were made incapable of holding any Ecclesiastical benefice." (*Hist. of his Own Times*, vol. i. p. 183.)

And even Mr. Keble confesses that, "nearly up to the time when Hooker wrote, numbers had been admitted to the ministry of the Church in England, with no better than Presbyterian Ordination: and it appears by *Travers's Supplication to the Council*, that such was the construction not uncommonly put upon the Statute of the 13th of Elizabeth, permitting those who had received Orders in any other form than that of the English Service-Book, on giving certain securities, to exercise their calling in England." (*Pref. to Hooker*, p. lxxvi.)

Even since the Restoration, the ministrations of those who had only Presbyterian Orders were for a long course of years, up to nearly the present time, habitually used by the Society for the Propagation of the Gospel, which is under the special direction of the Bench of Bishops.¶

* See Zurich Letters, published by Parker Society, *passim*.

† Strype's Whitgift, 406, 408; or Ox. ed. ii. 159, 173.

‡ See p. 33, above.

§ See Doctrine, &c. p. 29.

|| See Doctrine, &c. pp. 29, 30.

¶ *Ib.* p. 31.

And I will now add another case, that has lately been under my notice, that of Dr. De Laune, which is given in Dr. Birch's *Life of Archbishop Tillotson*, from a letter of Bishop Cosin, a witness of the case, in the following terms:—

"Dr. De Laune, who translated the English Liturgy into French, being collated to a living, and coming to the Bishop, then at Norwich, with his presentation, his Lordship asked him where he had his Orders. He answered, that he was ordained by the Presbytery at Leyden. The Bishop upon this advised him to take the opinion of counsel, whether by the laws of England he was capable of a benefice without being ordained by a bishop. The doctor replied, that he thought his Lordship would be unwilling to reordain him, if his counsel should say, that he was not otherwise capable of the living by law. The Bishop rejoined: 'Reordination we must not admit, no more than a rebaptization; but *in case you find it doubtful whether you be a priest capable to receive a benefice among us, or no*, I will do the same office for you, if you desire it, that I should do for one who doubts of his baptism, when all things belonging essentially unto it have not been duly observed in the administration of it, according to the rule in the Book of Common Prayer, *If thou beest not already*, &c. YET FOR MINE OWN PART, IF YOU WILL ADVENTURE THE ORDERS THAT YOU HAVE, I WILL ADMIT YOUR PRESENTATION, AND GIVE YOU INSTITUTION INTO THE LIVING HOWSOEVER.' But the title, which this presentation had from the patron, proving not good, there were no farther proceedings in it; yet AFTERWARDS DR. DE LAUNE WAS ADMITTED INTO ANOTHER BENEFICE WITHOUT ANY NEW ORDINATION." (*Birch's Life of Archbishop Tillotson*, 2d ed. 1753, pp. 170, 171.)

And the only one of our early divines, of any weight, whom I can find to have denied the legality of the practice, and that only on account of "*the laws of the realm*," is Archbishop Whitgift.

And that the statute and not the ecclesiastical law was the difficulty, *where any was felt*, we learn from a passage in Bishop Hall, who expressly tells us, in a work published in 1641:—

"The sticking at the admission of our brethren returning from Reformed Churches, was NOT IN CASE OF ORDINATION, *but of Institution:* THEY HAD BEEN ACKNOWLEDGED MINISTERS OF CHRIST, WITHOUT ANY OTHER HANDS LAID UPON THEM; but, *according to the laws of our land*, they were not *perhaps* capable of *Institution* to a benefice, unless they were so qualified as the Statutes of this realm do require. And, secondly, *I know those, more than one, that by virtue only of that ordination which they have brought with them from other Reformed Churches, have enjoyed spiritual promotions and livings*, WITHOUT ANY EXCEPTION AGAINST THE LAWFULNESS OF THEIR CALLING." (*Bishop Hall's Defence of the Humble Remonstrance*, Sect. 14, *Works*, ed. Pratt, vol. 9, pp. 690, 691.)

Now this practice of our Church from the Reformation to the Restoration, is the strongest possible proof that at least there was nothing in our Church's Formularies *against* the validity of such Orders, but on the contrary enough in its favor to justify such a course. And if so, *à fortiori*, our Church admitted their validity for ministering in *their own* communions. And it cannot be pretended, that while the Articles of our Church remained the same, any alteration was made in her doctrine on this subject by the mere introduction, at the Restoration, of the regulation requiring Episcopal Orders for those who ministered *in our Church*.

In considering the views of our divines subsequent to the reign of Elizabeth, we shall no doubt find some discrepancy of opinion among them on this subject. But still, we have an overwhelming majority in favor of the same view of the matter that prevailed before. It has been with some reason supposed that one of the first, if not the very first, to question the validity of the Orders of the Foreign Non-Episcopal Churches, was Laud. Certainly so early as 1604 he maintained this ground in the Divinity School at Oxford. When proceeding in that year to his degree of B.D., "his *Supposition*, when he answered in the Divinity Schools for his degree, concerning the efficacy of Baptism, was taken *verbatim* out of *Bellarmine;* and he then maintained, there could be no true Church without diocesan bishops, for which Dr. Holland, then Doctor of the Chair [Regius Professor of Divinity], openly reprehended him in the Schools for a seditious person, who would unchurch the Reformed Protestant Churches beyond seas, and now sow division between us and them, who were brethren, by this *novel Popish position.*" (*Prynne's Life of Laud*, p. 2.) And this is confirmed by Heylin himself, who says: "for which last [*i. e.* his position as to the necessity of bishops] he was shrewdly rattled by Dr. Holland above mentioned, as one that did endeavor to cast a bone of discord betwixt the Church of England and the Reformed Churches beyond the seas." (*Heylin's Life of Laud*, sub a. 1604.)

It is not a little remarkable, that the Popish doctrine of Baptism, and the indispensable necessity of the Episcopate to the existence of a true Church—the two doctrines for which the Bishop of Exeter has been so vehemently contending against his Metropolitan—should be the two principles with which Laud began his career. And I think we may derive instruction from the way in which an impartial investigator of our history at this period, our able historian Mr. Hallam, speaks of the reintroduction of the latter principle into our Church by Laud and his party:—

> "The system," he says, "pursued by Bancroft and his imitators, Bishops Neyle and Laud, with the approbation of the king, far opposed to the healing counsels of Burleigh and Bacon, was just such as low-born and little-minded men, raised to power by fortune's caprice, are ever found to pursue. They studiously aggravated every difference, and irritated every wound. . . . They began by preaching the divine right, as it is called, or absolute indispensability, of Episcopacy; *a doctrine of which the first traces, as I apprehend, are found about the end of Elizabeth's reign.* They insisted on the necessity of Episcopal succession regularly derived from the Apostles. They drew an inference from this tenet, that ordinations by presbyters were in all cases null. And as this affected all the Reformed Churches in Europe, except their own, the Lutherans not having preserved the succession of their bishops, while the Calvinists had altogether abolished that order, they began to speak of them, not as brethren of the same faith, united in the same cause, and distinguished only by differences little more material than those of political commonwealths (WHICH HAD BEEN THE LANGUAGE OF THE CHURCH OF ENGLAND EVER SINCE THE REFORMATION), but as aliens to whom they were not at all related, and schismatics with whom they held no communion; nay, as wanting the very essence of a Christian society. This again brought them nearer, by irresistible consequence, to the disciples of Rome, whom, with becoming charity, but against the received creed of the Puritans, and perhaps against their own Articles, they all acknowledged to be a part of the Catholic Church, while they were withholding that appellation, expressly or by inference, from Heidelberg and Geneva." (*Hallam's Constit. Hist.* vol. i. pp. 389, 390, 4th ed.)

Mr. Hallam's opinion of the first introduction of this notion at the end of Elizabeth's reign, is taken from the passage of Lord Bacon, which I before quoted on this subject;* in which he speaks of "some indiscreet persons" having been so "bold" as to pronounce those "ordained in foreign parts" to be "no lawful ministers."

And I have already shown that the more eminent of those who leaned to this new school, such as Bishop Andrews and Archbishop Bramhall, were far from condemning the Foreign Non-Episcopal communities as wanting in the *essentials* of a Church, or the Orders of their ministers as absolutely *invalid*.†

In the same place, I have added copious testimonies of the views of Archbishops Bancroft, Usher, Sancroft, Wake, Secker, and Howley, Bishops Hall, Davenant, Morton, George Downham, Cosin, and Tomline, Lord Bacon, Dean Field, and Sherlock, Archdeacon Mason, Drs. Crakanthorpe, Willet, and Claget, all showing their cordial recognition of the Foreign Non-Episcopal Churches as true Branches of the Church of Christ, and of their ministers as true ministers of that Church.‡

And to this list it would be easy to add largely; but it is obvious, that the consentient testimony of *such names* represents a weight of evidence in favor of such a point much greater than the mere *number* would indicate; and therefore any addition seems to be unnecessary.

Nevertheless, a few more shall be given here.

To the passage formerly quoted from Bishop Hall, the following may well be added:—

"The imputation pretended to be cast by this tenet [the Divine right of Episcopacy] upon all the Reformed Churches which want this government, I endeavored so to satisfy, that I might justly decline the envy which is intended to be thereby raised against us; for which cause, I professed that we do 'love and honor those our Sister-Churches, as the dear Spouse of Christ;' and give zealous testimonies of my well-wishing to them. Your uncharitableness offers to choke me with those *scandalous censures and disgraceful terms*, which some of ours have let fall upon those churches, and their eminent professors; which, I confess, it is more easy to be sorry for, than, on some hands, to excuse. The error of a few may not be imputed to all. My just defence is that no such consequent can be drawn from our opinion; forasmuch as the Divine or Apostolical right, which we hold, goes not so high as if there were an express command, that, upon an absolute necessity, there must be either an Episcopacy or no Church; but so far only, that it both may and ought to be. How fain would you here find me in a contradiction! *While I one-where, reckon Episcopacy amongst matters essential to the Church; anotherwhere deny it to be of the essence thereof! Wherein you willingly hide your eyes, that you may not see the distinction that I make expressly betwixt the Being and the Well-being of a Church;* affirming, that 'those Churches, to whom this power and faculty is denied, *lose nothing of the true essence of a Church*, though they miss something of the glory and perfection.' *No, brethren, it is enough for some of your friends, to hold their Discipline altogether essential to the very being of a Church; we dare not be so zealous.*" (*Bp. Hall's Def. of Humble Remonstrance*, Sec. 14. *Works*, vol. ix. p. 690.)

We here see, that he throws back upon *the Puritans* the *exclusive*

* See Doctrine, &c. p. 31.

† See Doctrine, &c. pp. 32, 33, where passages from Bishop Andrews and Archbishop Bramhall are given, fully proving this.

‡ *Ib.* pp. 34, 44.

doctrine of the indispensability of one particular form of church government, and disowns it; and also, that his general testimony to Episcopacy had been misunderstood and misrepresented, as if he had intended to deny the Foreign Non-Episcopal Churches to be true Churches; a fact which may show how easy it is to parade the appearance of a Catena of testimonies from our divines in favor of the exclusive doctrine, while, nevertheless, the authors of those testimonies meant nothing of the kind. I commend this to Chancellor Harington's consideration.

Again, it is worth our notice, that our learned and esteemed divine, Dr. Crakanthorp, not only justifies the Foreign Non-Episcopal Churches, as I have before shown, but distinctly admits that we are in communion with them, and that "in doctrine and the profession of the orthodox faith there is no difference between us." For in the 43d chapter of his *Defensio Ecclesiæ Anglicanæ*, entitled "Ecclesiam Anglicanam hæreticam esse, quia *communicat cum Reformatis Ecclesiis ultramarinis*, calumniatur Arch. Spal." &c., he says:—

"'Ecclesia,' inquis, 'Anglicana *communionem* publice et aperte profitetur cum Genevensi aliisque ultramarinis Ecclesiis. Etiam et Londini sunt regia concessione Gallis, Belgis, Italis, apertæ Ecclesiæ. Hæ vero omnes Calviniano veneno infectæ. Ipsa quoque Geneva, Puritanorum mater. Ab his Puritanismus in Anglia fovetur et promovetur. Hæ Anglicanam professionem et ritus abominantur: et tamen Anglicanæ Synagogæ sorores sunt dilectissimæ:' Quare cùm Anglicana cum his hæreticis Ecclesiis communionem teneat, erit et ipsa quoque hæretica. Imo nec Anglicana est, nec illæ hæreticæ; sed tu homo ex convitiis et mendaciis totus conflatus, et Anglicanæ et *illis sanctis Dei Ecclesiis* novus Shemi ore inverecundo oblatras. . . . Nec certe 'doctrinam illi aut professionem Anglicanam abominantur.' Calumnia hæc tua est, cujus si pudor tibi ullus inesset, pœnituisse te jamdudum oportuisset. *In doctrina et fidei orthodoxæ professione discordia inter nos nulla. Hac integra, in ritibus et disciplina discrimen ferendum utrique scimus.*" (*Crakanth. Defens. Eccles. Angl. contra Arch. Spalat.* 1625. 4to. c. 43, p. 253, *et seq.*)

Among our learned divines Dr. John White, brother of Bishop Francis White, takes a high place. In his *Way to the True Church*, first published in 1608, he expressly includes the Foreign Non-Episcopal Churches as forming with the Church of England the Protestant Church. For in meeting the Romish objection that "the Protestants' Church is not perfectly one, or uniform in dogmatical points of faith," he says, "we for our purgation name the *Harmony of Confessions*, wherein the particular Churches set down and name the Articles of their faith; the which *Confessions* if the Jesuit can show to jar, as he saith, in dogmatical points of faith, I am content you believe him in all the rest." (Ed. 1624, § 33, p. 75.) And he entirely repudiates the notion that ministerial succession is an essential note of the true Church. He says:—

"The succession required to make a Church Apostolic must be defined by the *doctrine*, and not by the *place* or *persons;* that is to say, they must be reputed the Apostles' successors which believe the Apostles' doctrine, *although they have not this outward succession of pastors* visibly following one another in one place throughout all ages, as the Jesuit saith it is in the Roman Church." "It is no disadvantage to the Protestants' Churches if, holding the Apostles' doctrine, they want external succession of place and persons, such as the Jesuit boasteth of: because the apostolicness of the Church is not defined by it, but *wheresoever the true faith contained in the Scriptures is professed and embraced, there is the whole and full nature of an Apostolic Church.*" (*Ib.* § 53, p. 210.) "The Jesuit objecteth, that 'God hath planted a Church to endure in all ages, wherein he will have a visible succession of teachers,' preserved from failing in the true faith; and therefore none are sent of God but such as come in this 'ordinary' manner, called and succeeding 'visibly,' and with 'peculiar consecration,' which Christ termeth entering in by the door. The antecedent whereof is false. For though God's ordinance be, that he have a Church, and teachers therein, in all ages, succeeding one another, and standing in the truth; *yet he hath made no law that this succession shall be 'visible,' or with 'peculiar consecration,' as the Jesuit meaneth them.*" "Yea, our very adversaries deny not but a man may be a lawful minister, though a bishop never consecrated him, but a simple priest, by dispensation; and whereas the *common opinion in the Church of Rome is that a bishop differeth not from a priest in order, but in jurisdiction only, hence it followeth, unavoidably, that jure divino a simple priest may ordain, because the power of ordaining belongeth not to jurisdiction but to order, as they call it.* The which point will serve to avoid all that the Jesuit hath said in this section, though we should say no more." (*Ib.* § 58, pp. 229, 230.)

This treatise was defended against the Romanists by his brother Francis, Bishop of Carlisle, in a work entitled: *The Orthodox Faith and way to the Church explained and justified*, in which he expressly vindicates the position, that "personal succession" is not an essential note of the Church (2d ed. 1624, p. 49), and that the Foreign "Protestant Churches" are at unity with the Church of England in all essential points. (*Ib.* pp. 124 and 132, 133.)

Another important testimony is that of the learned John Forbes —son of Bishop Patrick Forbes, and appointed Divinity Professor at Aberdeen in 1619, and ejected in 1640 on account of his adherence to the cause of Episcopacy and Charles I.—occurring in his *Irenicum*, first printed in 1629. And it will be the more esteemed, I suppose, by those who take the opposite view to that I am now maintaining, when I mention, that he distinctly advocates the *Jus Divinum* of the Episcopal form of church government. One of the propositions which he lays down, and defends at some length, is the following:—

"Ecclesia Orthodoxam tenens fidem, si careat Episcopo, sive Presbyterorum ordinario præfecto Diœcesano, laborat quidem defectu quodam œconomico: at non propterea desinit esse vera Ecclesia, neque excidit potestate illa Ecclesiastica, quam habent aliæ Ecclesiæ ab Episcopis gubernatæ. Quamvis optandum et annitendum, ut habeat Episcopum."

And on this proposition he remarks:—

"Gradus quidem Episcopalis est juris divini; sic tamen ut Ecclesia esse non desinat, sed esse possit, et sit quandoque vera Ecclesia Christiana, in qua non reperitur hic gradus .... Non ad esse, sed ad melius esse Ecclesiæ necessaria est hæc œconomia .... Valida est ordinatio quæ peragitur per presbyteros in eis Ecclesiis, in quibus non est Episcopus, aut ubi non est orthodoxus, sed notorius hæreticus et lupus: quamvis decentius fieret (si possibile) per orthodoxum Episcopum et Presbyteros; aut etiam per solos presbyteros, consentiente et concedente Episcopo .... Habent Presbyteri de jure divino ordinandi, sicut prædicandi et baptizandi, potestatem; quamvis hæc omnia exsequi debeant sub regimine et inspectione Episcopi, in locis ubi est Episcopus, sicut dictum est. In aliis autem locis, ubi Ecclesiæ communi tantùm Presbyterorum consilio administrantur, valida est et efficax ordinatio quæ fit per impositionem manuum solius Presbyterii. Quin et ubi est Episcopus, possunt Presbyteri ordinare, consentiente, licet non simul manus imponente,

Episcopo: cui propria de jure divino est sola authoritas et præfectura Episcopalis . . . . . . ordinare autem non possunt [presbyteri] sine particulari commissione ab Episcopo, vel a Presbyterorum Diœcesano Concilio in locis ubi non est Episcopus." (J. Forbes, *Irenicum*, lib. ii. c. xi. Prop. 13, *Op.* Amstel. 1703, vol. i. pp. 420–422.)

The Bishop of Exeter has referred to the 19th Article as supporting his views of the necessity of Episcopacy to constitute a Church. The following passage of our learned Bingham—the most deeply versed in ecclesiastical antiquity, perhaps, of any of our divines—will show how little notion he had that such a view could be extracted from it. After quoting this Article, and stating that none of our divines object to it on account of its not mentioning "bishops or their government," he adds:—

"For in all their disputes with the Papists, they never require more than *these two* notes of the Church. They say with Bishop Andrews, 'that though Episcopal government be of Divine institution, yet it is not so absolutely necessary, as that there can be no Church, nor sacraments, nor salvation without it. He is blind that sees not many Churches flourishing without it; and he must have a heart as hard as iron, that will deny them salvation. Something may be wanting, that is of Divine right, in the exterior regimen of the Church, and yet salvation be obtained therein.' Now this is *the case of the French Church*, which Bishop Andrews and his followers *allow to have all the necessary and essential notes of a true Church, though Episcopal government was never settled among them.*" (*French Church's Apol. for Church of England*, bk. 2, c. 2, *Works*, ix. 40, 41.)

In the debate on *Occasional Conformity*, in 1702, Dr. Sharp, Archbishop of York, stated, that "if he were abroad, he would willingly communicate with the Protestant Churches, where he should happen to be." (*Life of Abp. Sharp*, vol. i. p. 377.)

In the debate on the Union with Scotland, in 1707, Dr. Tenison, Archbishop of Canterbury, said, "he thought the narrow notions of all Churches had been their ruin, and that *he believed the Church of Scotland to be as true a Protestant Church as the Church of England*, though he could not say it was as perfect." (*Carstares*, 759, as quoted by Mr. Hallam, *Constit. Hist.* 4th ed. ii. 483.)

I will quote but one more testimony out of the vast body of evidence that might be given from our divines on this subject, and that shall be from Dr. John Scott, who, though no Low-Churchman, and taking very high views as to the Divine right of Episcopacy and the Episcopal succession, says:—

"A Church may be debarred of it by unavoidable necessities, in despite of its power, and against its consent, and under this circumstance I can by no means think such a Church to be separated from the Church Catholic; it is indeed an imperfect and defective part of the Catholic Church; *and if this defect of it be any way owing to its own* NEGLIGENCE, *it is a very great* FAULT *in it, as well as an unhappiness.* But though this instituted government is necessary to the *perfection* of a Church, yet it doth not therefore follow that it is necessary to the *being* of it. . . . . Why may we not reasonably suppose, that the Catholic Church will admit presbyters to govern and ordain, where there are no bishops to be had, since it hath admitted laymen to baptize, where there are neither bishops nor presbyters to be had? since the latter is as great a deflection from positive institution as the former." (*Christian Life*, 5th ed. 1747, vol. iii. pp. 310–313.)

Into his Lordship's remarks, occupying nearly the whole of the remainder of his pamphlet, upon the present state of the

Foreign Protestant Churches, and upon the individual members of those Churches who recently came over to this country, I shall not enter, because my object has been to discuss *principles*, not their particular application. To do justice to the subject would require a much more extended examination of it than his Lordship's *ex parte* statements afford, or than would be possible in this place.

I shall merely observe, that, *speaking generally*, the Public Confessions of those Churches are before the world; and that however much many of their members may have departed from their true meaning, it would be as unjust to renounce all brotherly communion with their sound members, as it would be for *them* to renounce all communion with every member of *our* Church, because of the Romish views of many of our clergy. And as to any who may have been forced to separate from those Churches on account of the corruptions prevailing in them, and form a separate body holding an orthodox confession of faith, such have a still stronger claim upon us for our sympathy and Christian fellowship.

But I may be permitted to ask his Lordship this question: *Was he, or was he not, a consenting party to the Letter sent in* 1835 *by the late Archbishop of Canterbury, in the name of himself and his* "BROTHER BISHOPS," *to* "*the Moderator of the Company of Pastors at Geneva*," *expressing their* "*high respect for the Protestant Churches on the Continent*," and speaking of *the Genevan Reformation* as a "noble achievement, which brought light out of darkness, and rescued their Church from the shackles of Papal domination and the tyrannical imposition of a corrupt faith, and a superstitious ritual," wrought by "illustrious men, who, under the direction of Almighty God, were the instruments of this happy deliverance," "an event not less glorious to Geneva than conducive to the success of the Reformation?"

It is scarcely to be supposed, that such a Letter should have been sent by the late Archbishop in the name of his "*brother bishops*" without the knowledge or assent of the Bishop of Exeter. And certainly incredible, that if he had dissented from it, his dissent should not have been made known to the public. If, therefore, such a Letter as this was sent with the sanction of the Right Reverend Prelate, with what face can he now turn round upon the present Archbishop, and assail him as he has for holding that the ministers of "the Protestant Churches on the Continent" are true ministers of Christ? He cannot venture to assert that the state of things in those Churches is worse now than it was then.

May I be permitted also to remind his Lordship, that it is not so many years since he himself was on a Committee formed for the purpose of obtaining aid for the Vaudois Pastors. Now if, as his Lordship here tells us, the administration of the Lord's Supper by such persons is "a profane mockery," that its effects are obtainable "only" through an Episcopal ministry,* and that persons

* Christ "gave to His Church—celebrating it as he celebrated, but only so—and by those whom *He authorized, but* ONLY *by them* [the meaning of which words the Bishop has himself told us]—a holy sacrament which should be," &c. (P. 83.)

not Episcopally ordained "have no other title" to the ministry "than their own presumption, or the presumption of men like themselves, who have dared to affect to confer it on them," (p. 83,) and that "we see not any promise of a blessing" to such a ministry (p. 87), then, surely, to be on the Committee of a Society formed for the purpose of aiding such "profane mockery" and "presumption," is an act for which it is difficult to account in one who has such high views of Christian duty. Certainly the claims of charity can be no sufficient defence. The only true charity would have been, to have warned them of the fatal delusion under which they were acting, and urged them, at the peril of their salvation and that of their flocks, to receive the imposition of Episcopal hands; and to have withheld any aid until this was done.

Nay more; I would ask his Lordship, where we can find his indignant protests against the course pursued for so many years by the Society for the Propagation of the Gospel (of which his Lordship is *ex-officio* a leading governor) of sending out missionaries not having Episcopal Orders? Such matters usually come before the public. But I am unable to find that there was any movement, on the part of his Lordship, on the subject. At any rate it must have been one of very recent date.

Why, then, may I ask, was all his indignation in this matter reserved for his present Metropolitan?

There is another point also which his Lordship will, I hope, permit me to bring under his attention. He has, in various parts of his present pamphlet, thrown out divers remarks about *Calvinism* and *Calvinists*, as something quite inconsistent with the doctrine of the Church of England. (See pp. 45, 46, &c.)

Let me remind him of the words in which a divine, whose authority he will respect, once rebuked a celebrated statesman for speaking slightingly of "Calvinists":—

> "To the peculiar tenets of that denomination of Christians, to which you appear to allude, I am very far from subscribing; but thus much I will say, that *no man, who knows what they really are, will ever treat them with contempt.* You, Sir, do not appear to have yet risen above THE VULGAREST PREJUDICES on this subject; *else you would have known, that opinions which have commended themselves to the full and firm conviction of* SOME OF THE ABLEST, AS WELL AS HOLIEST, MEN WHO HAVE EVER ADORNED OUR CHURCH, *are not to be thus blown down by 'the whiff and wind' of the smartest piece of rhetoric ever discharged in your honorable House.*"

Such were the terms in which the Rev. Dr. Phillpotts addressed the Right Hon. George Canning in 1825, in his "Letter" to him on the Roman Catholic Bill of that year. (Pp. 106, 107.) I may fairly hope, then, that the Bishop of Exeter will remember this indignant remonstrance of Dr. Phillpotts; and pause to reflect, before he singles out for his reproaches, or again endeavors, as he has of late been doing, to drive out of the Church those whose only crime it is to hold the same views with "SOME OF THE ABLEST, AS WELL AS HOLIEST, MEN WHO HAVE EVER ADORNED OUR CHURCH."

There remains but one point more for notice in his Lordship's

"Letter;" and that is one which, among all the extraordinary specimens we have lately had of his Lordship's qualifications for the high post he has assumed to himself in our Church, is perhaps entitled to the first place. It occurs in the last page of his "Letter." Unfortunately for his Lordship, a piece of information was brought him which he calls a "particular of very great moment in this discussion, with which I have only recently become acquainted," namely, "the form of Ordination used among Calvinists." And upon this the Bishop thus comments :—

"Our Church regards the Christian ministry as a commission from God himself, and confers it *in His name.* Not so the 'Reformed communities, so far as I can find. In *The Discipline of the Reformed Churches of France,*' 'The Form of Ordination' is as follows: 'That it may please God to vouchsafe grace unto this Elect Person, a short Prayer shall be conceived to this purpose: "O Lord God, we beseech Thee to endow with the gifts and graces of thy Holy Spirit this thy servant lawfully chosen according to that Order established in thy Church, and abundantly to enrich him with all abilities needful for his acceptable performance of the duties of his office to the glory of Thy Holy name, the edification of Thy Church, and his own salvation, whom *we now dedicate and consecrate unto Thee* by this our ministry."' Compare with this our own Ordinal: '*Receive the Holy Ghost* for the office and work of a priest in the Church of God, now committed unto thee by the imposition of our hands. Whose sins, &c., in the name of the Father, and of the Son, and of the Holy Ghost.' I stop not to discuss the causes of this difference. *It is enough to say, that they are* ESSENTIALLY DIFFERENT ; that the one professes to confer a commission from God *in His name,* whereas the other simply 'dedicates and consecrates unto God' the person ordained. THE PLAIN CONSEQUENCE IS, THAT THERE CAN BE NO INJUSTICE IN DENYING THAT THE LATTER HAS ANY COMMISSION FROM GOD ; HIS OWN ORDINATION DOES NOT PROFESS TO GIVE IT."

Now it is difficult to know in what terms to speak of such a passage as this. Were it not for the tone and position assumed by the writer, one might be inclined on several grounds to pass it by with the slightest possible notice, and throw a veil over it. But, under present circumstances, when his Lordship is misleading a host of our younger clergy to the borders of Rome, and teaching them to vilify the authorities of Church and State as ignorant or incompetent persons for not adopting his views of orthodoxy, it is absolutely necessary plainly to point attention to such proofs of the nature of the guidance to which they are submitting; especially as this "Letter" of his Lordship has received from his party the highest encomiums as a most able and masterly performance. Is there no kind friend whom his Lordship can consult, before he thus commits himself in a way that brings reproach upon the Church as well as himself?

Is his Lordship, then, really ignorant of the notorious fact that nearly twelve centuries passed over the Church before those words, "Receive the Holy Ghost," &c., were introduced into the Ordination Service? Does he really need to be informed, what was the character of the early Ordination Services of the Church, and that he has actually invalidated the ministry of the whole probably of the early Western Church, and left the ministry of the Greek Church to this day in a rather dubious position?

I shall have a few remarks to make presently on the correctness of his Lordship's statement as to what *is* done in the French Church. But I will first deal with it precisely as it stands.

Now first, as to the use of the formula, "Receive the Holy Ghost," &c., we have the authority of the learned Morinus, in his standard treatise on the subject of Ordinations, that it was unknown in the Church for *twelve centuries*. He says:—

"Dispiciamus an illa postrema manus impositio, cum qua jungitur illa formula, 'Accipe Spiritum Sanctum, quorum remiseritis peccata,' &c., sit formaliter vera et antiqua Sacerdotii forma, aut pars illius, quam Apostoli et antiqui nobis tradiderunt..... Tota illa ceremonia, et secundum materiam, et secundum formam, et secundum circumstantias, MILLE DUCENTIS ANNIS *incognita fuit in Ecclesia Dei.* Nulli rituales ante hoc tempus illius meminerunt, licet copiosi sint, et singulos ritus pauci momenti sigillatim describant. Imo nonnulli sunt eo tempore longe recentiores, et diffusi admodum, qui illam prætereunt." (*Morin. De Ordin.* Pt. 3, Exerc. 7, c. 2, ed. 1695, p. 106.)

"Verba illa, 'Accipe Spiritum Sanctum,' ab antiquis Latinis usurpata non fuisse; et consequenter nec Ordinationis Presbyteralis, nec cujusvis alterius, formam fuisse, præter argumenta jam allegata, ex omnium ritualium et autorum antiquorum, qui de officiis ecclesiasticis scripserunt, profundo silentio petita, demonstrant evidenter nonnulla alia quæ hic subjicimus." (*Ib.* c. 5, p. 118.)

The same learned author maintains at large:—

"Solam manuum impositionem Presbyteratus esse materiam." "Hanc solam omnis Ecclesia, Latina, Græca, Barbara, semper agnovit. Hanc solam commemorant omnes antiqui Rituales, Latini, Græci; omnes antiqui et recentiores Patres, Græci, Latini." (*Ib.* c. 1. pp. 102, 103.)

And he points to all the old Greek Rituals and Fathers as showing that in the ordination of a Presbyter *nothing more was necessary than imposition of hands and prayer.* He says:—

"Legantur et relegantur præcedentes Græcarum Ordinationum ἀκολουθίαι, seu rituales; legatur S. Clemens, Sanctus Dionysius, nihil aliud sedula lectione deprehendes præter manuum impositionem et orationem quod materiæ et formæ rationem induere possit. Sed consideretur præsertim S. Dionysius qui ritus istos diligenter persequitur, mystice et tropologice multis verbis explicat; versentur et revolvantur ipsius verba, nihil aliud præter manuum impositionem et orationem, aut si vis addere genuflexionem, tibi occurret, cui substantiale aliquid possis affingere." (*Ib.* c. 1, p. 104.)

And now let us see, from the words of some of the ancient Ordination Services of the Western Church, *what sort of prayers they were* which, at that time, accompanied the imposition of hands. The Bishop tells us, that the Service of the French Church, though it has retained the imposition of hands, yet, by only praying for spiritual gifts, and saying, "whom *we now dedicate and consecrate* unto thee by this our ministry," is *essentially* defective, and the party so ordained has no commission from God, and so, in his Lordship's view, is not really ordained at all.

In the great work of Morinus on this subject, written in the middle of the 17th century, are given some forms of Ordination from various very ancient Rituals of the Western Church. The first is from a MS. which was then eleven centuries old, which carries us back to the middle of the sixth century, and appears to have belonged to the Church of Poictiers. I need hardly say, that the laying on of hands, and offering up the prayers there given, form the whole service. And now let us see *what the prayers are.* The prayer "ad Presbyteros ordinandos" is this: "Exaudi nos Deus salutaris noster, et super hunc famulum tuum benedictionem Spiritus S. et gratiæ sacerdotalis effunde virtutem, ut quem tuæ pietatis suspectibus *offerimus consecrandum*, perpetua muneris tui largitate persequaris. Per Dominum." Then follows the prayer of "Consecration," which, after an opening in general terms, proceeds thus: "*Da quæsumus*, omnipotens Pater, in hoc famulo tuo illo *Presbyterii dignitatem:* Innova in visceribus ejus Spiritum sanctitatis," &c. Then comes the "Consummatio Presbyteri," which commences with the following exhortation to the people: "Sit nobis fratres communis oratio, ut his [hic] qui in adjutorium et utilitatem vestræ salutis eligetur, *Presbyteratus benedictionem divini indulgentia muneris consequatur*, et S. Spiritus sacerdotalia dona privilegio virtutum, ne impar loco deprehendatur obtineat per suum.* Per." And then follows the prayer of "Benediction:" "Sanctificationum omnium autor, *cujus vera consecratio, plena benedictio est*, Tu, Domine, super hunc famulum ill. *quem Presbyterii honore* DEDICAMUS, manum tuæ benedictionis in eum infunde, ut gravitate actuum et censura vivendi probet se esse seniorem," &c. &c.

And I may just add, that the prayers at the ordination of a deacon and the consecration of a bishop are of a similar kind, the words in the prayer of Consecration for a deacon being, if possible, a still more exact counterpart of those in the French Service— "Super hunc famulum tuum quæsumus, Domine, placatus intende, QUEM TUIS SACRIS SERVITURUM IN OFFICIUM DIACONI SUPPLICITER DEDICAMUS." (*Morin.* l. c. Pt. 2, pp. 214, 215.)

Here, then, we find nothing beyond a dedication of the person to the office, and humble prayer for the gifts of the Spirit to fit him for the right discharge of its duties. In a word, we have the precise form of Ordination which the Bishop tells us is essentially defective.

The next Ordinal given by Morinus is from a MS. then nine hundred years old, where the title to the Ordination Services is "Ordo qualiter in Romana sedis Apostolicæ Ecclesia Presbyteri, Diaconi vel Subdiaconi eligendi sunt." And here, again, the prayers are, as far as our present subject is concerned, exactly of the same kind, the same words indeed being used: "Quos tuæ pietatis aspectibus *offerimus consecrandos*"—"super hos famulos tuos *quos Presbyterii honore dedicamus*, manum tuæ benedictionis his infunde." (*Ib.* p. 217.)

The next is from a MS. then eight hundred years old, in which is given the "Ordo qualiter in Romana Ecclesia Diaconi et Presbyteri ordinandi sunt;" in which the same prayers are found. (*Ib.* p. 221.)

And these, in short, are followed by Ordination Services from various other very ancient MSS. belonging originally to different places in the Western Church, all of the same kind, and most of them in precisely the same words on the point we are now con-

* These two words *per suum* are probably added by a misprint.

sidering. So that here we see the general form of Ordination that prevailed for several centuries in the Western Church.

And the nature of these Services is in strict conformity with the testimony of the early Fathers, both Greek and Latin, as to what was considered necessary for Ordination, which they represent as being imposition of hands and prayer.

Thus Theodoret, telling us of the ordination of a hermit performed by the bishop of a neighboring city, who sought him out for the purpose, says that he entered the place where he was, and "laid his hand upon him and offered the prayer, and spake much to him," &c.*

And so Jerome says, that the ordination of the clergy is fulfilled, "not merely by the prayer of the voice over them, but by the imposition of the hand."†

And, to cite no more, the Apostolical Constitutions (as they are called) speak only of the imposition of hands and prayer in their account of the form of ordination for a presbyter; and the prayer of Consecration there given is merely a supplication to God for his grace to fit the person ordained for the duties of his office.‡ And in the Form given in these Constitutions for the appointment of a bishop, there is not even imposition of hands; which is, it should be observed, another testimony for the parity of Order in bishops and presbyters. After the people and presbyters present have been asked, whether they are satisfied with the person elected, and have testified in his favor, one of three bishops standing near the altar is to offer a prayer to God for a blessing upon him, some deacons holding the Gospels open upon his head. After the prayer, one of the bishops is to give him the eucharistic elements (τὴν θυσίαν), and the next morning he is enthroned by the rest of the bishops, all of them kissing him; and after the reading of certain portions of Holy Scripture, he gives the blessing, and preaches to the people, and then follows the Communion Service. (*Constit. Apostol.* lib. viii. cc. 4, *et seq.*)

In fact, his Lordship need not have gone farther than our own Bingham to have discovered his error; who expressly says, and quotes sufficient authorities to prove it, that "it is plain, the ancient Form was only imposition of hands and a Consecration-prayer." And having given the Consecration-prayer in the Apostolical Constitutions, he says:—

"Where we may observe, that it was not then thought necessary to express all or any of the offices of a presbyter in particular, but *only in general to pray for grace to be given to the priest then ordained, whereby he might be enabled to perform them. And this, with a solemn imposition of hands, was reckoned a sufficient form of consecration.*" (*Antiq.* bk. 2, c. 19, § 17.)

The French Service, therefore, is more consonant with the Forms of the earlier and purer period of the Church than our own.

* Τὴν χεῖρα ἐπέθηκε, καὶ τὴν εὐχὴν ἐπετέλεσε, καὶ πολλὰ μὲν πρὸς αὐτὸν ἔφη. Theodoret. Philotheus, seu Relig. Hist. c. 19, Op. Hal. 1771, tom. 3, p. 1232.

† Non solum ad imprecationem vocis, sed ad impositionem impletur manus. Hieron. Comment. in Is. c. 58, v. 10, Op. ed. Vallars. tom. 4, col. 694, 695.

‡ Constit. Apostol. lib. viii. c. 16.

And now let me remind his Lordship of the *consequences* of the doctrine he has thus propounded. He has shivered to atoms the whole doctrine of the Apostolical Succession, for he has left the whole Western Church without any Orders at all. He has not left us even my poor "Low Church" notion on the subject. I *did* think, we in the Church of England had something more to say in favor of the *regularity* of our Orders than other recently-constituted Bodies, who have been driven by circumstances to somewhat *irregular* courses; heartily as I repudiate the *Tractarian doctrine* of Apostolical Succession. But his Lordship has swept away even this. He is, upon his own showing, equally destitute of valid Orders with any of those whom he has so fiercely attacked in his Letter for "profane mockery" and "presumption;" for his golden chain of legitimate succession, instead of reaching to the Apostles, runs back only a third of the way. And what is more, I am afraid there is no Church on earth that can help him out of his dilemma. For the Greek form of Ordination, even if it could be proved to have been uninterruptedly used, is far from coming up to his standard. For the Bishop in the Greek Church does not do more than recognize God's supposed call of the ordained person to the office of presbyter, and *His use* of the Ordainer's ministry for the external consecration of such person to that office.

The Greek Bishop, on laying his hand upon the head of the person to be ordained a presbyter, says: "The Divine grace, which healeth that which is weak, and supplieth the wants of that which is defective, promoteth this most pious deacon to be a presbyter. Let us therefore pray over him, that the grace of the most Holy Spirit may come upon him." And in the Prayer occur these words—"to whom *Thou* hast vouchsafed that he should be promoted by me." (ὃν ηὐδόκησας προχειρισθῆναι παρ' ἐμοῦ.)

And the Form for consecrating a Bishop is of a similar kind. And in the prayer at the Ordination of a deacon, any power or commission in the Ordainer to communicate grace by the imposition of his hands is distinctly repudiated, for it is said: "Fill him with all faith and love, &c., for *not by the imposition of my hands*, but by the superintending agency of thy rich mercies (ἐν τῇ ἐπισκοπῇ τῶν πλουσίων σου οἰκτιρμῶν) is grace given to *those worthy of thee.*"

I take this from the last edition of the 'Αρχιερατικὸν (printed at the Patriarchal press at Constantinople in 1820 for the use of the Greek Bishops), which I obtained direct from Constantinople.

This, no doubt, the Bishop will think much *better* than such a Form as that he has referred to, or the old Services of the Western Church; and as the validity of his own Orders stands *self-condemned*, he may like to avail himself of the superior privileges of the Greek Church, to which certainly there can be no objection. It will be but reasonable.

But before I dismiss this subject, I must add one word as to the correctness of the Bishop's statement with relation to the French Church. He complains that the French Church does not profess to confer a commission from God *in his name*. Now if his

Lordship had looked only to the page previous to that from which he has quoted, he would have found that Canon 5 directs, that "the Assembly remonstrating to him [the person to be ordained] the duty of that office whereunto he is called, shall farther declare that power which is GIVEN HIM IN THE NAME OF JESUS CHRIST, to minister both in the Word and Sacraments."*

And farther, it would have been well, if his Lordship had recollected, that the original of the Canon he was quoting was *in French*, and therefore that before he made it the subject of such a serious charge against the whole Reformed French Church, it would have been wise to have ascertained how it stood in the original. The words in the original are not "whom we now dedicate and consecrate unto Thee by this our ministry," but, "who *is* now dedicated and consecrated by our ministry" (est maintenant dédié et consacré par nôtre ministére);† which is very similar to the Greek Form.

Such, then, is the character of his Lordship's censure upon the Form of Ordination in the French Reformed Church. He is evidently totally unacquainted with the Ordination-Services of the Primitive Church for many centuries; he assumes the indispensable necessity of the particular Form that happens to occur in our own Service, which was not introduced till the 12th century, and he flings his random reproaches at other Churches in a way that makes them so recoil upon himself and his own Church as to deprive both of any valid Orders.

It is, however, it must be confessed, nothing more than what might be expected as the consequence of that deeply-rooted evil from which our Church is, and has long been, suffering. Church, State, and Universities long combined to treat all such knowledge as of no more value than an old almanac. And the result has been, as might be expected, the present state of profound, chaotic, and hopeless confusion in our Church.

But his Lordship has one more charge to bring against the French Reformed Church. He says:—

"In conformity with these different views of the nature of the Christian ministry, is the view taken of the indelibility of Holy Orders. We regard them as *simply indelible;* even degradation, though it disables the party from exercising any ministry, does not erase the *character*. Not so the 'Reformed'—whose XIth Canon is, 'Such as are chosen unto the ministry of the Gospel must know, that they be in that office for term of life; unless they be *discharged upon good and certain considerations, and that by the Provincial Synod.*'"

Now, in the first place, this Canon does not touch the question of the indelibility of the character imparted by Holy Orders, for it does not state in what condition the person is who is discharged from the ministry. And in all Churches there is a power in the Church to take away the "office" of minister in that Church on good and sufficient grounds. And if his Lordship means to intimate, that the person thus discharged would so have lost his Orders in the French Church by this discharge, that if at any

* Quick's Synodicon, vol. i. p. xvii.

† Conformité de la Discipline Ecclesiastique des Protestans de France, &c. 1678, 4to. By M. Larroque, whose name is appended to the Dedicatory Epistle.

subsequent time he was found fit and competent to fulfil the duties of the office, he would have to be reordained, the 53d French Canon shows his mistake; for it enacts, that "ministers deposed" "for slighter faults, upon confession of them, they may be restored by the Provincial Synod, but with this condition, to serve in another Province, and not in their own." (Quick, *Synod.* i. xxvi.)

And as to the Bishop's statement of the doctrine of our Church on the subject, I shall merely place by the side of it the following remarks of our learned Ecclesiastical antiquary Bingham.

"The full import of the phrase, and the adequate notion of reducing a clergyman to lay-communion, is totally degrading and depriving him of his Orders; that is, the power and authority of his clerical office and function, and reducing him to the state and quality and simple condition of a layman. . . . . . *This supposes a power in the Church, not only of conferring Clerical Orders at first to men,* and promoting them from laymen to be bishops, or presbyters, or deacons; *but also a power of recalling these offices, and divesting them of all power and authority belonging to them, by degrading clergymen upon just reasons, and reducing them to the state and quality of laymen again.* This is undoubtedly the true meaning of all those ancient canons and writers, which speak so often of degrading clergymen for their offences, and allowing them only to communicate in the quality of laymen. Hereby they were deprived of their order and office, and power and authority, and even the name and title of clergymen; and reputed and treated as private Christians, wholly divested of all their former dignity, and clerical powers and privileges, and reduced entirely to the state and condition of laymen." "The plain result of this discourse is, that reducing a clergyman to the communion of laymen was a total deprivation and divesting him of his office and Orders. So that if he now pretended to act as a minister, his actions were reputed null and void, and as no other than the actions of a layman. The learned Dr. Forbes has rightly observed this (*Iren.* lib. 2. c. 11) in the ancient discipline, and I cannot better express it than in his words: 'He that is deposed with a plenary and perfect deposition, cannot now validly exercise the offices that belong to his order, because he *wants his order and the power of his order.* He is now nothing but a mere layman, and in so much a worse condition than other laymen, because the restitution of such an one to his office is a much more difficult thing than the promotion of other laymen.'" "It may perhaps be said, there was still an inherent power and authority in such deposed clerks, and that their deposition did not totally annul their ordinations: for they still retained the indelible character of their respective Orders; and therefore they might be ministers still, and their ministerial actions stand good and authentic, notwithstanding any power and authority in the Church to depose and degrade them. *But as this is* NEXT TO A CONTRADICTION IN ITSELF, *that a man should be deposed from his order and yet retain his order still,* with all the spiritual power belonging to it; so it implies such a notion of that which is commonly called the indelible character of ordination, *as no ancient writer ever thought of. For the notion that the ancients had of the indelible character of ordination, was no more than they had of the indelible character of baptism;* that as the outward form of baptism, washing or immersion in water, though but a transient act, served forever to distinguish a Christian from a mere heathen or Jew; so as that, though he apostatized from the Christian faith into Judaism or Gentilism, he should still retain so much of the Christian character, as, upon his conversion and return to the faith, not to need a second baptism; in like manner the outward form of ordination, which is imposition of hands designing a man to any clerical office, though it be but a transient act, was sufficient to distinguish such an one from a mere layman, who never had any such ceremony of Ordination; so that by this mark or character of his office once received, though he should afterward forfeit his office and all the power and honor belonging to it, he would always remain distinguished in some measure from those who never had such an office; and though he should be wholly divested of his office and power, and reduced to the simple capacity and condition of a layman, yet *so much of the marks and footsteps of his former office would remain upon him, as that if he should be recalled again to his office, though he might need a new commission, he would not need this outward character or ceremony of a new ordination.* There is no one [who] has explained or illustrated *the sense of the ancients* upon this point with more accuracy than the learned Dr. Forbes: and therefore, for farther confirmation, I shall here transcribe his words: 'There remains (says he) some distinguishing character in a man that is deposed, by which he is distinguished from other laymen; but to make this distinction, it is not necessary there should be *any form impressed,* but a transient act, that is long ago past, is sufficient, viz., that he was once a person ordained. The character that remains in a deposed person, *is not the character of any present office or power,* but only some footstep or mark of an honor that is past, and of a power that he once had; by which footstep he is distinguished from other laymen, who never were ordained; and may, after a sufficient penance performed, if he be found fit, and the advantage of the Church so require, be restored again without a new Ordination.'" (*Antiq.* bk. xvii. c. 2, §§ 3–5. *Works,* vol. 6, pp. 350–354, ed. 1844.)

It is unnecessary to say, that there is nothing in the Canons of the French Church opposed to this, and that it leaves the doctrine which the Bishop seems desirous of inculcating entirely destitute of foundation.

—One word in conclusion. If this matter were a mere theoretical question, or one of little practical import, I should not have thought it worth the space I have here devoted to it. But it is not so. The circumstances of the times demand more than ever the cordial intercommunion and mutual good-will of all who hold the true faith. Romanism is making a last effort to regain her lost dominion and reassume her empire over the nations of the earth. Her emissaries are everywhere, especially in the strongholds of Protestantism; spreading around us those corrupt principles by which she hopes to ensnare the unwary, and gradually draw them into her toils. Infidelity, as ever, is making the best use of the dissensions prevailing among the followers of Christ to cast reproach upon the Christian faith. How are these foes to be met?

We have been recently told, and told even from a quarter where such language is all but incomprehensible—our own Episcopal Bench—that the latter especially is to be met, and can only be successfully met, by urging upon our people the "*authority of our Church,*" and that the Episcopal Church, throughout Christendom, is so completely the exclusive channel of all Divine grace to men, that all we can hope for other communions is, that it "may overflow its channels for their benefit."* To show the total opposition of such sentiments to the principles of our Reformers, would be a work of supererogation; nor is this the place for it. But I point attention to these statements as showing how deeply the poison has entered into the very soul of our Church, and is rankling in her heart's core.

These are the principles from which Popery took its rise. The substitution of the authority of the Church for the supremacy of Holy Scripture is the foundation-stone of Popery. Take it away, and

* See the Bishop of Oxford's recent Charge, pp. 38–42, and 81, *et seq.*

the whole system crumbles to atoms. The authority of the Church is another phrase for the authority of the Apostolically-descended priesthood. The supremacy of this priesthood involves the committal into their hands of the interpretation of Holy Scripture and unlimited power over the consciences of mankind. And thus there arises a vast body of men, endowed since the fourth century with large possessions, to whose care religion is intrusted, upon whom mankind are to depend for a knowledge of the faith, and whose spiritual directions they are to follow at the peril of their salvation. Worldly-minded and ambitious men crowd into it to partake of its wealth and honors. Satan's emissaries make their way into its ranks in order to corrupt the true faith. Will "the grace of the Apostolical succession" keep such men out? or convert them when in? Facts prove the contrary. What reason have we to expect that even the *majority* of such a priesthood will remain true to the pure faith of Christ? None. Much for a contrary expectation. And if they do not, what becomes of the faith of Christ? It is distorted by perverse interpretations of Holy Writ, overlaid with errors, and immersed in an ocean of corrupt rites and practices. The power of the priest being the corner-stone on which the system rests, the main object is to provide for its support. He becomes, therefore, all in all. He converts the feast of the commemoration of Christ's sacrifice into a real sacrifice, in which he is exhibited as possessing a superhuman power of changing the bread and wine into the real body and blood of Christ, and then offering them up again to the Father as the sinner's advocate. He claims a power even in the other world, of releasing from the pains of hell the soul of the sinner. He secures the salvation of all who will obey his directions. He is not, he will confess, divine; but divine power has been confided to him.

And how does the world receive all this? The priesthood find a large proportion of mankind prepared to admit every superstition and every perversion of the true faith, everything, in short, but real religion; the willing captives of a religion adapted to please the senses of human nature. And when universal dominion is thus placed in their hands, what reason is there to suppose they will not grasp it? They might be the envy of a Cæsar or an Alexander. For their prize is unbounded empire over the souls as well as bodies of mankind. Who can wonder, that a priesthood thus gifted should swell out into gigantic proportions, and that as its numbers and influence increase, its corruptions of the true faith increase in a proportionate ratio; that its pretensions and its errors go on multiplying with its years, until they reach the climax at which the measure of their iniquities is filled up, and the Divine forbearance reaches its limit! It soon becomes far too potent for any earthly power to cope with; its roots are spread throughout all lands, and its boughs extend to the ends of the earth; it is a vast upas tree, under whose poisonous influence the world must remain until the hour—and it is a *promised* hour—when it "shall be consumed with the spirit of *His* mouth, and destroyed with the brightness of *His* coming."

Such are the natural and necessary effects of setting up the authority of man in the place of that of God, man's teaching in the room of God's word. And if ever this principle regains its lost dominion in our Church, her relapse into Popery will speedily follow. In fact, her allowance of such a principle involves in itself her self-condemnation; for her doctrines are held by a very small minority of the apostolically-descended priesthood.

How, then, are we to meet the wiles of Popery, the assaults of Infidelity? By the united efforts of all who "hold the Head." They who hold the true faith, and have been admitted by baptism among the followers of Christ, and are living as such, are undoubtedly members of His body. And *ubi tres, ibi ecclesia, licet laici*, said a Father of the second century. "Where two or three are gathered together in My name," said our blessed Lord, "there am I in the midst of them to bless them." And those to whom He s joined are beyond all doubt members of His Church.

True; He who is the God of order, and not of confusion, no doubt looks with disapprobation upon all unnecessary schisms and divisions in His Church, and therefore, doubtless, there are communities whom, though we recognize as brethren and as partakers of the Divine blessing in their labors, we believe to be involved in the sin of unnecessarily dividing the Christian Church, and whose encouragement of strife and disorder among the followers of Christ we cannot aid in promoting; and still less give up our own Apostolical rule of government for theirs. But we see with thankfulness the Divine blessing resting upon their labors, we own them as brethren, and we say to any objector: "Enviest thou for our sakes? Would God that all the Lord's people were prophets." Nay, though circumstances necessarily prevent intercommunion in ministerial offices, there may still be somewhat of united effort in the cause of God. Nor must it be forgotten, that our Church may have given, in various ways, too much ground for such secessions from her communion.

To the Protestant Churches of other lands no such objection attaches. Alas! that the claims of those Churches upon the countenance and support of the more favored Church of England have been so little regarded! How different might have been their present state, if our Church, *true to her first principles*, had held fraternal communion with them, counselling them as a friend, and throwing the shield of British protection over them when in adversity from the enmity of the bitter foes by which they have been from the first encompassed. But they have been left almost without a helping hand from us. And, so far as Europe is concerned, our efforts for the cause of the Reformed faith, which through the power and influence God has given us might have been spread throughout the whole Continent, have been confined to our own little Island; and even there in so imperfect a manner as to have left a large portion of our population destitute of even the ordinary means of grace.

What has been the result? Popery and Infidelity are lifting their heads, and advancing with rapid strides. The cause of the true Reformed faith on the Continent is at the lowest ebb, and in the last stage of weakness and exhaustion. Popery already seems to see the reward of its long and persevering and insidious labors almost within its grasp.

How, then, is this state of things to be met? If we take the advice of the new school that have risen up among us, we are to wrap ourselves up in the dignity of an Apostolically-descended Episcopate, and repudiate all intercourse with any but those who can advance the same claim to the title of a Church. That is, we are to cast off all the Protestant Bodies that have not retained our form of church government, as having no part or lot in the Church of Christ, as Bodies not entitled to our fraternal regard.

Is it too much to hope, that the earnest response of our Church will be, We have not so learned Christ! that it will rise to the exigencies of the present crisis, and, casting off the trammels with which the agents of Popery among us would fain fetter its energies, will make common cause with all the genuine disciples of the true faith; that no Diotrephes "loving to have the pre-eminence," who "doth not himself receive the brethren, and forbiddeth them that would, and casteth them out of the Church," will be suffered to stand in the way of that true Catholic communion which ought to exist among "all those that love our Lord Jesus Christ in sincerity." Grave as were the charges laid against some of the Seven Churches of Asia in the Apocalyptic Epistles to them, we find them still numbered, with all their imperfections, among the Churches of Christ. And shall we suppose, that a diversity in the form of government adopted is a greater sin than a corrupt state of faith and practice?

Let our Church, then, gird herself to the conflict by rallying round her all the adherents of the genuine Reformed faith, and plant her standard with an unwavering hand on the rock of God's word. Her ancient banner, the undivided supremacy of the Holy Scriptures, must be again unfurled; and under it the contest must be waged. It may be too late to do much that might have been done at former periods. But there is still the opportunity left to make an effort for the cause of Protestant truth in Europe against the dangers by which it is encompassed.

Our country has much to answer for in the encouragement, direct and indirect, given by her to Popery both here and elsewhere. And she is now reaping the fruits of her suicidal policy, and beginning to feel the pressure of the iron yoke of Papal tyranny. May she be wise in time; and learn the value of that Protestant faith to which, under God, she owes so many blessings! May she exert the influence which God has given her, for the protection of that faith throughout the world! The power that is used in the cause of God will receive a blessing that will react upon her own welfare. And above all, may she jealously guard that sacred deposit of truth committed by God's mercy to her own keeping; and never suffer the blood-bought inheritance of freedom from spiritual slavery, bequeathed to her by her "noble army of martyrs," to be snatched from her, either by treachery within, or open aggression from without.

www.ingramcontent.com/pod-product-compliance
Lightning Source LLC
LaVergne TN
LVHW021410110826
845150LV00007B/1864